CALL COLLECT,
ASK FOR BIRDMAN

CALL COLLECT, ASK FOR BIRDMAN

The Record-Breaking Attempt to Sight 700 Species of North American Birds Within One Year

James M. Vardaman

ST. MARTIN'S PRESS • NEW YORK

For information, write:
St. Martin's Press, Inc., 175 Fifth Avenue, New York, N.Y. 10010.
Manufactured in the United States of America

Library of Congress Cataloging in Publication Data

Vardaman, James M
Call collect, ask for Birdman.

1. Bird watching. I. Title.
QL677.5.V37 598'.07'23424 80-14060
ISBN 0-312-11425-7

Design by Nancy Dale Muldoon

10 9 8 7 6 5 4 3 2 1
First Edition

CONTENTS

CALL COLLECT,
ASK FOR BIRDMAN

1

MAKING THE PLAN

"Is 700 possible?"

This question was the start of the greatest one-year adventure of my life. It came in June 1977 from the editor of *Birding,* the official journal of the American Birding Association (known as the ABA). In that month's issue he was asking whether it was possible, in one calendar year, to sight 700 species of birds in North America north of Mexico, including strips extending 100 miles from each coast (or halfway to another country, whichever is closer)—a huge chunk of the world we call the ABA area. Among birders such a game or contest is called a Big Year, and the rules are set and the records are kept by the ABA.

There was good reason to doubt that the feat was possible. According to ABA records at that time, only 816 species had ever been recorded in the ABA area. Four of these, Labrador Duck, Great Auk, Passenger Pigeon, and Carolina Parakeet, are definitely extinct, and Ivory-billed Woodpecker is thought to be extinct because there have been no verified sightings of it since the 1940s. Of the remainder, only 645 breed in the area, so fifty-five species would have to be seen when they came on regular or accidental visits. The record for a Big Year, 657 species, was held by Scott Robinson, an accomplished birder from Pittsburgh, Pennsylvania, who spent almost all of 1976 setting it. Seeing 700 species in one year was the birding equivalent of the three-and-a-half-minute mile, the eight-foot high jump, or the twenty-foot pole vault.

The challenge of the project appealed to me immediately. Of course, I wanted to see the birds, but all my life whenever someone said to me, "You can't do that," my answer had always been, "You just watch me." This would be a challenge in natural science—to know or learn enough about bird habits, habitats, characteristics, and markings to find the birds in the first place and then to identify them. It would also be a challenge in organization—to get to the right place at the right time over an area that contained about 10,000,000 square miles and to do it 700 times in 365 days. This meant making complicated and ever-changing arrangements with guides, witnesses, planes, boats, autos, and motels, while at the same time meeting pressing family and business responsibilities.

I thought about the question for several months. Birding has been my hobby since I joined the Boy Scouts in 1933, and I was good enough at it to have run up a life list (the number of species seen during a lifetime) of 430. But was I good enough to play in the birding big leagues? Maybe. A Big Year of 700 species wasn't just a test of birding expertise; it was a race against the calendar and a test against the challenges described above. As a forester, I had been a natural scientist for almost forty years; I had organized a consulting forestry firm that became the largest in the United States; I was persistent, single-minded, and determined. Would this be enough?

While deciding whether to take the challenge, I spent a lot of time studying the reports that previous record holders had written about their activities and soon noticed that most of them did not begin serious planning for their efforts until they were well into the year and had realized that a big total was a possibility. It occurred to me that very careful planning might produce a much higher yield. As might be expected, all previous record holders had relied heavily on help from other birders to locate good birding spots and to learn when rarities showed up, but there was little evidence that any of them made extensive use of birding professionals. Since I was a professional forester and knew what a difference I could make in the yield of a forest property, I was sure that the birding pros could make a big difference in the yield of a Big Year.

Careful planning and extensive use of birding pros could not only make 700 possible but also make it possible in a relatively short time. This was very important because time was my most precious commodity. Kenn Kaufman, the 1973 record holder, spent fifty-and-a-half weeks birding, if you count the time he spent traveling to where the birds were. I couldn't do this. My wife Virginia and I have six children ranging in age from seventeen to six, and I couldn't even think of leaving them alone for a full year. In addition, I am president of a consulting forestry firm with 125 employees and thirty-nine branches in twelve states, and just about everything I own is tied up in this practice, so I couldn't abandon that either. How much such a venture would cost was also important; although I make a good living, I am a long way from being independently wealthy. Therefore, in the fall of 1977, it was obvious that the only way I could go for 700 was to make a very detailed plan in advance, a plan that would show how much time I would be away from Jackson, Mississippi, where I live, and how much money would be needed.

My first step was to decide to go ABA all the way: ABA Checklist of Birds, ABA bird names, ABA area, ABA rules, and so on. This seemed only appropriate. ABA had been founded in 1969 especially to serve the needs of those who loved the hobby or game or sport of bird watching (or birding, a better and shorter name). Its 4,000-plus members are persons very much like me; it places great emphasis on the fun of listing (life lists, state lists, Big Year lists, Big Day lists); its excellent magazine is devoted to describing how to find and identify birds; and the editor had planted the idea in my mind in the first place. (Anyone interested in watching birds will enjoy membership in ABA; its address is P.O. Box 4335, Austin, Texas 78765). There were alternatives—maybe better ones—but planning the project would be complicated enough without having to deal with several different frameworks.

I bought a copy of the ABA Checklist of Birds to discover what species were listed and why. It revealed that, for a naturally occurring species to be included, there must be the following supporting evidence:

1. a specimen identified by a qualified authority and evidence that the specimen was obtained in the ABA area, or
2. photographs or tape recordings that clearly show definitive characteristics, or
3. a sight record backed by detailed observations prepared independently by three experienced observers and accepted by the ABA Checklist Committee.

Introduced species, either deliberately released or escaped from captivity, could be included only after they had been breeding in the wild for ten years and increasing in abundance or maintaining a stable population without direct help from humans.

The introduction to the Checklist contained these statements about another type of species that I might see:

> Each year dozens of species of foreign birds escape from captivity within our borders, some through poor packaging or careless handling at ports of entry, others through inadequate restriction at private and public collections. Most of these are unrecorded and difficult if not impossible to trace, and after a bird has gone through a complete moult there is no way a field observer can suspect a captive history unless the bird remains unusually tame. Often encountered in the wild are foreign waterfowl, cagebirds, and birds of prey that have escaped from their owners. These exotics deserve no place on a list of North American birds.
>
> For [deciding whether to count] a foreign bird whose origin is in doubt, many factors must be considered, such as geographic range, normal migratory pattern, the chances of its surviving the trip from its native land, specific weather

conditions at and preceding the time of first sighting, the bird's overall condition, and likelihood of its having been kept in captivity.

These requirements seemed reasonable to me, but the procedure for getting approval to count certain birds raised some problems. The Checklist Committee was made up of ten outstanding bird authorities, but I knew from business experience that a committee of ten was often too large for fast action. Furthermore, the committee did not have formal meetings at regular intervals; it usually "met" through telephone calls and correspondence. Although it tried to bring the Checklist up to date each year, its members were active and successful persons who, at times, might have to postpone volunteer work. Finally, the committee would not act until a matter was brought before it by one of its members, and no individual was responsible for surveying the entire birding world to spot matters the committee should act upon. Therefore, naturally occurring or introduced species might not be added to the list or foreign species approved for counting for months after I needed a decision. This being the situation, I decided to count species in any doubtful category only after the most careful study, to publish the reasons why I counted them, and then to allow readers of this book to decide whether or not I should have counted them.

I also decided that each of my sightings should be witnessed and signed for by a credible authority. In forestry I was an acknowledged expert, but in birding I was, by some standards, a rank amateur. There was little point in going to the trouble of seeing 700 species if some of the sightings could be successfully questioned. (My sighting ledger is reproduced in Appendix B (pp. 207–234); the witnesses who have signed it almost constitute a "Who's Who in North American Birding.")

The first time I looked over the Checklist, I was struck by the number of unfamiliar names. Middendorff's Grasshopper Warbler, for example, was not in any of my field guides; in forty-five years of birding, I had never even heard of it. It was clear that I needed to learn a great deal more about ABA birds and, in particular, about when, where, and how often they could be found in the area.

The first person to come to my rescue was ABA's Executive Secretary, Dr. James A. Tucker of Austin, Texas. Jim was one of ABA's founders, and his enthusiasm and hard work (with no pay in the beginning) almost certainly were responsible for ABA's survival and growth. In addition to being a top birder, he knew the names and qualifications of all serious birders and how to get in touch with them. He suggested corresponding with a preliminary planning group of about forty persons, and by late 1978, this group had grown to more than seventy-five people located all over North America.

The planning group began its work by devising a number code to show how often each species occurred in the ABA area as a whole. After months of discussion and correspondence, we developed the following codes and indicated the number of species that fall into each category.

Code	*Specifications of Code*	*Number of Species*
1	Can be found in one day at predictable times and places	643
2	Known to be present in certain places at certain times but may require more than one day to find	27
3	60–90 percent chance of occurring each year	23
4	30–50 percent chance of occurring each year	19
5	10–20 percent chance of occurring each year	14
6	Less than 10 percent chance of occurring each year	21
7	No real chance of occurring each year	64
		811

This classification made the goal of seeing 700 seem much harder to reach. Since Code 6 and Code 7 birds probably wouldn't show up and since I couldn't go outside the area, catch them, and bring them back, my task was not seeing 700 species of a possible 811, but seeing 700 of a possible 726, or 96.4 percent of all species that were even remotely likely to come into the area in any year.

The next step was to pinpoint where and when each species would occur. We divided the ABA area into fifteen regions and, across the top of a big sheet, headed columns with each region and then divided each column into four parts for the seasons of the year. Then opposite each species we moved across the sheet entering "1" under each region and season where the species was Code 1. So as not to drown in a sea of numbers, we used only the smallest code number applicable to the species. For example, for Snowy Owl we entered "1" under all seasons in Alaska, where the bird was easy to find, and did not try to show by numbers that Snowy Owls sometimes come to the Lake States and New England in winter or that one spent the winter near Shreveport, Louisiana, several years ago. If a species was never Code 1, we tried higher numbers until one fit.

The complete chart of 811 species appears in Appendix A (pp. 193–206). It contains the distilled bird-finding knowledge of the leading birders of ABA and is a unique guide for anyone who wants to know where and when to search for each species with the greatest likelihood of finding it. So far as we know, this is the first attempt to show by numbers how rare some species are in the ABA area.

The big chart showed several quirks of bird distribution that would complicate planning an itinerary. Caribbean Coot and American Flamingo occur only in Florida in winter, so I had to go there in January unless I wanted to run the risk of waiting until December. Colima Warbler and Lucifer Hummingbird occur only in Big Bend National Park, Texas, but Colima Warblers can be found easily only in spring when they are singing (and they quit as summer wears on), whereas Lucifer Hummingbirds can be found easily only in summer when they are nesting and the agaves are blooming; therefore, two trips to Big Bend would be needed. Crested Mynas occur only at Vancouver, British Columbia; Spotted Orioles only near Miami; Five-striped Sparrows only in southern Arizona; and Baird's Sparrows only in the Dakotas in summer and Arizona in winter. Nevertheless, it would be possible to plan trips to see them efficiently, since each of these Code 1 species could be easily seen in these areas.

One other resource was extremely valuable in locating the birds at the beginning of the year: the Christmas Bird Counts conducted in the last half of December under auspices of the National Audubon Society. At each point (its location remains the same year after year), organized parties of observers search a circle fifteen miles in diameter and record numbers of each species seen. The amount of data gathered is enormous. In 1978 there were 1,269 counts with 31,140 participants who counted 103,403,790 birds. In ten counts there were more than 100 observers. Some counts have been made for more than seventy-five years, so past records revealed how predictable certain species were, and the most recent counts revealed the presence of rare species. (Christmas Bird Counts are fun. Each participant must contribute a small fee to pay for publication of the results in *American Birds,* a monthly magazine, and 30,000 or more persons wouldn't pay to give up a whole day of the Christmas season unless they were a *lot* of fun. You can get more information about them from the National Audubon Society, 950 Third Ave., New York, New York 10022.)

Code 3, 4, and 5 birds presented a tougher problem. Since they did not occur in the ABA area every year, planning trips to see them was impossible, but I could go to the areas where their occurrence was most likely and wait for them to appear. The chart revealed that chances to see many of them were good during migrations in western Alaska, Attu (the westernmost Aleutian Island), and St. Lawrence Island (only forty-five miles from Siberia). Going to these places in the spring and fall could pay handsome dividends. But it was obvious that accidental sightings were not frequent enough elsewhere to make the same strategy worthwhile; some other mechanism would have to be worked out for them.

The only way to learn about accidentals in such a vast area was to mobilize an army of volunteer observers who would call me when a rare bird showed up. Somehow I had to get birders everywhere interested enough in the project to help me; it could succeed only as a joint venture, not as an individual effort. Fortunately, Jon Rickert's valuable book, *A Guide to North American Bird Clubs,* was published in 1978 and contained addresses of about 850 clubs, and my planning group plus key figures in the ABA and the National Audubon Society made a total of about 300 more individuals. I decided that the key to mobilizing these observers was a periodic newsletter that would start with the planning stage and give a detailed account of each leg. We decided to call it *Vardaman's Gold Sheet,* a variation on our forestry newsletter, *Vardaman's Green Sheet.* Since it had to provide an easy way to get in touch with me, many issues would contain the same plea: "CALL COLLECT 601-354-3123, ASK FOR BIRD-MAN." The telephone was connected to a twenty-four-hour answering device. (Ultimately, there were twenty-eight issues of the newsletter, and it helped to add about twenty species to my total.)

By late 1978 we had gathered enough data about the birds to know where they would be, and it was time to look at other aspects. I listed each day of the year on a chart three-and-a-half feet square and laid out what seemed to be a satisfactory itinerary on it. If I traveled at night as much as possible, the trips that could be planned would require 145 days, with the bulk of them falling in January and in the period between April 15 and June 20. The longest period I would be away from home was thirty-eight days from May 13 to June 20. And many of my absences would fall on Saturdays, Sundays, and holidays, since those were the days when most birders would be available to help me. I guessed that an additional fifteen days would be needed, one at a time, for chasing rarities. Therefore, the project would consume less than half the days in the year, and it began to seem more and more possible for me.

To estimate the cost, June (Mrs. Robert S.) Simmons of Delta Air Lines in Jackson prepared the schedules for all plane flights for the entire year and figured their costs. Since there were very large travel costs in a forestry practice like ours, we needed no help in developing other expense estimates. The grand total we came up with was $35,000, a figure we could live with.

Next I asked my associates in James M. Vardaman & Co., Inc., to allow me time off to carry out the project, to continue my salary without change, and to pay my expenses. A favorable decision from them was vital; the best-laid plan in the world would be worthless if I didn't have the time or the money to carry it out. In return for their support, I suggested that the firm would receive publicity that could not be obtained by other means, and I also agreed to assign to it all royalties from any book that might come from the project. The try for 700 had to be a sound business venture; I was not an eccentric millionaire indulging a whim. Although I own a controlling interest in the firm, the other stockholders had to be considered, and since all employees participated in the profit-sharing plan, each would be contributing $300 to $400 of his own money to finance my Big Year.

At first the decision seemed to be an easy one. Bob Cantwell, an experienced writer and a special contributor to *Sports Illustrated,* had told me that he would cover my Big Year, that he would go along on the January trips, and that the magazine would probably carry three articles during the year. The publicity seemed to be assured. But while the Vardaman board was considering my request, Bob died suddenly, and *Sports Illustrated*'s interest died with him. It would certainly take several months to develop interest elsewhere, and a large investment in time and money might go up in smoke if something happened to me after I had spent months chasing birds, but before I had reached

Robinson's record. Although it now required faith to believe there would be sufficient return on their investment, the Vardaman board members approved my request. Their faith would be tested.

My wife Virginia had the final say. She was accustomed to taking care of our home and children when I traveled on business, but I was usually away for only a day or two at a time, and I could always fly home in a few hours. Now I would be gone almost half the year, including one stretch of six weeks, and, while on Attu, might not be able to get home in less than a week. During almost twenty years of marriage, we had never been apart so much. She studied the plan and finally approved it. But it was hard to comprehend fully and in advance how great its demands would be, and the project was destined to have an effect on our marriage.

Soon after Virginia gave her assent, the glorious adventure began.

2

THE BIG YEAR STARTS IN SOUTH FLORIDA

Since most species arrive in their winter quarters by January 1 and stay there until spring migration begins, you can start a Big Year anywhere. I chose south Florida for mine because Caribbean Coot and American Flamingo, two rare Code 1 birds, are usually found on Christmas Bird Counts there, and I wanted to get them in the bag as soon as possible. Several other species occur only in south Florida and could be picked up at the same time. We designated these as "targets" for the trip, meaning that we would concentrate on finding them and thereby eliminate the need for a second trip after them.

Thinking that an unusual adventure deserved an unusual start, John Edscorn suggested that we go after a Barn Owl just as the New Year arrived. He reported that the species was abundant in winter along the highways south of Miami, so we left our motel at Homestead, Florida, at 11:15 P.M. on New Year's Eve and headed south on Highway 27. In the center of Florida City, four blocks from the police station, we pulled into a service station to switch something from the back seat into the trunk. As soon as he opened the door, John heard a Barn Owl calling from the vacant lot diagonally across the intersection. We drove opposite the bird, which was hidden somewhere in a tall palm, waited thirty-five minutes for 1979 to arrive, and counted it one second into the Big Year. John thought the calling owl was a young bird, and during our wait, we heard others calling and saw one fly to a neighboring tree, stay a moment, and fly away. We had flushed three Killdeers when we parked to wait for the New Year, and I had hoped to get two species quickly, but we couldn't find them after we tallied the owl. Too keyed up to sleep, we drove south on Highway 27 looking for other birds but found nothing more than another Barn Owl perched on a powerline.

Soon after dawn, with the temperature at 70 degrees and a brisk wind, we drove around the fringes of Homestead. When I spotted two black birds out of the corner of my eye and called out, "Two grackles in a bush on your side," John slammed on the brakes and backed up quickly. They were two Smooth-billed Anis, still sitting in the bush almost close enough to touch, the first new addition to my life list, and my first quick-but-wrong identification of the year.

By the time the sun had warmed the earth enough to allow vultures to soar, we were at Royal Palm Hammock in Everglades National Park scanning the skies for Short-tailed Hawk. Ten minutes after we got the telescopes set up, Phil Warren of Fremont, North Carolina, a former Air Force pilot being further trained by Eastern Airlines in Miami, drove up and said there was a very dark hawk perched in a tree up the road. We couldn't find his hawk again, so we drove to the visitor center and, in the parking lot, ran into Charlie Clark, an experienced birder and a former resident of Chicago. He reported having seen a Short-tailed Hawk a few minutes earlier, and then, almost as though on cue from a stage director, an adult Short-tailed Hawk soared over our heads at an altitude of about 200 feet, and stayed about three minutes. For a few seconds I had the hawk and a Wood Stork in the field of my binoculars at the same time. Ten minutes later Phil spotted another hawk sitting in the top of a twenty-five-foot tree, and we and six or seven others studied it at leisure through telescopes. With Phil following us, we picked up two more on the road to Flamingo.

Small craft warnings were flying at Flamingo, and it took

us three hours to find a boat captain willing to go out and a boat flat enough to negotiate the very shallow waters of Florida Bay, where we hoped to find the rarest bird of the trip. During the delay we saw a Scarlet Ibis (an ineligible species not on the ABA Checklist) from the porch of Flamingo Lodge. By 3:30 P.M. John, Phil, and I were banging along at twenty-five miles per hour in a fiberglass skiff with a 70-horsepower motor. We ran for twenty minutes, stopped to sweep the horizon, and found our quarry perhaps two miles ahead, four bright pink blobs sticking out of the shimmering water. We whooped. There could be no mistake; they were four American Flamingos. With the sun directly behind us, we eased up to within fifty yards of them and stopped when they began a stately walk away. We'll never forget the sight: four brilliant pink birds, bright sun, warm blue water full of grass just below the surface. We ended the first day with seventy-six species.

The next morning was windy, over 70 degrees, and cloudy. Soon after dawn we watched about forty noisy, fast-flying Canary-winged Parakeets (ineligible) leave their roost in the palms at the Miami Public Library. Then we searched in vain for Spotted Oriole and Red-whiskered Bulbul (unfortunately, you can't make an appointment with a bird) and finally headed west on the Tamiami Trail, U.S. Highway 41. Paul Sykes had said we would find Snail Kites along the canal on the north side of the highway from L67-A to Miccosukkee Village. He was right. We found eight altogether, one eating a snail, and all completely oblivious to us, the fishermen below them, and the heavy highway traffic.

Next we headed northeast through increasing rain showers, picked up a Burrowing Owl at Pembroke Pines Airport, and struggled to Vero Beach in the blinding rain that signalled the approach of a cold front. We were lucky to add ten new birds.

By early morning on January 3 the temperature had dropped 40 degrees, a strong northwest wind was blowing, and the Atlantic Ocean was steaming like a kettle of boiling water. From our fifth-floor balcony in an oceanside motel, we had hoped to see Northern Gannet over the ocean, but the steam eliminated any chance; we could hardly see a bird more than a quarter-mile out. Driving to Port St. Lucie, we got the Caribbean Coot found on the Christmas Bird Count there; the white of its frontal shield extended higher than does my receding hairline.

After missing a Lesser Black-backed Gull that had been seen at Cocoa Beach, we found a Limpkin near Lakeland at Saddle Creek Park, where abandoned mining pits have filled with water and produced an ideal habitat for these birds. We ended this leg of my Big Year in St. Petersburg with several Ringed Turtle Doves near a feeder and two Budgerigars on a high powerline in a busy shopping center on the beach.

The trip was a great success in that we got all eight target birds: Smooth-billed Ani, Short-tailed Hawk, American Flamingo, Snail Kite, Caribbean Coot, Limpkin, Ringed Turtle Dove, and Budgerigar. There were two unexpected species in Everglades National Park, Swainson's Hawk and White-winged Dove, but all the others on our trip list of 105 species were those that are common in south Florida in January. I also got an indication of how much car travel would be involved in the year; we drove 850 miles in three long days.

During this Florida trip, I found out several things about birding pros. I expected John to know exactly where to find certain species, and he did. I was very surprised, however, to discover how keen his eyesight and his hearing were; I thought I was good in these departments, but he saw and heard 50 percent more than I did. I was also surprised at his commitment to birds, a commitment so intense that it had changed his whole life. In his late forties, after twenty years as an agent for Southern Farm Bureau Insurance Company and with a wife and five children, he quit and became a birding professional. That takes courage. His wife told me that, in the five years since then, they have never regretted the decision and all the changes it must have caused.

Since in some ways south Florida is like a huge zoo, I also ran smack into the problem of how to handle introduced species and learned the benefits and limitations of following ABA policy on them. For expert advice on this subject, I turned to Dr. Oscar T. Owre, Maytag Professor of Ornithology, University of Miami, and our greatest expert on introduced birds of southern Florida. I learned much of what follows from his writings and from my conversations with him.

Humans have completely changed the environment in southeastern Florida, having their biggest effect on what is known as the Atlantic Coastal Ridge, a slightly elevated strip of land about 100 miles long that runs from north of Palm Beach to south of Homestead and is ten to twenty miles wide between the Everglades and the Atlantic. This is where most of the people live, the Gold Coast; from 1930 to 1970 the population there grew from 200,000 to 2,000,000. To make the kind of suburbs these people wanted to live in, developers usually removed all the natural cover of pines and tropical hammock and replaced it with exotic plants with showy flowers or desirable fruit. Thousands of species of plants were imported from all over the world. Now the area is a vast tropical garden producing variety and abundance of food for birds 365 days a year.

As the human population exploded in the salubrious Gold Coast climate, residents began to keep birds in outside cages and backyard aviaries, and zoos and tourist attractions featuring birds became popular. With the expansion of commercial aviation came the development of Miami as headquarters for many bird importers; the birds could be flown up from the tropics and easily held while they were being sold. The numbers were large; in 1971 more than 500,000 cage birds (not counting canaries and parrots) passed through Miami. Many of these birds accidentally escaped from their various owners. Others were deliberately released by those who sought to introduce a new species; the Budgerigar was established in St. Petersburg as a tourist attraction.

With such a bountiful habitat and such large numbers of birds escaping and being released each year, many exotic species established a toehold in the wild. Spotted Oriole, Red-whiskered Bulbul, Blue-gray Tanager, Ringed Turtle Dove, and Budgerigar made it to the ABA Checklist. Dr. Owre has discovered evidence that others (Canary-winged Parakeet, Red-crowned Parrot, Rose-ringed Parakeet, Monk Parakeet, Java Sparrow, and Indian Hill Myna) are breeding there and reported that still others (Orange-fronted Parakeet, Brown-throated Parakeet, Orange-chinned Parakeet, Orange-winged Amazon, White-fronted Amazon, and Brazilian Cardinal) are flying wild in the area.

When I encountered this situation, I was glad to have the ABA Checklist to guide me in deciding which ones to count. In all my previous birding I had never counted birds seen in a zoo or others that were obviously pets or escapees, and I didn't intend to start in 1979. On the other hand, I didn't have the time or the resources to determine on my own the exact status of each species. The ABA Checklist solved most of these problems for me; you might say that it was a publication of research by qualified authorities into the status of species.

But the Checklist also had its limitations. Because the Checklist Committee was composed of volunteers and had no money to pay for research, it couldn't keep pace with developments in each species. Canary-winged Parakeets illustrated the problem. The species was observed in Miami in 1945, and about fifty birds came to one roost there in 1969. In 1970 they were seen in Homestead, Fort Lauderdale, and Islamorada. In 1971 at least 200 were reported in Coconut Grove; in 1972 the wild population in metropolitan Miami was estimated to be between 1,500 and 2,000; that winter about 700 roosted in the Coconut Grove-Coral Gables area; Dr. Owre told me that, in 1979, the population in south Florida seemed to be almost 5,000. These facts convinced me that the species was established. I decided not to count it on my Big Year list because I had adopted the ABA Checklist at the very beginning, but I counted it on my life list since this was a personal matter with me, one in which I was the sole rule-maker.

The Blue-gray Tanager was another illustration. Although it was on the Checklist (I would try to locate one in November because it was on the Checklist), no one, not even the pros or the best amateurs of the area, could tell me where to find one. I was convinced that the species was gone and that any individual I saw in future years should be treated as an escapee unless there was proof to the contrary.

Information from Dr. Owre made it easy to decide not to count the Scarlet Ibis at Flamingo. Owre said that Carter Bundy, a Pan American Airways employee, brought fifteen to twenty Scarlet Ibis eggs from the tropics many years ago and placed them in White Ibis nests at Greynold's Park near Miami. Banding the young birds that hatched from these eggs was not permitted, so no one knew how many of them became adults, and there was no way to track their later movements. There must not have been enough of both sexes, however, for the Scarlets that did survive began to interbreed with the Whites and produced offspring that were deep pink. The bird I saw was more deep pink than scarlet. Therefore, although I was not sure what it was (unestablished introduction, hybrid, pink White Ibis?), I was sure that it couldn't be counted.

3

FIRST WESTERN SWING

The temperature is twelve degrees, the wind is blowing forty miles an hour, the wind chill factor is −44 degrees, falling and blowing snow at times reduces visibility to zero, and Warren Harden says this is a good day for finding longspurs. This was the situation in Norman, Oklahoma, on January 13. When we started walking across a big field of sparse, ankle-high grass, my bald head got cold even inside my down hood; when I put my hands before my face, my fingers nearly froze inside two pairs of gloves. I was ready to go back to the car long before we saw the first bird. But Warren was right; it *was* a good day to find longspurs. The cold and wind made them as reluctant as I was, so instead of flying away they allowed us to walk within a few feet. In a big field across the road from a new apartment complex, we got two species, Smith's and Chestnut-collared, and later, on the shoulder of I-40 toward Amarillo, we saw Lapland Longspurs.

Before we left Norman, we stopped at Linda Steiner's feeder and saw Harris's Sparrow, which we encountered many times later in the day. American Tree Sparrows were everywhere.

Driving on to Oklahoma City in spite of blizzard warnings on the radio, we found Lake Hefner almost frozen over, but the remaining patches of open water were full of Common Mergansers and Common Goldeneyes. John Shackford was on the north side of the lake and helped us locate several Glaucous Gulls.

As we headed west through flat, open country where you could see for miles, the snow stopped, but the strong north wind and bitter cold continued. Along the road on the dam of Foss Reservoir, we clocked a young Bald Eagle at thirty-five miles an hour as he sailed along the road without moving even his wings. Near Elk City we stopped to watch the birds clustered around a small cattle shelter open on the south end and were surprised to see about twenty Common Bobwhites settle down for the night inside the shelter with two cows. They had the right idea—it was probably the warmest place within miles. The sun set behind a row of cottonwood trees covered with thin ice; they looked like they were made of diamonds.

January 14 was cloudless and cold. West of Canyon, Texas, the whole country was full of Lapland Longspurs and Horned Larks, not hundreds, not thousands, but literally clouds of them. Warren spotted McCown's Longspurs in several flocks, but our best look at this species came when three of them walked across a hard-surfaced road about 150 feet ahead of our car. Ten minutes later we saw a female Lark Bunting in the fence row alongside the road.

Having wrapped up all four longspurs, we drove to Palo Duro Canyon, a huge gully 600 feet deep in the high plains southeast of Amarillo. There I saw my first Townsend's Solitaire ever, three Golden Eagles, a Canyon Wren almost close enough to touch, and, on the way back to Amarillo, a Ferruginous Hawk on a roadside fence post. In these two days, we saw sixty-seven species, forty-three of which were new for the year. I saw everything I went after, and Warren, a thirty-six-year-old protégé of Dr. George M. Sutton, had everything perfectly organized. One of his most helpful acts was to take me by the University of Oklahoma Museum before we went out and to show me skins of all four longspurs in winter plumage. Warren has an unusual combination of abilities; he is a professional trombonist with the Oklahoma Symphony Orchestra, but he also leads birding and nature tours to the Arctic, Central and South America, and the Galapagos Islands and may be our greatest expert on longspurs.

In the mountains west of Denver, January 15, at an altitude of over 11,000 feet, I not only saw a White-tailed Ptarmigan, I also watched Dr. Clait Braun catch one with a noose on the end of a long pole and band her, and I even held the snow-white grouse in my hands for a few seconds. A short while earlier, Clait, Dr. Ron Ryder, and I had parked at the side of the road behind a snowplow and many cars full of skiers. We buckled on snowshoes; pulled on down parkas, hoods, and gloves; and headed across the rolling mountains above timberline. In a strong wind, bright sunshine alternated with snow showers. I don't know how even an expert like Clait found the birds. After an early-morning feeding on the buds of willows three or four feet tall, only the tops of which protruded above the snow, the Ptarmigan had settled to roost *under* the snow, and no sign of them was visible to an untrained eye. Nevertheless, Clait flushed ten of them and captured the only unbanded one. To my surprise, I made it to the capture site and back without falling down in my first experience on snowshoes.

Early that afternoon at the house and office of Mr. and Mrs. Bob Swanlund on top of Squaw Mountain, I saw Steller's Jay, Clark's Nutcracker, Gray Jay, Mountain Chickadee, Northern Raven, and all three Rosy Finches. At an elevation of 11,500 feet where the night before the temperature was 7 degrees and the wind velocity was eighty miles an hour, the Swanlunds operate radio relays for sixteen government agencies and feed the birds 1,000 pounds of millet a year. The finches fed with feverish urgency, and it was easy to get a good look since they were only four feet away on the other side of the window.

At sunrise on January 16 I was at Ron Ryder's house in Fort Collins watching Evening Grosbeaks at his feeder. Soon thereafter, he, Clait, and I drove to a lake in City Park where, among the crowded ducks and geese in the small area of open water, we spotted one Eurasian Wigeon, my first unusual species. Then Clait and I drove through the high plains east of Fort Collins for two hours hoping to spot a Prairie Falcon, but all we got was a Merlin around a farm headquarters and a Common Snipe along a creek. Although we saw only forty-four species in Colorado, twenty-seven were new for the year and brought my total to 177.

Both Ron and Clait have impressive credentials as biological scientists. Ron is Professor of Wildlife Biology at Colorado State University, has written more than seventy-five articles and reports on birds, and has been president of most ornithological organizations in his area. Clait, one of Ron's former students, is a Wildlife Research Biologist at Colorado Division of Wildlife in Fort Collins, has been a serious birder since 1960, probably knows more about grouse of the Great Plains than anyone because of Colorado's intensive research on them, and is a thoroughly engaging companion.

On the Oklahoma-Texas-Colorado leg, in addition to the birds mentioned above, I added the following new species for the year:

Canada Goose
Snow Goose
Mallard
American Wigeon
Wood Duck
Canvasback
Hooded Merganser
Rough-legged Hawk
Greater Roadrunner
Horned Lark
Scrub Jay
Black-billed Magpie
Black-capped Chickadee
Carolina Chickadee
Tufted Titmouse
Red-breasted Nuthatch
Pygmy Nuthatch
North American Dipper
Bewick's Wren
Curve-billed Thrasher
Eastern Bluebird
Mountain Bluebird
Golden-crowned Kinglet
Bohemian Waxwing
Western Meadowlark
Brewer's Blackbird
Great-tailed Grackle
Cassin's Finch
House Finch
Pine Siskin
American Goldfinch
Rufous-sided Towhee
Brown Towhee
Northern Junco
Gray-headed Junco
Field Sparrow
White-crowned Sparrow
Fox Sparrow
Lincoln's Sparrow
Song Sparrow

Across the street from Walt Anderson's office in Colusa, California, is the levee guarding the town from floods of the Sacramento River. Atop this levee at daybreak, January 17, Walt and I got Yellow-billed Magpie and Great Horned Owl. Birds were everywhere and in greater numbers per square mile than I had ever seen. Walt and I had eleven species before sunrise, forty-four at 9:00 A.M., seventy-five before lunch, and ninety-six at dark.

Walt has been a naturalist all his life but became serious about birding when he worked for the United States Fish and Wildlife Service on the National Bison Range in Montana. He graduated in wildlife biology from Washington State University and got a master's degree in the same field from the University of Arizona. In addition to experience as a biologist at federal refuges in Oregon, Washington, and Alaska, he has led tours to Mexico and Alaska.

In midmorning we went by outboard motor boat to the edge of Butte Sink, a 600-acre field flooded every winter ankle-deep to waist-deep in water. At times in the past, local birders have used aerial photos to estimate that this temporary lake contained 1,750,000 geese and ducks; we guessed that 500,000 were present during our visit. The most spectacular birds were white—huge flocks of Snow Geese, Ross's Geese, and Whistling Swans, many arriving over the Sink so high we couldn't see them with the naked eye and then dropping out of the sky as if shot.

Early in the day there were four species of blackbirds in the same tree, Yellow-headed, Red-winged, Tricolored, and Brewer's, and two new woodpeckers, Acorn and Lewis's, alongside the road within a few minutes of each other. As rain clouds gathered in late afternoon, we took a thirty-minute walk up a small canyon in Sutter Buttes and found Say's Phoebe, Rufous-crowned Sparrow, Varied Thrush, and Phainopepla—a pleasant way to end an exciting day.

Rich Stallcup and I had the biggest day of the year, with 111 species seen by both of us January 18 at Point Reyes, California, and vicinity. Near Bolinas, California, the highway has a wide lagoon on one side and steep slopes covered with chaparral on the other, so two very different habitats are clearly visible from roadside parking areas. To give you an idea of what this means, here is an excerpt from our chronological log of sightings: Canvasback, Wrentit, Black-bellied Plover. I have never before or since seen so many species from one observation post; Rich said that it was easy to see or hear forty species in one hour and that a total of eighty was possible in a full day.

Next came a remarkable bird-finding feat: Rich picked one accidental Common Skylark out of a flock of about 250 Lapland Longspurs and Horned Larks. The locale was a rain-soaked pasture full of cows at Point Reyes National Seashore. Slick bare spots, hoof prints six inches deep in the soft ground, and other common features of cow pastures made the going so treacherous that I had all I could handle to keep from falling or stepping in something. After searching for fifteen minutes, Rich called out, "There it goes. Did you see the different one?" I said, "No," but thought to myself, "Is he kidding? All I saw was a flock of small birds flying rapidly back and forth, around and around, up and down, and then disappearing as they lit." In a few minutes, however, he had the bird in the telescope in full sunlight, and I was able to examine it for several minutes with the field guide in my hands.

We ended the day with telescopes at Richardson Bay near Tiburon. Huge rafts of ducks and grebes seemed to stretch almost to the horizon, occasionally stirred into excitement as a harbor seal scared sections of a raft into flight.

This was my first experience with birding in a crowd of people. The shore of Richardson Bay was always full of pedestrians and joggers, and I was amazed at the great interest all of them showed in birding. Nearly every one of them stopped and asked what we were doing. When we said we were studying birds, they usually asked a flood of questions, and most of them wanted to look through the telescope. The superintendent of a small sewage plant adjacent to our observation point walked up and asked us to identify an unusual bird at one of his ponds; it was a Sora. What a change there has been since I began birding forty-five years ago; back then, most people who saw me looking through binoculars thought I was crazy!

At sunrise on January 19, we spotted a Merlin on a telephone pole next to the motel parking lot, and there were ten to fifteen species of shorebirds, ducks, and grebes in the flats below it. Thirty minutes later, back at Richardson Bay again, we found a Tufted Duck in the nearest raft of Canvasbacks. Then driving south along the coast highway below Half Moon Bay, we got Surfbird on the first rocks we looked at and two distant Marbled Murrelets off Pigeon Point. One lone Brant and the first Heermann's Gulls (the most beautiful gull so far) were in the harbor at Moss Landing.

Thanks to Rich's good telescope work, the harbor and Point Pinos at Monterey produced Arctic Loon, Brandt's Cormorant, Thin-billed Murre, Rhinoceros Auklet, Pigeon Guillemot, Wandering Tattler, Black Oystercatcher, and four Manx Shearwaters. One brilliant male Hermit Warbler and four Band-tailed Pigeons were in the pines in the hills above town.

There was a cold, strong, east wind on the morning of January 20, and we could see nothing unusual in Monterey Bay. What we needed was a twelve-knot wind from the northwest. Turning to the hills, Rich called a California Thrasher out of the chaparral, and I recorded my first sightings for the year of Hairy Woodpecker, Purple Finch, and Brown Creeper, although all of them occur regularly at my residence in Jackson, Mississippi.

The whole eight-day western swing left me in wonder at the skills of birding professionals. Although they know where to go and could get me there faster than I could make it on my own, that was not the big plus in using them. The remarkable contribution of all the men mentioned so far was their almost incredible eyesight and hearing. John Edscorn, my first guide, was always correct in identifying mere silhouettes on a telephone wire a half-mile away; Rich Stallcup, my last guide, immediately identified birds that flashed before our headlights as we drove to Muir Woods north of San Francisco before daybreak. Such unique skills enable a pro to sweep every locality with speed, accuracy, and thoroughness, and I realized how right I had been in deciding to use them in my race against the calendar.

In the California portion of the western swing, in addition to the birds mentioned above, I added the following new species for the year:

Red-throated Loon
Eared Grebe
Western Grebe
Pelagic Cormorant
Greater White-fronted Goose
Gadwall
Cinnamon Teal
Redhead
Greater Scaup
Barrow's Goldeneye
Bufflehead
White-winged Scoter
Surf Scoter
Black Scoter
White-tailed Kite
Cooper's Hawk
California Quail
Ring-necked Pheasant
Sandhill Crane
Virginia Rail
Sora
Black-necked Stilt
Snowy Plover
Whimbrel
Long-billed Curlew
Greater Yellowlegs
Mew Gull
Anna's Hummingbird
Common Flicker
Downy Woodpecker
Nuttall's Woodpecker
Black Phoebe
Chestnut-backed Chickadee
Plain Titmouse
Bushtit
Pygmy Nuthatch
Winter Wren
Marsh Wren
Rock Wren
Hermit Thrush
Western Bluebird
Ruby-crowned Kinglet
Water Pipit
Hutton's Vireo
Black-and-White Warbler
Orange-crowned Warbler
Townsend's Warbler
Lesser Goldfinch
Lark Sparrow
Golden-crowned Sparrow

4

CANADA AND PELAGIC TRIPS

In the year up to this point there had been plenty of excitement and frustration. The swings through Florida and the West had thrilled me with the spirit of the chase, but after each of them, I had to return home to take care of pressing business matters. Of the first twenty-four days I had spent only ten days birding. Therefore, I was full of anticipation when my sixteen-year-old son John and I took off January 25 for my first visit to the Maritime Provinces of Canada and my first experience with birds of the open ocean. We soon ran into the stone wall of bad weather. The Bangor, Maine, airport was closed by a violent winter storm most of the day, so we wasted the first day of our trip, remaining in Boston as unhappy guests of an unhappy airline. Things began to look up, however, when Davis Finch met us in Bangor on January 26 and drove us to Elm Lodge in Milltown, New Brunswick, where we enjoyed excellent food and rooms with the comfort of 1979 and the atmosphere of 1879 or 1779.

Davis Finch is, in the opinion of his peers, one of the three or four best birders in North America. He was first captured by birds at the age of nine, but they didn't get a firm grip on him until after he had carved out a career as a college teacher. He graduated from Yale in 1959 with a major in French, later did graduate work there, and held a Fulbright fellowship. Then he taught French for six years at Yale and four years at Vassar. Since 1971, however, he has been a birding professional and is now a partner in Northeast Birding with Will Russell and Rich Stallcup.

Peter Vickery of Massachusetts Audubon Society joined us the next morning as we headed toward Saint John, New Brunswick, in a steady, blowing, cold rain. The first bird to appear out of the half-light at Maces Bay was Great Black-backed Gull, and quickly thereafter we saw Purple Sandpiper, Iceland Gull, Common Eider, Oldsquaw, and Red-necked Grebe, a species we had looked hard for in California. Just as we left the area, Peter found a flock of twenty Snow Buntings about twenty yards away in the front yard of a house by the side of the road. In a few minutes Davis spotted a Pine Grosbeak at even closer range.

At Saint John we boarded the *Sir Robert Bond,* a 300-foot ferry ship to Digby, Nova Scotia, forty-five miles south over the Bay of Fundy, and I got my first taste of pelagic birding. For almost four hours, we stood amidships on the starboard side thirty feet above water level and stared at fifty square miles of heaving gray water, trying to see and identify fast-flying birds ranging in size from a small dove to a large duck. Even when Davis or Peter spotted a bird, he had a hard time describing its location to a greenhorn like me because there are no landmarks or reference points, nothing but water, water, and more water. Furthermore, flying birds often disappeared behind big waves, and sitting birds dove to feed or to escape the ship. These problems were aggravated by a 38-degree temperature, a steady breeze, and cold steel decks that made boots with felt liners essential. Worse weather would have made me want to stay home. I found it tiring, boring, and very difficult birding, but it was all worth it when I finally got good looks at Thick-billed Murre, Razorbill, and Dovekie.

In Digby Harbor, Davis quickly picked out a Lesser Black-backed Gull, a Code 2 bird that I had received many calls about. One Lesser Black-backed Gull has wintered at Digby for the last seven years or so. If it has been the same individual each year, how does it know it is supposed to go to Digby when October arrives, and how long do gulls live anyhow? If it isn't the same individual, how do the gulls arrange for a replacement every year but never send more than one?

Good luck in finding the gull allowed time for a fast drive southwest to Brier Island. With one eye on the road and the other out the window, Davis spotted six White-winged Crossbills clustered in the top of a small spruce, and then Peter found a Northern Shrike "teed-up" on a tree top 100 yards off the highway. Two short ferry crossings along the way produced good sightings of Black Guillemots. As the sun set and the rain began again, John drove us to Yarmouth and a meal of the best scallops I ever ate.

January 28 was a seven-hour vigil on an upper deck of the *Marine Evangeline,* a 361-foot ferry ship on the 200-mile run across the Atlantic Ocean from Yarmouth to Portland, Maine. Seas were calm, and no one was seasick. Birds were few and far between; we sometimes stood and watched as long as thirty minutes between sightings and then saw no more than a single bird. As the day wore on, we all got a little anxious because there had been nothing more than a few Northern Fulmars and murres. Then out of nowhere came a Northern Gannet, a bird I had missed in Florida and was worried about. It was in full white plumage and flew alongside about 200 yards away before slowly drawing away from the ship.

We still needed Atlantic Puffin, however; it was the target bird for the day. With less than an hour of daylight left, Davis leaned over the side and, with the cold wind in his face, stared through his binoculars at the water ahead of the bow without taking a break to rest his eyes. After thirty-five minutes of this, he shouted, "There it is, on the water, at 11:30 o'clock about fifty yards from the ship! It's a puffin, I think." I found the bird, and a puffin it was, and I got a species that might have required a return trip later this year.

Davis's determination to find a puffin and his complete concentration in "pulling" that bird out of the water were, I thought, marks of a true professional.

Pelagic birding proved how badly I needed a good pair of binoculars. For years I had been using a 7 × 35 glass with a zoom mechanism that allowed me to shift to 12 power. I knew the zoom feature was almost worthless; the gear was usually out of order, and the image fuzzy at 12 power anyhow. On the ocean I discovered two other severe limitations: the field of view was only 5.5 degrees, and the ocular lenses were set deep inside plastic eye-pieces. Since I have to wear eyeglasses to see anything more than the difference between night and day, my pupils were a long way from the ocular lenses. The combination of these features meant that I was trying to spot birds by the rough equivalent of looking through a rifle barrel, and this made pelagic birding almost impossible. I solved these problems by buying a lightweight 7 × 35 Nikon glass with a 7.3-degree field of view and ocular lenses nearly flush with the end of the barrel. I got one other advantage: I can focus on an object only twelve feet away.

January 29 was the Day of the Owls. The night before, we had learned through the intelligence network serving all avid birders that several Great Gray Owls had been seen in coastal New England, so we decided to scrap other plans and hunt for this hard-to-get species. Dennis Abbott met us at 7:00 A.M. and guided us to the woods where he had studied one owl for several hours a day on several days running and even recovered one of its pellets. Eight other birders from all over New England arrived soon thereafter, and although all of us searched the woods thoroughly for three and a half hours, we met with no success. Elisabeth Phinney of Portsmouth, New Hampshire, and I saw a Peregrine Falcon, but I didn't count the bird for the year because she had to leave before I could get her to sign my sighting ledger as a witness.

We then drove a short distance to Salisbury Beach State Park, where, in a circle with a radius of 200 yards and in less than thirty minutes, I saw three hawks and three owls. There was nothing special about a Northern Harrier, an American Kestrel, and a Rough-legged Hawk in such a situation. But I got excited about the owls: a Long-eared roosting about six feet off the ground in a small shrub, a Short-eared hunting over the marshes, and a Snowy first sitting on a hump of ice about fifty yards away and then flying directly overhead.

The most excitement, however, came at the Audubon Society's Ipswich River Sanctuary at Topsfield, Massachusetts. Walking a short distance in front of me, Davis suddenly dropped to the ground and pointed to a Great Gray Owl sitting about ten feet above ground in a thirty-foot tree only forty yards from us. It certainly saw our group of eight birders long before we saw it, but it seemed completely unafraid of us and did not take alarm when another group of thirteen birders came up behind us. The huge bird, without moving except to turn its head, completely dominated its surroundings. It seemed to be larger than the tree it was sitting in, the embodiment of the remote far north wilderness suddenly come to civilization and overpowering it.

We ended the day with a Mute Swan standing on a frozen pond and an unsuccessful search for Black-headed Gull. On the trip we saw fifty-nine species, of which twenty-six were new for the year for a total of 294. During January, I birded in nine states, two Canadian provinces, and five time zones.

On this trip, in addition to the birds mentioned above, I added the following new species for the year:

Great Cormorant
American Black Duck
Black-legged Kittiwake
White-breasted Nuthatch

5

THE FIRST CHASE AND SOUTH TEXAS

"Jim, this is Paul Sykes. There's a Key West Quail Dove in Everglades National Park. I saw the bird this morning and can tell you exactly how to find it."

These few words over the phone in the early evening of February 3 started my first "chase" of the year. By 8:00 P.M. Larry Balch of Chicago had agreed to go to Miami immediately and be on the ground looking for the bird by sunup, and Benton Basham of Chattanooga had decided to drive to Atlanta and fly down from there with me. I knew everything was going to work when my alarm failed to go off at 1:30 A.M. on February 4 but I woke up anyhow. After landing in Miami and driving for more than an hour, Benton and I, following Paul's directions, walked in about a half-mile on Snake Bite Trail near the park headquarters and we found Larry with the dove in his telescope and Bill and Jan Bolte and Wally George of Fort Lauderdale looking at it through binoculars and camera sights. At 9:45 A.M., in a cloud of mosquitoes in the low trees and tangled undergrowth of the Everglades, our chase ended in success.

The dove was beautiful in itself, slightly larger than a Mourning Dove, mainly rufous above with greenish and purplish irridescence on its crown, hindneck, and upper mantle and a white stripe below the eye. It was very tame. It sat, walked, fed, and flew in a small area within fifty feet of us (where it seemed to have stayed for several days) and appeared to be undisturbed by the seven of us and the large number of birders who had come to see it on February 3. But it was also beautiful to us because it is rare. This was only the third one seen in the United States in this century; the other sightings were in Florida in 1964 and 1966, and even in its natural range in the Bahamas, the dove is rarely seen on most of the islands.

We then drove to Flamingo, chartered a fast boat, and rode out over a glassy Florida Bay to see the Flamingos. There were four of them again, one slightly smaller and paler, and they seemed to be the same ones I saw January 1. They were a welcome sight to Larry because they brought his life list to 705; the dove had earlier brought Benton's to 705. As we headed back to Miami, I added Blue-gray Gnatcatcher, Northern Parula Warbler, and Indigo Bunting to my list for the year. In Kendall, Florida, we got Red-whiskered Bulbul but missed Spotted Oriole.

This whirlwind trip contained in one package what are, for me, the excitement, the joy, and the frustration of birding. The excitement came from the electrifying news that a real rarity had appeared, the frantic preparations to get planes, cars, and witnesses converging on the spot at the same time, and finally the frightening possibility that the bird would disappear before I saw it. The joy came from traveling over 1,250 miles to a point marked only by two trenches dug with the heel of Paul Sykes's boot in the damp earth of a primitive road cut through the huge Everglades swamp, and then finding one single bird smaller than a pigeon. The frustration came from missing for the second time Spotted Oriole, a species that occurs in large numbers in Kendall, is seen by many birders every day, and is reported to be very easily found in all the yards and parks of the city.

Gene Blacklock, coordinator of Environmental Education and Museum Curator at the Welder Wildlife Foundation, Sinton, Texas, my fourteen-year-old daughter Kimble, and I spent most of February 9 northeast of Corpus Christi, Texas, looking for and missing Greater Prairie Chicken. A flight delay was part of the reason we did not get to the booming grounds until 9:30 A.M., and early in the year the courtship displays do not last long. We visited and revisited several grounds during the day without a sign of a chicken.

Things went well at the Aransas Refuge, however; we got Wild Turkey near the headquarters and Whooping Crane from one of the roads, thereby saving the time required by the boat trip. Later in the day, Kimble spotted my first Mottled Ducks of the year, and we saw four pairs of Crested Caracaras and several soaring White-tailed Hawks.

At 5:00 A.M. on February 10, we were on our way to Santa Ana National Wildlife Refuge in search of four Hook-billed Kites reported there. Gene was certain that we actually saw the species, twice flying over the trees at long range and once sitting for a second in a nearby tree during a long walk through woods full of tree snails, the kite's only food. I was almost certain, but not certain enough to count the bird; in each sighting I failed to see enough to eliminate positively all other species. This was supreme frustration; we spent six hours either standing on lookouts or walking through the bare woods and, in the process, missed a chance to go to Falcon Dam for perhaps ten more new birds for the year.

Two hours after dark in 60-degree weather, we drove the roads of Bentsen Rio Grande Valley Park and saw and heard nothing. Then Gene put his tape recorder on the hood of the car and played a series of Pauraque calls. We got an immediate answer from close at hand. He played them again, and there were several answers. We repeated the same process with Screech Owl calls and got the same results. In less than fifteen minutes the roads were full of the bright red eyes of Pauraques and the ghostly figures of Common Screech Owls. One owl sat on a roadside sign and let us approach until our front bumper was only ten feet from him. The experience of calling strange, wild birds out of a warm, dark night captivated Kimble for the first time and charmed me for the umpteenth time.

February 11 was a day of little birds. After seeing such big birds as Mexican Crow, White-necked Raven, and Reddish

Egret in and near Brownsville, we headed back to Corpus Christi and hunted field after field along the highway for Sprague's Pipit. It occurs only singly in grass more than ankle deep and flushes perhaps seventy-five feet ahead of you. Then it flies around in circles like a longspur, drops suddenly into the grass, disappears immediately, and then apparently runs faster than a man can walk until it is far away from the place where you think it is. With time running out, we arrived at a dump near Gene's office and chased several birds back and forth across a huge pasture nearby until my tongue was hanging out. Just as I was about to surrender, one let us get close enough to examine it carefully. Without the help of someone like Gene, I'm sure I would have missed the bird and may never have noticed it at all. Compared to the pipit, the Grasshopper Sparrow we got on the way back to the car was a cinch. As we ended the day at Welder Wildlife Refuge, a beautiful 7800-acre area, Gene jumped a Le Conte's Sparrow that sat in a mesquite bush in full sunlight facing us for two or three minutes.

On this Texas trip we saw 146 species, of which forty-two were new for the year, so my total rose to 343. In addition to the birds mentioned above, I added the following new species for the year:

Least Grebe
Olivaceous Cormorant
White-faced Ibis
Black-bellied Whistling Duck
Blue-winged Teal
Harris's Hawk
Plain Chachalaca
Clapper Rail
Lesser Yellowlegs
Spotted Sandpiper
Red Knot
Stilt Sandpiper
Gull-billed Tern
Inca Dove
White-tipped Dove
Barred Owl
Golden-fronted Woodpecker
Yellow-bellied Sapsucker
Ladder-backed Woodpecker
Tropical Kingbird
Greater Kiskadee
Purple Martin
Green Jay
Cactus Wren
Long-billed Thrasher
Altamira Oriole
Bronzed Cowbird
Pyrrhuloxia
Olive Sparrow
Vesper Sparrow
Swamp Sparrow

Of the 168 species coded higher than 1, I had seen only three at this point: Lesser Black-backed Gull and Great Gray Owl (Code 2), and Key West Quail Dove (Code 7). Hook-billed Kite is only a Code 3, and many United States birders have never heard of species coded higher than 2. Therefore, although my list seemed to be near the halfway mark, in reality I had barely started. You can see why many birding experts thought I was attempting the impossible.

At this point my sighting ledger contained 343 signatures. From the first I kept a record of each sighting, thinking that some sightings of a greenhorn like me would need verification. I got a loose-leaf notebook that contained clear plastic envelopes large enough to hold eight-and-a-half-by eleven-inch sheets and listed all ABA species with spaces opposite them to record date, place, and signature of the witness of each first sighting. Such a ledger might prevent arguments about whether I really saw certain species, but it also unexpectedly produced an enormous amount of pleasure. Even when I had been at the project only six weeks and had fewer than half the signatures I would ultimately have, my ledger was already an irresistible invitation to day-dreaming, to remembering those who signed it and the events surrounding their signatures, and to relive some of the most enjoyable hours of my life. In no time, the ledger became one of my treasures.

6

FIRST BIRDING IN ARIZONA

Although it was still early in the year, I began to feel the pressure of a Big Year. There were signs that the waves of migration were not far off. A Barred Owl was incubating eggs in Texas; ducks were beginning courtship displays everywhere; Purple Martins were north of Corpus Christi; the dawn bird songs were growing so loud in Jackson that the secretaries in our office mentioned them. Soon would begin the feverish quest to see all migrants as they passed through singing and in nuptial plumage. Those I missed would have to be chased over their huge northern nesting grounds or picked up with great difficulty as they returned in the fall, silent and nondescript.

It was already clear how easy it was to miss a common bird. I had spent four hours looking for a Spotted Oriole in Kendall, Florida, and six hours looking for a Chipping Sparrow in Jackson, Mississippi, and failed both times. How much more of this was in store?

It was also clear how important the pelagic birds were: shearwaters, petrels, albatrosses, skuas, auklets, and murrelets. About fifty of these species could be seen only from boats fifty or so miles out in either the Pacific Ocean or the Atlantic north of Miami. Organized boat trips left from several ports on each coast during the seasons when pelagic birding was at its best, but many of them were scheduled for the same weekend, and I could not be in San Diego, California, and Ocean City, Maryland, at the same time, or in either of them while I was in Alaska.

To reduce the pressure, my fourteen-year-old son Stewart and I met Kenn Kaufman at 4:30 A.M., February 23, in Tucson, Arizona, and began a three-day hunt for nine target species and as many others as possible. At sunup with a heavy frost on the ground we were in the grasslands east of Patagonia coursing back and forth through patches of Andropogon grass looking for Baird's Sparrow, a target species. We spent almost an hour in two separate walks without jumping a single sparrow or new species of any kind. A fifteen-inch snowfall and near-zero temperatures in December and similar weather in late January either wiped out the sparrows or chased them south into Mexico. As we left the area in disappointment, our spirits got a lift when five Pronghorns appeared from behind a slight rise about 150 yards from the car.

We drove slowly back toward Patagonia with the windows down in spite of the chill and jammed on the brakes each time one of us saw or heard something unusual. There were many birds around a ranch headquarters, and in less than ten minutes, we added Gray-breasted Jay and Brown-headed Woodpecker to my year's list and Curve-billed Thrasher, Bewick's Wren, American Robin, Say's Phoebe, Rock Wren, and Lewis's Woodpecker to our trip list. A short distance down the road, I saw the year's first Chipping Sparrow, a species that is usually a cinch in Jackson, Mississippi, but one I had missed on several occasions since January 1. Just before we reached Patagonia, we parked and walked up a dry, rocky ravine that Kenn said was ideal habitat for Black-chinned Sparrows. He was right; it took only five minutes to find one.

Our next stop was one of the best-known birding spots in Arizona, The Nature Conservancy's Patagonia-Sonoita Creek Sanctuary southwest of the town of Patagonia, a 312-acre tract that extends along Sonoita Creek for one and a half miles. Most of it is covered with a stand of huge cottonwood trees ninety feet tall and two feet in diameter, some of the largest trees I saw in Arizona. By noon the temperature was near 60 degrees, and we combined birding with a picnic lunch of Vienna sausages, crackers, and cookies on the hood of the car. I enjoyed it as much as Stewart did. We had hoped to see several species of small flycatchers, but all we got for the year were Verdin, Green-tailed Towhee, and Gila Woodpecker.

With Kenn driving while Stewart and I dozed, we arrived at the headquarters of a large ranch north of Nogales at 2:00 P.M. and spent an hour searching the ponds, pastures, and wooded areas for small flycatchers or perhaps an early migrant. We found nothing until we ran into several Violet-green Swallows on the way out.

Kenn had been worried about Pinyon Jays all day. He said they were large and noisy and traveled in flocks, but somehow we had missed them that morning. Since they might be tough to find outside Arizona, we returned to Patagonia and headed east over our route of the early morning with the windows down. Suddenly Kenn spoke softly, "Stop the car. I hear them." I got out and heard nothing. He said, "I'm sure they're on top of this ridge on my side of the road. Let's go up and see." He was right again. After climbing up 100 feet and then walking a quarter mile, we found fifty of them feeding on acorns.

By this time I was very tired. Stewart and I had not reached our motel until 11:30 P.M. the night before and then had started out with Kenn at 4:30 A.M. I was physically ready to call it a day, but it was only 4:00 P.M., and there were two hours of daylight left. We went back to the Sonoita Creek Sanctuary and walked along the abandoned railroad right-of-way. Just at dusk we found what we had been looking for since mid-morning, Hammond's Flycatcher, and in a few more minutes, Bridled Titmouse. No one had to urge us to go to bed at 9:00 P.M.

Soon after sunup on February 24, we checked the sanctuary again and found nothing new. We then drove to Nogales, and while Kenn was calling several local birders to see whether there were any rarities around, Stewart walked to the Mexican border on the main street, stuck his arm through the turnstile, and became the second Vardaman child to get at least partway into a foreign country. The Nogales birders reported no rarities, so we drove to Tucson. About halfway there we spotted a flock of Gambel's Quail along the highway.

We grabbed take-out hamburgers at a McDonald's in Tucson and then drove to the eastern edge of the city to a spot along the river near the Tanque Verde Guest Ranch, where our family had spent a short spring vacation in 1974. In two hours we found four new birds for the year: Abert's Towhee, Black-throated Sparrow, Rufous-winged Sparrow, and White-throated Swift. Since the Catalina Mountains were close by, we drove up into them as fast as the traffic and winding roads would permit, and in less than an hour after leaving the river, we saw some snow, a Tassel-eared Squirrel, and the first Mexican Junco and Red Crossbill of the year.

We ended the day's birding at a sewage treatment plant west of Tucson where the sprinklers and ponds created an oasis in the desert. The grounds were full of birds, but the only new one was a brilliant male Vermilion Flycatcher. By 7:00 P.M. we were at our motel in Phoenix where Stewart and I had a dinner engagement with my high-school sweetheart and her husband.

Kenn got us going before dawn February 25; he said we must be on the ground if we wanted to catch the thrashers singing. It was chilly and windy. On a perfectly flat salt-bush desert ten miles south of Phoenix, there was nothing to obstruct the view for miles in any direction except a few scattered mesquite trees less than eight feet tall, and there seemed to be no birds at all. As the sun rose, however, we discovered that the ground and bushes were full of small birds, and we soon added Black-tailed Gnatcatcher, Sage Sparrow, and Brewer's Sparrow. Then we heard the first distant thrasher song. I could barely hear it and saw nothing at all. But Kenn set up the telescope and, by very careful searching, eventually spotted Bendire's Thrasher and then Le Conte's Thrasher singing from the tops of mesquites.

Then came the highlight of the trip. We drove to the home of Mrs. Retha A. Beveridge, northwest of Phoenix, where she had a hummingbird feeder only twenty inches away from a large picture window. The window was covered with a plastic film that reflected light, so people inside could see out but the birds outside couldn't see in. This feature allowed Stewart to hold his camera against the window and take pictures of a Costa's Hummingbird, a new bird for the year, that came to the feeder twice. I was just as enchanted as he was, for I have never seen any hummingbird at such close range for such a long period. We saw Inca Doves in Mrs. Beveridge's yard at the same time and spotted a Northern Mockingbird nearby.

We ended the birding soon after noon at a ranch west of Phoenix with the first Crissal Thrasher of the year and then dashed for the airport. We got five of the target species we were hunting for, twenty-seven new species for the year, and 103 for the trip list. As I boarded the plane, my total was 370.

My success on this trip was certainly due in large part to Kenn Kaufman. Like all birding pros, Kenn has extraordinarily keen eyes and ears and his own style. He lives in Arizona because he likes warm climates, but he picked Tucson because the University of Arizona there has a great ornithology library that is open twenty hours a day. That Kenn has absorbed much of this library shows in his birding. He has learned all about the habitats of Arizona, where they are located, and what birds are present in each one at any one time. Therefore, when he wants to see a certain species, he goes directly to the correct habitat and then searches it deliberately, patiently, and very intensively until he comes up with the bird. He couldn't keep the snow and cold from chasing off the Baird's Sparrows, but if the birds had been there, he surely would have found them. These abilities make him invaluable to any birder with limited time.

"The White-cheeked Pintail is back at Laguna Atascosa."

George Clayton of Houston, Texas, called me with this third-hand report the morning after I got back from Arizona, and when John Arvin confirmed it later in the day with the refuge manager, I caught a plane for McAllen, Texas, and my second "chase" of the year was on, this time after this duck from the Bahamas, a Code 5 bird. I lost. John and I arrived at Laguna Atascosa National Wildlife Refuge about sunup on February 28, and we knew we were the first visitors of the day because coyote tracks were superimposed on all the other tracks in the sandy roads. During the next five hours, we examined the duck's favorite marsh four times from the roads and slogged across it three times through ankle-deep mud and water. We also searched all similar habitats nearby. The bird is distinctively marked and easy to identify, and we saw nothing that even remotely resembled it.

The bird we hunted for was almost surely the same one that showed up last November and then vanished soon after Christmas. John said that the species had never been recorded in Texas before, so he thought that the same bird was merely wandering around the area. It had plenty of room to wander; there are 7,000 acres of water and marsh in the refuge total of 45,000 acres and additional areas on adjacent private lands. Our task was to find one lone duck among the hundreds of thousands scattered over a huge area, so you can understand why we missed it. This was frustrating because it apparently did not wander during November and December; hundreds of birders, without leaving their cars, had little trouble finding it in the ditch along the road and the adjacent marsh.

So as not to come up empty-handed for the day, we broke off the hunt at noon and drove to Santa Ana National Wildlife Refuge to look for Hook-billed Kites again. Here our task was to find two birds (a pair and, so far as we knew, the only two in the United States) on only 2,000 acres. But these birds are shy and elusive, and since they eat snails found on trunks and lower branches of trees, they seldom fly high in the sky. The 2,000 acres were covered with a dense growth of small trees, bushes, and vines where visibility was often less than fifty feet. We missed again.

We found one good species, however: Tropical Parula Warbler, a Code 3 bird, and four new ones for the year: American Bittern, Groove-billed Ani, Solitary Vireo, and Black-throated Green Warbler. At the end of February, my list for the year stood at 375.

7
PLANS AND CHASES

As soon as I began to miss common species, I became uneasy about whether the original itinerary provided enough chances to see all Code 1 birds, especially those I was unfamiliar with. When I discussed how to find certain species with members of my planning group, I discovered that no one knew everything about all species and that, when two people knew a species well, they often had different ideas about how to find it most easily. If some changes in the itinerary were required, I needed to know about them before the birds came streaming northward in spring migration. To solve problems of this kind, the original planning group seemed too large and too informal (especially since it was a volunteer group), so, in mid-February, I appointed a formal Strategy Council made up of these members:

Will Russell, Seal Harbor, Maine, a partner in Northeast Birding, a bird tour group, and a student of bird distribution and abundance in the ABA area all his life.

Paul W. Sykes, Jr., Delray Beach, Florida, a U.S. Fish and Wildlife Service biologist working with endangered species and a birder with the second highest ABA list.

Lawrence G. Balch, Chicago, Illinois, a college mathematics teacher, the operator of bird tours to Alaska, and a birder with the fourth highest ABA list.

John C. Arvin, McAllen, Texas, a birding professional who has lived in the Rio Grande valley for more than twenty-five years and who often leads tours to Mexico.

Kenn Kaufman, Tucson, Arizona, holder of the Big Year record from

1973 to 1976; the editor of *Continental Birdlife,* a bi-monthly journal of North American ornithology; and the outstanding bird pro of Arizona.

Richard W. Stallcup, Inverness, California, a partner in Northeast Birding, president of Western Field Ornithologists, and author of *Pelagic Birds of Monterey Bay, California.*

These men were not only birding experts but were also located around the perimeter of the ABA area where accidentals were most likely to occur. Furthermore, like all top listers, Sykes and Balch maintained private, informal, national intelligence networks to get quick news about rare birds. Each had birding friends all over the ABA area who would call them whenever a rarity showed up, and both kept these friendships active by means of frequent telephone calls. While birders were becoming interested in my project and therefore willing to respond to my plea, "Call Collect, Ask for Birdman," these two networks and all six of these men would help ensure that I learned whenever accidentals appeared.

When we missed four of the nine target birds of the Arizona trip, I decided that we needed to review the itinerary quickly, so I called the Strategy Council to a session in Jackson, Mississippi, March 3 and 4. During work sessions that ran for hours, we prepared an itinerary for the rest of the year and then checked it against the complete list of unseen birds (except Codes 6 and7) to make sure that I would be in position to see all Codes 1 and 2 and have a good chance at all others.

At the end of this long session, someone mentioned that a Siberian Chickadee was coming to a feeder at Edmonton, Alberta. Thinking that the itinerary provided enough chances for me to see the species, I asked, more or less to be making conversation, "Should I chase it?" There was a dead silence, followed by laughter; then Larry Balch spoke up, "Well, nobody on this council has ever seen one." I called Delta Air Lines for reservations.

I traveled 5,000 miles to Edmonton, Alberta, and got help from five other birders to see one bird only five inches long, the Siberian Chickadee. Even though it was only a Code 2 bird, I chased it because it was nearly impossible to reach its normal range and find it once you get there.

There also seemed to be only a small chance of failure; the bird had been in McKenzie Ravine and coming to the same feeder for four months. I took it as a good omen when, as I settled into my seat in Minneapolis for the long flight to Edmonton, I heard someone call my name and looked up to see Davis Finch and Cloe Mifsud, a freelance editor from New York, on their way to see the same bird.

By 7:45 A.M. of March 7 we had joined Wayne Neily, a biologist from Winnipeg, and two birders from Edmonton, Eric Tull, an environmental consultant, and Terry Thormin, a foreground artist at the Provincial Museum of Alberta. For an hour we stood in the snow on the edge of the ravine, strained our eyes at the feeder attached to a window about forty feet away, and listened in vain for chickadee calls from the dense timber below. All this effort produced nothing but one Black-capped Chickadee.

Finally, we decided to search the ravine, a formidable task. The sides were covered with snow and dropped at a 45-degree angle to a flat bottom about twenty feet wide and 100 feet below us. I made it to the bottom without breaking my neck only by hanging on to spruce and aspen trees at every step. We found nothing on the way down or in the bottom, so all of us headed back up. I discovered I was not in shape for climbing slopes, especially snow-covered ones, and I was breathing so hard when I reached the top that I hoped someone would suggest that we wait for the bird to come to the feeder.

Before the suggestion came, however, Eric shouted from below, "I've got it," and there was a mad scramble down again, with me making about fifteen feet of it on the seat of my pants. All of us soon had our glasses on the Siberian Chickadee, perhaps the hardest-to-see North American breeder. Very pale, brown-capped, the "Little Ghost of McKenzie Ravine" was spending the winter with eight or ten

Black-capped Chickadees 1,500 miles from its normal range. It was as tame as chickadees are apt to be, and we got to study it well not only at this time but also about a half-hour later at the feeder and once again when we returned to the ravine in the afternoon to search for Black-backed Three-toed Woodpecker.

This tiny bird of the far north would have been easy to overlook. It was not a pink or green chickadee that would stand out like a neon sign demanding attention from any casual observer. It was just a paler chickadee that was brown where others in the same flock were black, and its actions were like those of chickadees everywhere. We were lucky that the man who operated the feeder was a careful observer and spotted a real rarity. Birding needs many others like him; all the leading birders I've met said that if we could double the number of careful observers in the field, we might triple or quadruple the number of rarities found.

A rare bird like a Siberian Chickadee could appear to any birder anywhere anytime. Its presence so very far from its normal range was totally unexpected. You might expect a bird to wander from the Bahamas to the east coast of Florida or from Central America to our Gulf Coast, but how and why would one fly 1,500 miles over millions of possible wintering places just as suitable as residential Edmonton—and much closer to home?

Next we drove to the north side of the Industrial Airport and, in the open spaces around a railroad yard, found a flock of Gray Partridges. After dark we tried for owls along a road across a bog west of Edmonton, but the wind was blowing so hard that it drowned out other sounds. Getting under way well before dawn on March 8, we made a 200-mile circuit out to the west. Soon after full daylight we encountered a male Spruce Grouse feeding on the shoulder of the road. It was unbelievably tame; I walked to within ten feet of it before it flew. A short time later we found my first Common Redpoll close enough to see well.

The most abundant birds in Edmonton were Bohemian

Waxwings. The 1978 Christmas Bird Count showed more than 18,000 of them, and we continually saw flocks of fifty to 250. How many other cities of the world can claim this distinction? Black-billed Magpies were common, but all other birds were scarce. Counting Rock Doves, House Sparrows, and one Starling, we saw only sixteen species in one and a half days.

I quit birding in Edmonton at noon on March 8 and resumed it exactly twenty-four hours later with Paul Sykes in Delray Beach, Florida, about 3,750 miles away. During this twenty-four-hour period, I not only traveled between the two cities but also flew from Atlanta to Jackson, introduced myself to Virginia and the children, bathed, shaved, changed clothes, slept, and flew back to Atlanta. You can see that, without commercial jet planes, a Big Year of 700 species would be impossible.

Paul and I tried for Spotted Oriole and then for Little Gull at Fort Pierce and missed both. Just as we got ready for bed, we got Chuck-will's-widow outside Paul's house. Before dawn of March 10 we were at Loxahatchee National Wildlife Refuge walking toward a water impoundment area near the southeast corner and were greeted upon arrival by a female Masked Duck swimming in the canal inside the fence, only seventy-five feet away and completely oblivious to us. A few minutes later we spotted Purple Gallinule and Least Bittern. We returned to Delray Beach, and at 8:42 A.M., to my great relief, I finally saw a Spotted Oriole. Then our luck ran out. Although we drove another 250 miles near Lake Okeechobee hunting for Swallow-tailed Kite and Fulvous Whistling Duck, we saw many birds but nothing new. We ran up a list of 73 species with ease, but only five were new, bringing my total to 384.

Paul's success in leading me to the Masked Duck helped me learn some things I had been doing wrong for years. Time and time again I had searched for Masked Duck in the rafts of ducks on ponds and marshes on the Texas coast once the sun was well up. I never saw it because, in the first place,

I was looking in the wrong state; in recent years it has been found most regularly in Florida. In the second place, it rarely ventures onto open water or consorts with other ducks; it skulks among cattails and other vegetation like a gallinule. In the third place, it is active only at night or after sunset or before sunrise; it seldom shows itself during usual birding hours. If I had taken the time to study the Masked Duck's life style as much as Paul has, I would have seen it long ago. This is another illustration of what an outstanding birding pro can teach an amateur.

In both Edmonton and Delray Beach I heard reports about three Whooper Swans on Lake Ontario near Toronto, and since these beautiful European swans are often bred in captivity, I called Richard Ryan in New Jersey, my authority on birds that may have escaped from zoos or breeders.

I chose him to sort out the foreign birds because he has been in the zoo business for twenty years, has made several trips collecting live birds in Central America for zoo exhibits, and served two years as a manager for an import company specializing in birds and reptiles. For the past fifteen years he has been Director of the Turtle Back Zoo, West Orange, New Jersey, and a regular contributor to *Birding* on escaped, released, and introduced birds. Dick reported that he was 99 percent sure they were wild birds. He said that he had talked to all nearby breeders and found no swans missing, that the swans were worth about $450 each, and that every breeder he knew would have raised a hue and cry if he had lost even one. In addition, he said that the birds were not banded, and that immature birds such as these were much more likely to wander than adults. After calling Dr. D. R. Gunn of Oakville, Ontario, to verify that they were still there, I hopped a plane for Canada again.

Davis Finch and I arrived simultaneously in Toronto in midafternoon on March 16 and then discovered that Paul Sykes's plane from Miami was so late that he wouldn't arrive until 5:00 P.M. Afraid to wait for him, we dashed to Oakville, picked up Piet Van Dyken as a guide, and drove to the boat ramp at a small city park on the shore of Lake Ontario. There were our birds, three immature Whooper Swans near the shoreline with one adult Whistling Swan, six or eight Canada Geese, twenty-five or thirty Mallards, and two Buffleheads. Since we found our target birds so quickly, we rushed back to the airport, found Paul while he was looking for us inside the terminal, overcame the rush-hour traffic in time for him to see the birds before sundown, and then got him back to the airport for an 8:20 P.M. plane to Edmonton. The Whooper Swan was 716 on his list, so he tied Paul DuMont for top spot among ABA birders in Toronto and then passed him when he got the Siberian Chickadee in Edmonton March 17.

Whooper Swans breed near the North Pole and almost never show up near populated parts of North America. According to Davis, one was collected in Maine many, many years ago and there have been a few sightings on the westernmost Aleutian Islands in more recent times. Since the nearest breeding ground for the species is probably Iceland, these birds were even farther from their normal range than the chickadee was. And since they are raised in captivity, they might have been escapees, which would, under ABA rules, make them ineligible in a Big Year. I counted the Whooper Swans in spite of this because of Dick Ryan's judgment and other factors.

Swan families usually stay together from the end of one breeding season until the start of the next. All the experts told me that, being immatures, these three birds probably came from the same nest and were separated from their parents in some way, perhaps even lost (if that's possible for a bird). They were first spotted in the harbor at Hamilton, Ontario, in early December and then disappeared until they showed up in their present location a few days before Dr. Gunn photographed them December 28. They and the other species in the same flock wandered up and down the coast but seemed to return often to the place where we saw them because someone was scattering corn on the shore at this point.

The Whistling Swan had been with them from the beginning, and its presence was also unusual; Dr. Gunn told us that Whistling Swans almost never wintered in Toronto. It was surely a wild bird; Dick Ryan reported that he knew of no breeders of this species and that it was rarely kept in captivity. I wondered how the four swans got together in the first place. And did the old whistler lead the three young whoopers, or did it just tag along on their wanderings?

But it was hard for me to believe that three birds, so large and so valuable and all from the same brood, had escaped from captivity over three months ago without being missed and hunted by their owner. It was also hard for me to believe that any owner of such birds would allow them to reach full size without banding them. That they allowed me to come close to them did not detract from their wildness; I got much closer to the Key West Quail Dove in Florida and the Spruce Grouse in Alberta.

Whooper Swans do not breed their first summer after hatching; they merely return to their normal summer range and consort with other Whoopers of the same age. How would these birds ever find their way back? Were the urge to return and the directions implanted in their genes?

I went all the way to Toronto to add one bird to my list and knew before I went that there was little chance to see more. Why did I go? Because I was after 700, not to do the best I could or to break the existing record, but to see 700 species. And since I had only 726 possibilities, I had to chase Whooper Swans and Siberian Chickadees; the chances of seeing them again in 1979 were almost zero.

In my chases of rarities up to this point, three things intrigued me. The first was that someone could give me such good directions to the location of one single bird that I could travel thousands of miles and still find it. Although I couldn't make an appointment with a bird and therefore it would not be expecting me, I had better luck finding birds than I would have in finding humans under the same conditions. The second thing was how long these rare wanderers remained in areas where they suddenly appeared. The Siberian Chickadee had spent almost six months in Edmonton; the Whooper Swans had been near Toronto for almost three months; the Key West Quail Dove was still in the Everglades six weeks after I saw it. The third thing was how slowly and yet how rapidly the news of rarities could spread through the birding world. On one hand, I didn't hear about the chickadee until five months after its discovery; yet on the other, I got news of the dove only ten days after it was found.

A reporter who interviewed me when I returned from Alberta thought that humans' effect on birds had been completely adverse and asked me whether I had noticed it. I am not sure about our total impact on birds, but it is clear that we have created ideal habitats for many species, which in turn has caused greater concentrations of them. The Bohemian Waxwings were abundant in Edmonton because food was plentiful on ornamental trees and shrubs there; they were much less numerous outside the city. White-necked Ravens, Mexican Crows, and several gulls occur in great numbers at the city dump of Brownsville, Texas, and dumps and sewage treatment plants are favorite birding spots everywhere. The geese and ducks I got in Oklahoma, Texas, and Colorado were there because humans, in one way or another, kept the water from freezing; the Spotted Oriole can't make it anywhere except among the lawns and gardens of Florida cities. Even in the Patagonia-Sonoita Creek Sanctuary in Arizona, the abandoned railroad bed and the tangle of brush under the adjacent telephone lines were the best places for some species and increased the variety of habitats offered by the sanctuary. Humans and some birds certainly get along well together.

8

SPRING MIGRATION BEGINS

An adult male Garganey came to Riverside, California, gave many local birders a chance to see a rare visitor from Europe, and then left without my permission. I heard of his arrival through calls from Ed Johnson, president of Riverside Audubon Society, and Guy McCaskie, Imperial Beach, California, and flew there directly from a timber-cruising job near Albany, Georgia. From soon after sunup until almost noon on March 29, Ed and Donna Johnson, Dorothy Tribbett, Virginia Patterson, Mildred Smith, and I inspected carefully and often every duck in three big ponds filled with Green-winged and Cinnamon Teals, Northern Shovelers, Common Pintails, and other species, finally flushing most of them by getting too close. The Garganey was nowhere to be seen. The only new birds we turned up for the year were Barn Swallow and Western Kingbird.

Hoping to make my trip pay off by finding Yellow-headed Parrot, we spent the short time left in the Los Angeles Arboretum near Pasadena. We missed again. An arboretum supervisor with some knowledge of birds told me that a flock of Amazon parrots lives in the surrounding area and visits the arboretum every day, usually in the early morning but never on a predictable schedule. He said they are very noisy and are easily heard when they are nearby; whenever we listened, all we could hear was the public-address announcer at the Santa Anita Racetrack across the road. We did, however, find two more new ones for the year at the arboretum: Northern Oriole and Spotted Dove.

My lack of luck in Los Angeles made the plane trip back to Jackson seem three or four times as long as the one going out. Although new birds were always welcome, I just couldn't get excited about the four we got. After all, Northern Oriole nests in a neighbor's yard; Barn Swallows raise a brood in every highway culvert and bridge in Mississippi; Western Kingbirds are all over the West; Spotted Doves are so common in the Los Angeles area that they can probably be picked up by driving the freeways. But because Yellow-headed Parrot occurs only in Los Angeles, I had to go back into the center of the metropolitan area to search for one species when I could have been elsewhere getting several. And I also wondered whether I had missed Garganey for the year; it was a Code 3 bird, and although I might have a chance to see it in Alaska, it had not been spotted there in 1978 by my tour group. Sometimes you win, sometimes you lose, sometimes the birds are predictable, sometimes they aren't—I could only be philosophical about my luck and comfort myself with the thought that this was what made the project a challenge.

During March I added only fifteen new birds to raise my total to 390. But one of them, Northern Oriole, a very common species all over the United States and not worth going all the way to Los Angeles to see, deserves a momentary digression because it illustrates a key point of the ABA Checklist.

Northern Oriole does not appear in any bird field guides I own. In my books, birds now called by this name are called either Baltimore or Bullock's Orioles and are treated as two species. If you will look at pictures of them, you can see one reason why this distinction was made. The plumages are so different that most birders have no difficulty in separating them quickly. Some think that these differences arose because one population was split in two by glaciers of the Ice Age, and each half went its separate way in evolution. Yet Baltimore and Bullock's Orioles are now considered to be one species, Northern Oriole, and this brings up questions important to all birders: What is a species, and how do species get lumped or split?

A species is made up of all individuals that interbreed readily and produce fertile offspring, or that would do so if opportunity permitted. When this kind of breeding takes place, the offspring will show characteristics of both parents with all kinds of variations in between, and these variations will show up generation after generation.

It is not enough for two individuals to produce offspring; the offspring must also be fertile. Although the mating of a horse and a donkey will produce offspring (mules), mules are not fertile, so horses and donkeys belong to separate species. And finally, it is not even enough for the offspring to be fertile. They must also be able to breed freely with either parent type and spread their genes among the population of both parent types where they meet.

In a paper written in 1938, Dr. George M. Sutton noted the possible hybridization between Baltimore and Bullock's Orioles, and this work led to an extensive study of the matter by Drs. Charles G. Sibley and Lester L. Short, Jr. These two scientists collected adult orioles in the Great Plains during the breeding seasons of 1954 and 1957 and studied them, along with others collected earlier. In all there were 634 specimens, 602 adult males from thirty-nine localities and thirty-two females from seventeen localities, all from the zone where ranges of the two species overlapped. Sibley and Short discovered that, in this zone, most of the orioles were hybrids with all gradations between parent types present. This meant that there were no barriers to interbreeding, that their genetic heritage was much the same, and that, therefore, the two were actually one species. If the zone had contained mostly pure parent types with only a few hybrids, this would have meant that there were some barriers to interbreeding and that the two parent types were probably different enough genetically to be considered separate species. Sibley and Short recommended that the two be lumped into one, and the American Ornithologists' Union (AOU), accepted their recommendation in 1973. The authors of field guides will undoubtedly make this change as new editions are published. Since I saw both Baltimore and Bullock's Orioles, I could have counted them as two species if I had tried my Big Year in 1972.

Scientists have an easy time when they can observe the results of interbreeding, but this isn't possible when two populations are separated, as are the Scrub Jays of Florida and California. In such a case, in addition to evidence revealed by specimens, they must rely on likeness in behavior, type of displays, kinds of sounds the birds make, types of ectoparasites on their bodies, ecological requirements, methods of feeding, types of nests, structure of their egg-white proteins, or other distinguishing traits yet to be discovered. Ornithological research goes on continuously and produces new facts that change old ways of looking at things. By their insatiable curiosity, the very scientists who decided that Baltimore and Bullock's Orioles were one species may discover new information that would indicate that their earlier conclusions were incorrect, and the present one species will be split in two again. They won't be vacillating or indulging whims in their ivory towers; they will be recognizing new and important scientific discoveries.

One of the world's most distinguished ornithologists demonstrated what great lengths these researchers will go to. Dr. Wesley E. Lanyon, Chairman of the Department of Ornithology, American Museum of Natural History, New York, did some of his early work on whether Eastern and Western Meadowlarks were separate species. Although their songs were different, these two birds seemed quite alike in every other way to a routine birder like me. I had often wondered why they were listed as separate species. To find out for sure, Dr. Lanyon, between 1966 and 1978, induced twenty-five captive meadowlarks to pair and produce forty-four clutches of 158 eggs. Mixed matings (one Eastern and one Western) resulted in 90 percent fertility, whereas the fertility of eggs of matings of hybrids was only 10 percent. It was easy for an

Eastern and a Western Meadowlark to produce offspring, but 90 percent of the eggs of these hybrid offspring were infertile (never hatched). Although a small fraction of the offspring were fertile, it was obvious that there were barriers to interbreeding and that the parent types were different enough genetically to be considered separate species.

Most professional ornithologists in North America belong to the American Ornithologists' Union (AOU), the most prestigious ornithological society in the United States, founded at the American Museum of Natural History in 1883, and with a present membership of more than 3,000. Dr. Lanyon is a past president of it. Scientists publish their findings in *The Auk,* AOU's quarterly journal, in articles often too technical for ordinary birders to enjoy or even understand. That doesn't mean they are unimportant. The findings of these ornithologists are on the point of humanity's probe into the unknown and should carry great weight. Using all its scientific data, the AOU has been publishing a checklist of bird species for many years and brings it up to date at frequent intervals; the ABA follows the AOU lead in this matter.

Ruth Downey goes birding almost 365 mornings a year in the bottom-land hardwoods lining the Pearl River in Jackson, Mississippi, and as a result she knows more than anyone else about what species are present there each day and exactly where they can be found. To give me my first local taste of the spring migration, Ruth, Frances Wills, and I spent three hours in Riverside Park in Jackson on April 6 and got Brown-headed Nuthatch, Wood Thrush, Red-eyed Vireo, and three warblers, Prothonotary, Pine, and Yellow-throated.

On April 9, soon after 8:00 A.M., my eleven-year-old daughter Emily and I drove to Attwater Prairie Chicken Refuge near Eagle Lake, Texas, picked up Wayne Shifflett, the manager, and no more than fifteen minutes later climbed an observation tower to see four Greater Prairie Chickens on the booming grounds about 100 yards away. Compared to my fruitless search for hours on a cold, windy day in mid-February, getting the bird this way seemed like child's play. And, as an extra bonus, when we returned to the headquarters, there was a Scissor-tailed Flycatcher perched on the parking lot fence.

At noon Emily and I met John Arvin in San Antonio and headed immediately for the north edge of the city, to Friedrich Park, an area of more than 200 acres of virgin Texas hill country covered with large patches of oaks and junipers. Although we looked hard until 4:00 P.M., the woods were still as a tomb, and we found only one Nashville Warbler. But since there was still plenty of daylight, we drove south on Texas Highway 16 to the McMullen County line and saw Cave Swallows and Barn Swallows building nests under a highway bridge.

Hardly an auspicious beginning, but in the next two days we hit the birding equivalent of a grand-slam home run. Look at these sightings:

April 10	6:30 A.M.	Golden-cheeked Warbler
	8:43 A.M.	Black-capped Vireo
	4:30 P.M.	Cassin's Sparrow
	5:01 P.M.	White-cheeked Pintail (Code 5)
	5:45 P.M.	Wilson's Phalarope
April 11	10:39 A.M.	Hook-billed Kite (Code 3)
	1:13 P.M.	Red-billed Pigeon (Code 2)
	1:14 P.M.	Ringed Kingfisher
	1:29 P.M.	Brown Jay
	1:46 P.M.	Black-headed Oriole

A combination of luck and timing was responsible for this fine series of sightings.

At first light on April 10 we were back in Friedrich Park, and this time there were Golden-cheeked Warblers everywhere. John "pished" up a male and female almost before they woke up, and even though it was cool, windy, and foggy, we soon heard many males singing. (Pishing is making noises with your mouth that sound like you are saying, "Pisssh,

pisssh, pisssh." These sounds excite the curiosity of many birds, and they will come quite close to investigate them, thereby giving you a good look at birds otherwise hard to see.) Climbing to the ridge top, we began scrambling through thick brush and over rocky slopes chasing distant vireo songs. After two hours of this hard work, we suddenly heard close at hand a Black-capped Vireo singing his heart out, and although he dodged us for a while in the thickets, he finally perched on top of a bush at eye level about twenty feet away and sang until we almost got tired of looking at him. He was just about the prettiest vireo I ever saw.

Elated at such quick success, we headed for Laguna Atascosa National Wildlife Refuge at faster-than-legal speed. The marshes that John and I slogged through in February were now dry, and the few remaining ducks and shorebirds were concentrated in small areas. While driving toward one of them along the road by the shore of the bay, we saw a Cassin's Sparrow do his "skylark" routine, flying up from a perch and then gliding down, singing all the time. Soon we reached a large pond and began to examine every duck on it. We saw nothing but American Coots, Blue-winged Teals, and Northern Shovelers. We walked slowly around the pond. One lone duck jumped up, and John shouted, "There he is." Sure enough, there he was, flying across our path and then away from us: the White-cheeked Pintail, the second rarest bird I had seen so far, a bird that I had worked so hard to find and had finally given up on. As we continued around the pond, we saw him again, sitting on the water and feeding.

Sensing that we might be in the middle of a lucky streak, (sometimes birding seems like a poker game), we started off early on April 11, arriving at Santa Ana National Wildlife Refuge well before 7:00 A.M. and began to walk the trails, Vireo Loop, Dicliptera, and Pintail Lake. We found nothing. We then drove the entire tour route, walked around the Cattail Lake, and found nothing. From on top of the levee, we searched the skies and still found nothing. By this time the temperature was above 90 degrees, and we had walked more than six miles and driven for two hours. Emily, tired and bored, was asleep on the back seat. John said there was only one spot left, a small area near the northeast corner of the refuge, so we drove there and climbed the fence. In less than five minutes, we found our quarry, the Hook-billed Kite, another rarity that I had already missed twice. The bird flew up from a small tree and then wheeled over us not more than forty feet off the ground, so close that the long hook on its beak was clearly visible.

Certain now that our luck was running strong, we raced for Falcon Dam seventy miles away even though our birding time there would have to be limited to two and a half hours. We left the car and Emily at the parking lot below the dam and practically jogged a mile down the dirt road leading south to an old campground on the water's edge. Ten minutes after we started down a path through the tangled underbrush and small trees along the Rio Grande, we flushed two Red-billed Pigeons from a tree over our heads and then got to study the one that stopped in a tree about thirty feet above us. While we were doing this, a Ringed Kingfisher flew by over the water. Fifteen minutes later we encountered a small flock of Brown Jays that got excited and came almost close enough to touch when John gave an owl call. And just before our time ran out, two Black-headed Orioles began to call and then came into plain view in the small tree above us. John saw one Green Kingfisher, and we heard three or four, but I failed to see one clearly enough to count it.

This Texas trip was a birder's dream. Outside Alaska, I would probably not see so many rarities and hard-to-get birds in such a short time. Besides that, I could feel the mighty surge of spring migration building. All birds were in full song once again; many summer residents had arrived; courtship and mating, the most important and frantic bird activities, were going on all around us. We got a total of 125 species, including twenty-two new ones, to raise my total to 418. In addition to the birds mentioned above, I added the following new species for the year:

- Broad-winged Hawk
- Solitary Sandpiper
- Wilson's Phalarope
- Chimney Swift
- Black-chinned Hummingbird
- Wied's Crested Flycatcher
- Bank Swallow
- Cliff Swallow
- Carolina Wren

9

GROUSE DURING MATING SEASON

Grouse of the Great Plains do their courting and mating about dawn or, when the moon is full, all night long. For most species, all this activity takes place on leks (also called booming, strutting, or dancing grounds). All the leks I saw were level and covered with low grass or scattered sage bushes. Each male selected a territory about fifty to seventy-five feet in diameter and defended its invisible boundary against all other males by vigorous displays and ritual combat (I never saw any real fighting). Each territory seemed to adjoin those next to it, so twenty to thirty males on the same lek used a total of three or four acres. Although the females feeding nearby seemed completely oblivious to the male hoopla, they must have been taking it all in, for each eventually moved into the territory of one of the males and mating took place. On leks the birds are easy to see because they make a lot of noise and have but one thing on their minds. Once they leave the leks, they become difficult to find; you can spend days looking for them without success. These considerations sent me and my eleven-year-old son David to Colorado, where we met Jane and George Clayton of Houston, Texas, and Dr. Clait Braun of Fort Collins and began three days of tumbling out of bed at 3:45 A.M.

Bright stars, a heavy frost, and 20-degree temperatures greeted us April 20 in Kremmling, and Rick Hoffman and Kellen Duncan of Colorado Division of Wildlife guided us to a Sage Grouse lek north of town. As we eased toward it at 4:56 A.M. with headlights off, we could see eight or ten big males displaying furiously, their white ruffs almost shining in the half-light.

An hour later, this time accompanied by a big liver-and-white pointer, we worked our way slowly up a mountainside north of Kremmling, playing from time to time a tape of Blue Grouse calls. There were no answers, but the dog finally found a male sitting completely still about ten feet up in a small pine tree. The bird allowed all of us to approach within twenty feet before flying. After returning to town for a huge breakfast, we headed for Denver and found three Sage Thrashers in a sage-brush pasture by the roadside.

Since the Claytons had never seen White-tailed Ptarmigan, we detoured by Guanella Pass and, out of breath and with pounding hearts from the altitude of over 11,500 feet, searched a large area of the mountainside for an hour. We found nothing and headed for the car. Less than 100 yards from it, I almost stepped on an unbanded male, and Clait did his remarkable act again, catching the bird with a noose on a pole while all of us watched in wonder. This time we took pictures of everyone holding the bird. Later in the day, southwest of Denver, a male Prairie Falcon flew directly over us.

The next morning, Rick Kahn, also of the Colorado Division of Wildlife, guided us in a search for Sharp-tailed Grouse near Castle Rock. There were no birds on the first two leks we visited, but after walking in a mile to the third, we found nine males at about 6:30 A.M.

Rick left us, and we began the long drive to Springfield, Colorado, the only place in the state where Lesser Prairie Chickens can be easily found. Anyone who has made this trip knows how the Great Plains got the name; the gently rolling grassland stretches to the horizon in every direction with nothing to block the view except power poles and fence posts, and an occasional windmill or grain storage bin. Mountain Plovers like these wide open spaces and can often be seen sitting on fence posts along the highway. But they all seemed to be elsewhere during the entire drive down and back, and we saw only one Mountain Plover (and thank goodness for it) near the entrance to the state refuge at Two Buttes. Around the refuge headquarters we also got Scaled Quail.

At 4:52 A.M. on April 22 we were at a lek about ten miles southeast of Campo watching nine male Lesser Prairie Chickens. Even at this early hour two other carloads of birders were ahead of us, and another came up as we drove off. Alongside the highway north of Lamar, we got both Semipalmated and Baird's Sandpipers on the shore of an irrigation reservoir. This ended a 1,150-mile swing through Colorado, where with beautiful weather I got ten new species for a total of 428 for the year.

Although the Claytons made our party more efficient because both are excellent birders, I was especially glad to have them along for other reasons. George (now Director of Research at Baylor Medical School) and I grew up together in Memphis and caught the birding disease from one of the greatest amateur ornithologists, Ben B. Coffey. I was a member of the wedding party when Jane and George married. Finally, they introduced me to the ABA, and I first got the idea of trying for 700 during a visit to their second home on Galveston Island.

One of the birds we saw in Colorado was Common Flicker, and it illustrates a key point about how birds get their common names. The field guides I used do not identify Common Flicker as a separate species; instead, mine list three flickers: Yellow-shafted, Red-shafted, and Gilded. What has happened now is that scientists have discovered the same sort of interbreeding among these three as between Baltimore and Bullock's Orioles (see pp. 54–55), so they lumped them into one species and then had to find a new name since none of the old ones was suitable. But why did they select the name Common Flicker?

For most purposes, the job of providing a standard nomenclature of both English and scientific names is handled by the AOU Committee on Classification and Nomenclature. Chaired by Dr. Eugene Eisenmann, the committee is composed of nine distinguished taxonomists. Dr. Eisenmann is like many birding pros in that his consuming interest in birds changed his whole life. Having graduated as a Doctor of Jurisprudence from Harvard, he practiced law in New York for about twenty years. But birds, which had captured his interest as a boy, would not let him go, and he finally switched to full-time ornithology as Research Associate in the American Museum of Natural History. He is the author of *The Species of Middle American Birds,* until recently a member of the International Commission on Zoological Nomenclature, and an authority on neotropical birds. His committee meets at least once a year, and its members carry on a voluminous correspondence with experts concerned with each potential change. Findings are published as Supplements to the AOU Checklist of North American Birds. Most of the lumpings, splittings, and name changes that shook up the bird world in recent times appeared in the 32nd Supplement in *The Auk* of April 1973.

In this Supplement, the committee announced that it would use the following guidelines in selecting English names:

1. *Provide a specific modifier when the same group name is used for another species of this hemisphere.* For example, it adopted Common Flicker for North American birds because there are other species of flickers in Central America, and Gray Catbird for North American birds because there is a black catbird in Mexico.
2. *Facilitate conformity with international usage that is already supported by much American usage.* Examples are Merlin for the old Pigeon Hawk, American Kestrel for the old Sparrow Hawk, and Storm-petrels for some species to separate them from those simply called Petrels.
3. *Avoid names with misleading taxonomic implications.* The committee adopted Wood Stork for Wood Ibis because the bird is a stork and not an ibis, and Upland Sandpiper for Upland Plover because the bird is a sandpiper and not a plover.

4. *Prevent confusion with another species bearing the same name.* The committee substituted Montezuma Quail for Harlequin Quail because there is another harlequin quail in Africa with an earlier claim to the name.
5. *Conform with usage in the breeding region of a species that merely migrates or wanders to our area.* Flesh-footed Shearwater was adopted for the old Pale-footed Shearwater because Flesh-footed is used in Australia where the bird is a common breeder.
6. *Substitute a short but more meaningful modifier when possible.* Examples are Great Egret for Common Egret and Black Scoter for Common Scoter (the bird is black and the *least* common scoter).

There will surely be more name changes in the future. But when they do occur, they will not be the result of mere whimsy; scientists will change them in an attempt to improve our communication by improving our common language.

10
SPRING MIGRATION IN FULL SWING

The Strategy Council set up some exciting days for me when it scheduled me to work the spring migration on the upper Texas coast. The great variety of habitat there produces many species, the migration itself produces large numbers of each species, and a combination of weather and the long flight produces birds in strange places. For example, in Texas I saw a Scarlet Tanager sitting in a pasture four miles from the nearest tree, a Water Pipit on the Basin parking lot in Big Bend, and a flock of Cattle Egrets along the Rio Grande at Santa Elena Canyon.

It all began thirty-six hours after Colorado with just enough time to go by Jackson and pick up clean clothes and a car. At 3:00 P.M. on April 23 I met John M. Read near Vinton, Louisiana, and headed to Gum Cove in search of the Black Francolin. Introduced south of Vinton years ago, this game bird looks somewhat like a big black Common Bobwhite, has a song that to me doesn't sound like a bird at all but like two pieces of metal clinking together, and can be easily seen alongside the roads that run through the huge fields and pastures. Although John and I heard its distinctive call north of the Intracoastal Waterway, we had to cross the cable-drawn ferry before we saw one. Just after we saw the Black Francolin, the first King Rail of the year walked across the road in front of us. That night I drove to High Island, Texas, and joined a Victor Emanuel Nature Tours group of fourteen persons led by Victor Emanuel and John Rowlett.

After dawn on April 24 we drove north of Silsbee and got the species usually found in southern piney woods: Red-cockaded Woodpecker, Bachman's Sparrow, Brown-headed Nuthatch, Kentucky Warbler, Hooded Warbler, and Blue Grosbeak. All these birds were active and singing away in early morning, the traditional time for birding.

But in Smith Woods and Boy Scout Woods at High Island, it was a different story. There were few birds in early morning and little singing at any time; the birds that had filled the trees the day before usually left during the night on the next leg of their flight. Peak birding time was late afternoon when birds that left Central America the previous evening were just finishing their twenty-hour flight across the Gulf. Sometimes you could see them dropping out of the sky into the trees, and you could always observe a great increase in the number of individuals present. In the afternoon of April 24 these woods were full of warblers (Blackburnian, Worm-eating, Blackpoll, Blue-winged, Golden-winged, Cerulean, Chestnut-sided, Tennessee, Bay-breasted, Magnolia, Ovenbird, and American Redstart) and thrushes (Wood, Swainson's, Gray-cheeked, and Veery). One large mulberry tree, a riot of color, was loaded with both ripening fruit and about 100 Scarlet Tanagers, Rose-breasted Grosbeaks, and Eastern Kingbirds.

At mid-morning on April 25 we took the first rail-buggy trip of the day at Anahuac National Wildlife Refuge. The controversial rail-buggy has a front end like that of a farm tractor and a back end that is an eight foot by ten foot box for passengers with a floor four feet above ground. This box is mounted on four rubber tires about three feet wide, pulls a rubber-tired wagon about twelve feet long, and moves over the mud, water, and marsh grass at about two miles per hour.

Some say that rail-buggy trips damage the rails or the habitat, but I doubt it for several reasons. First, the speed of the buggy is less than that of a person walking. Second, except in a few places, the very wide wheels keep the buggy on top of the vegetation and do not allow it to make ruts in the marsh; I could see no tracks from previous seasons. Third, the area traversed by the buggy is less than 640 acres, whereas the area of identical habitat surrounding it contains hundreds of thousands of acres.

Our ride lasted an hour. Passengers stood (it was too bumpy to be comfortable sitting on a wooden bench) and held tightly to the sides to keep from falling off, keeping their eyes trained on the areas immediately ahead and on either side of the buggy. Whenever a bird jumped up, everyone shouted. The rails appeared suddenly. They ran along tracks through the marsh or flew short distances and were very close, so everyone got a good look sooner or later. We saw many Sedge Wrens, six or seven Yellow Rails, one Black Rail, and many Virginia Rails and Soras. Since we saw a King Rail on the way to the refuge and a Clapper Rail later at Bolivar Flats, we got all six United States rails in one day.

Before dawn on April 26 John Rowlett and I headed off by ourselves to search for additional species. By looking carefully at the wet croplands and flooded rice fields along the road toward Anahuac Refuge, we found three Buff-breasted Sandpipers (more than 300 had been present the day before) and six or seven Hudsonian Godwits among hundreds of other shorebirds. After a quick breakfast at Winnie, we drove several miles east on the road toward Port Arthur and saw many Fulvous Whistling Ducks circling over the fields. Then, wasting no time, we drove to Bolivar Flats, waded for thirty minutes across the salt marsh behind the beach, and finally flushed one of the last remaining Sharp-tailed Sparrows wintering there.

At first light the next day the whole group was in the tour bus at the Dickinson Airport watching fifteen Greater Prairie Chicken cocks going through their display routines. Two of them were so carried away that they were actually standing on the concrete runway. Our view of the action was outstanding because the lek was mowed and very close to the parking area, and Victor used a parabolic mike and earphones to bring the booming to each of us. We then drove a short distance to the southernmost breeding colony of Henslow's Sparrows, and I got a good look at a male on top of a small bush, singing with great gusto a song that he is justly not famous for.

This was my first experience with an organized tour, and even though this year I was interested almost solely in seeing new species for the year and in doing so as quickly as possible, I found the tour highly satisfactory. I had expected (and did encounter) delays when some group members wanted to study species that I had already seen, but this was more than offset by the tremendous advantage of having a woods or shore full of migrants searched by fourteen birders all anxious to help me. All members of the group were experienced birders and probably had life lists of 400 or better. One of them, Bjorn Christopherson of Copenhagen, Denmark, had been birding in the United States for twenty years, had a life list of over 500 for the ABA area and became the first foreigner to sign my sighting ledger when he was my witness for Little Tern. Most members were about my age, but there was a woman in her twenties and a couple in their thirties. They told me they chose the tour for the same reason I did; their experience had shown that you could see many more birds in much less time and for much less money with a guide than you could by yourself.

And the guides on this tour were some of the best in the business. Victor Emanuel, the tour leader, has a degree in zoology and botany from the University of Texas and a master's degree in government from Harvard, and he is another of those who have finally been captured by the birds. He has been president of Texas Ornithological Society and is founder and compiler of the record-breaking Christmas Bird Count at Freeport, Texas. John Rowlett was one of the three editors of Oberholser's *The Bird Life of Texas,* and after spending several days with him, I was convinced that he has two sets of eyes and two sets of ears. Rose Ann Rowlett,

John's sister, has a B.A. in botany from the University of Texas; an M.A. in ornithology from California State University; extensive birding experience in Texas, the Southwest, and the American tropics; and charm without limit. David Wolf has a B.A. in biology from Stephen F. Austin State University, has been birding Texas since childhood, and gets credit for the second United States record for Rufous-capped Warbler and the first United States record for Aztec Thrush.

Because the Henslow Sparrow was the last species I really needed on the coast, David Wolf and I left the tour and headed by plane to Big Bend National Park. But since we had only one day, April 28, we pushed ourselves to the limit—and very nearly reached it. Leaving Terlingua at 5:00 A.M., we drove to Santa Elena Canyon and walked near a point where the Rio Grande River, about 100 yards wide, completely fills the space between two perpendicular rock cliffs rising perhaps 1,500 feet above it. Even the softest bird song seemed to be magnified by bouncing off these rock walls; a White-winged Dove calling above us sounded like a whole pack of wolves. A few yards east of this point, in a strip of tamarisk trees and cane less than fifty yards wide, we found a Rufous-capped Warbler, the main target of our trip, a Code 4 bird. Our trip was a winner before 7:00 A.M. And I became even more convinced that I could see any bird that I chased; all I needed to reach my goal was news that a species was present.

On our way to the Basin, we stopped at an abandoned ranch house and spotted several Varied Buntings. Leaving the Basin at midmorning in a cool breeze, we began the five-mile walk to Boot Spring. Soon after we started out, I began to thank the Lord we didn't have to walk all the way. The trail was so full of rocks that you had to watch every step, and it rose so steadily that, even in stretches that appeared to be flat, you could feel the strain of climbing a hill. About three and a half miles up, we heard the first singing male Colima Warbler and began to hunt for him. It took almost two hours to spot his distinctive marks. The slopes were very steep, the growth of trees and brush was very thick, and either the bird was a ventriloquist or the rock walls made him seem like one. After what felt like five hours rather than two, we finally found him on the ground beside the trail.

By the time we got back to the car, it was very warm, and I was so tired that I might have quit if David had told me then that we still had two more miles to go. Searching for Lucifer Hummingbird, we walked first to the sewer ponds below the Basin campground and found nothing. Then we crossed the wash, climbed up through the brush to Campground Canyon, struggled about one-third of the way up it, and still found nothing but hot, dry winds and a dozen cactus thorns that passed through my pants and stuck in my leg. On the way back to the car, one wash was so steep that I had no trouble going down it on the seat of my pants in a shower of loose rocks.

Missing the hummingbird was a disappointment, but we still got the three birds just described plus Scott's Oriole, Cassin's Kingbird, Poor-will, Bell's Vireo, Ash-throated Flycatcher, Western Flycatcher, Zone-tailed Hawk, and Hepatic Tanager. In all of Texas I got sixty-two new birds for the year, bringing my total to 490. In addition to the birds mentioned above, I added the following new species:

Piping Plover
Lesser Golden Plover
Upland Sandpiper
Pectoral Sandpiper
Black Tern
Black-billed Cuckoo
Common Nighthawk
Acadian Flycatcher
Eastern Pewee
Yellow-throated Vireo
Philadelphia Vireo
Yellow Warbler
Northern Waterthrush
Yellow-breasted Chat
Orchard Oriole
Summer Tanager
Dickcissel

Stopping in Jackson just long enough to see my family and get a fresh supply of clean clothes, I flew to south Florida to work the migration there. The May 3 boat trip from Daytona Beach on the *Sea Bea* (Ed Fleischer, captain) was notable because of both seasickness and rare birds. Seasickness struck first and was a new experience for me. The forty-eight-foot boat was pitching so much in the swells of an eighteen-knot wind that everyone had to hold on to something all the time, and I lost my breakfast about one and a half hours out and had to prove that my stomach was really empty three more times before 11 A.M.

Although we traveled at a speed of eighteen knots, it took us two and a half hours to run from the harbor to where the target birds were, and we saw almost no birds during these periods going and coming. Occupied as I was, I might have missed something, but my companions, Paul Sykes, Guy McCaskie, Jon Dunn, Kenn Kaufman, and Dr. Oliver K. Scott, are among the sharpest eyes in American birding and didn't miss a thing. By the time we were fifty miles out, we had seen Arctic Tern, Audubon's Shearwater, and Bridled Terns flying by and also sitting on driftwood. About sixty-five miles out, we began to "chum," which means traveling in a big circle and throwing meat scraps over the stern, and this drew Wilson's Storm Petrels and a Pomarine Jaeger.

Far out at sea, the star of the show was Black-capped Petrel (Code 3). At one time we had fourteen of these big, rare petrels around the boat, and most of the time there were at least one or two close by. As we headed for home, the captain set out two fishing lines, and, at the first strike, Guy McCaskie scored another first, reeling in a six-pound bluefish. Pausing only minutes at the dock, and thanking heaven for firm ground, I drove with Dr. Scott to Lakeland, picked up John Edscorn, and then saw White-rumped Sandpiper at the St. Petersburg dump at sunset.

After a long drive and a few hours of sleep at a roadside motel, we were at Taylor Slough in Everglades National Park soon after sunrise May 4 but unfortunately missed Seaside Sparrow; ten to twelve inches of rain north of the park about a week earlier apparently flooded them out of their usual habitats. Next we worked the woods in a city park on Key Biscayne in Miami and picked up several common migrants and Florida specialties. Then, very tired from the pelagic trip, loss of sleep, and driving, the three of us drove to Key Largo. Dr. and Mrs. V. Thomas Austin had made arrangements for us to stay at the lodge of Ocean Reef Club, and I spent the most restful evening of the year so far. Mrs. Austin also showed us White-crowned Pigeon and Prairie Warbler near her home.

It took us three hours on the morning of May 5 to find Mangrove Cuckoo on Sugarloaf Key, and after lunch Al Weintraub flew us to the Dry Tortugas. The place was awash with birders: sixty-two persons on a Northeast Birding Tour, thirty or so on a Sierra Club tour, Paul Sykes and Rob Thorn, Larry Balch and three friends from Chicago, and several others. In no time we found two Brown Boobies perched among the Magnificent Frigatebirds on Bush Key, Sooty Terns and Brown Noddies in great numbers, and an assortment of common migrants inside the fort. It was hot and sticky, and there was no sign that another grand-slam home run was just ahead of us.

About 6:30 P.M. Paul Sykes returned from a small-boat tour of areas not visible from the fort and reported the presence of two exciting species. Everyone raced for the boats, and Rich Biss, Alan Anderson, Homer Eshbaugh, and Larry Balch asked us to share theirs. After creeping around to the back side of Bush Key in water only two feet deep, we saw our first target sitting among the frigatebirds: an immature Red-footed Booby, a Code 6 bird and the second rarest I had ever seen. We watched him preening for five minutes or so and then turned toward Middle Key, an acre of sand several miles away. Even at that distance and in fading light, we could see two adult Masked Boobies, huge white birds with black accents that seemed almost as big as the key they were sitting on. We approached within 100 yards of this Code 3 species before we returned to the fort, laughing and joking all the way like Super Bowl winners. I had two drinks of bourbon, ate a can of Vienna sausages and a box of crackers for supper, spread a two-inch pad of foam rubber on a concrete fueling dock, and slept under one blanket in my clothes. The night was beautiful, with a half-moon, a steady breeze, no insects, and continuous background music from the nesting terns on Bush Key. Despite these pleasures, I discovered before dawn that a thin foam-rubber mat couldn't protect me very much from a concrete dock.

While I was eating a can of peaches for breakfast on May 6, Will Russell shouted, "Jim, come quick! We've got Black Noddy." I rushed to the old piers northeast of the fort and joined about fifty birders looking at one Black Noddy, a Code 4 species, sitting and flying with about fifty Brown Noddies. I could hardly believe my good luck: three rarities in less than twelve hours, one of them a Code 6 bird, and, with almost eight months to go, a great start for a Big Year.

We flew to Sugarloaf Key before noon and, that afternoon, drove around until we got to observe at leisure a Mangrove Cuckoo in a small tree on the side of the road about fifteen feet from the car window. Apparently the best way to get this species is to drive the roads of the south part of Sugarloaf Key. We saw and heard Antillean Nighthawk (an ineligible species) around the motel that night.

The following morning Paul Sykes, Larry Balch, and their associates joined us in trying to find a Melodious Grassquit reportedly seen on No Name Key, but we found nothing more unusual than three Bobolinks. After searching unsuccessfully for new migrants on Islamorada and Key Largo, we returned to Everglades National Park and scanned the sky above Royal Palm Hammock until several Swallow-tailed Kites came up to hunt.

Dr. Scott added both good company and birding expertise to the trip. Having retired several years ago as the first pediatrician in Casper, Wyoming, he now operates a huge cattle ranch there with his sons. He grew up in Massachusetts, started birding under the legendary Ludlow Griscom, and has an ABA life list of over 650. We got more birds because of him. Our total trip count was 109 species, twenty-three of them new for the year, bringing my total to 514. In addition to the birds mentioned above, I added these new species on the Florida trip:

Gray Kingbird
Black-whiskered Vireo
Cape May Warbler
Black-throated Blue Warbler

11

MOPPING UP IN TEXAS AND CALIFORNIA

May 10 brought another triumph for John Arvin and an unexpected bonus of excitement for me. It was midmorning and we were walking through the woods along the Rio Grande River below Falcon Dam. Suddenly, a bird flushed ahead of us and flew a short distance to a dead limb about fifty feet away. By moving slowly and quietly toward her, we soon had her in plain view. It was a Hook-billed Kite, a Code 3 bird. With the bright sun behind us, we could see all her distinctive markings, especially the striking white eye and long hooked bill. We examined her at leisure as she perched on the branch, and then three times she uttered the cry used only near the nest. In less than five minutes John had found her nest, an open network of sticks about thirty feet up in a willow, and then we quickly moved on to avoid disturbing the lady. So far as we know, this is only the fourth Hook-billed Kite's nest found in the United States, and John has found two of them.

Only thirty-six hours after I finished in Florida, my last scheduled trip to the Rio Grande Valley began with John early on May 9 in a coastal prairie east of Brownsville, Texas, the habitat of Botteri's Sparrow. We soon heard one singing and picked him up easily with the telescope. Next we drove to an Audubon Society sanctuary containing many palm trees and, in about thirty minutes, found three warblers I had missed in Florida or on the upper Texas coast, Wilson's,

Canada, and Mourning. The woods were quiet and contained only two small loose flocks of migrating warblers, and I thought we were lucky to get all three so easily.

Next stop was Steve Benn's backyard in Brownsville. Steve started birding under John and became well known among birders when he discovered a nest of Yellow-green Vireos in his yard several years ago. At Steve's feeder a Buff-bellied Hummingbird could be found almost 100 percent of the daylight hours, and the male I saw perched at eye level was so accustomed to humans that he let me approach to within three feet. I was so close that I felt he could almost touch my nose with his long red bill.

Before noon we found Olive-sided Flycatcher at the northeast corner of Santa Ana National Wildlife Refuge, and then we searched for Hooded Oriole around McAllen, but with no luck. Since we were far ahead of schedule, we decided to look in Anzalduas Park near Mission for Rose-throated Becard. After an hour and a half of fighting through brush on this sultry afternoon, we found only the paths made by illegal immigrants coming across the border from Mexico. After that hard work, we put in two hours that any birder would enjoy. Arriving at Bentsen-Rio Grande Park about 5:30, we parked at a campsite next to the nest-hole of an Elf Owl. I mixed a bourbon-and-water in an empty pineapple-juice can, climbed on the hood of the car, leaned back against the windshield, and passed the cocktail hour watching for the owl and discussing birds with John and John Sterling, a young birder from California who happened by. The owl came to the entrance at 6:45 and let us have a good look but did not come out again; after waiting another half-hour, we headed west toward our motel near Falcon Dam. On the highway to Rio Grande City, when it was so dark that we had to use a big spotlight plugged into the car's cigarette lighter, we got Lesser Nighthawk. About an hour later, I enjoyed another benefit of using local guides. John stopped at a tiny secluded restaurant in a small town so completely dark that I wanted a bodyguard, and I ate the best Mexican food of my life.

At dawn the next day we met Bob Farris of Tulsa, Oklahoma, near the parking lot below Falcon Dam and walked along the roads and trails by the river to an old campground over a mile away. Just as John said, "When we were here last week at this time, the Ferruginous Pygmy Owl was singing," the rare little owl began to sing. He sang without stopping, and by following the call we finally spotted him near the top of a hackberry. In trying to get a better look at the owl, John moved to the river's edge and discovered a Green Kingfisher just as the owl flew. Two target birds at the same spot and in less than five minutes' time! From the same spot we heard Red-billed Pigeons singing at full volume and Brown Jays calling at several locations. Later, after Bob Farris left us, came the Hook-billed-Kite sighting described above, and later still, about 200 yards from the kite's nest, we spotted both Yellow-bellied and Sulphur-bellied Flycatchers.

Birding traffic in the valley was markedly lower than it had been on my earlier trip. During April there were birders by the carload behind every tree; one month later we saw exactly one lone birder. This surprised me because, of course, the birds were still there, even more conspicuous because of singing and courtship, and they were on nesting territories, in the most predictable locations of the year. With a guide like John, any birder, in one twenty-four-hour period, could be sure to see Elf and Ferruginous Pygmy Owls, Hook-billed Kite, Green and Ringed Kingfishers, Red-billed Pigeon, Black-headed and Altamira Orioles, and Pauraque—not a bad day's work.

We saw 109 species, twelve of them new for the year, bringing my total to 526.

Although my long spring trip to Alaska would begin in a few days and I wanted to spend some time with my family, I still needed some summer residents of the Far West that might be gone before I had another chance. The only solution was to reduce my time at home to only forty-eight hours, leave early for Alaska, and spend a few days in California with Rich Stallcup. I would get mighty homesick before I quit birding again.

The California trip began early May 13 in the hills of Tilden Regional Park in Berkeley, a varied habitat that produced many western species in a small area where the walking was easy and the scenery beautiful. In an hour and fifteen minutes I added to my list for the year Black-headed Grosbeak, Warbling Vireo, Western Pewee, Western Tanager, Allen's Hummingbird, and Black-throated Gray Warbler. These sightings exhausted our possibilities here, so we headed east into different habitats. Soon after lunch in a dry, hot valley south of Livermore, we found Black-chinned Sparrows singing on one side of the road and a flock of Lawrence's Goldfinches on the other and a singing Lazuli Bunting several miles farther. We continued east to Yosemite National Park, where high mountains and dense forests contained a completely different set of birds. Our trip across the intensively cultivated San Joaquin Valley was hot and uneventful except for a flock of about 150 American White Pelicans soaring above a wildlife refuge.

In the yard of our motel at El Portal, several Anna's Hummingbirds were coming to feeders, and while I was registering inside the motel office, Rich spotted a Northern Goshawk that soared overhead and then disappeared behind the mountaintop before I could get out to see it. By 5:00 P.M. we had driven into Yosemite National Park where, at least for a while, birding had to take a back seat to standing in awe of some of the most spectacular scenery in the United States. It didn't take us long to combine both, however; we crossed the bridge in the spray of Yosemite Falls, stretched out on the ground with our heads propped on rocks, and watched White-throated and Black Swifts coursing 3,000 feet above us in front of North Dome. On the way back to supper at the motel, we stopped by the roadside, climbed a short distance up a ravine full of rocks big as houses, and got Calliope Hummingbird, a target species for the trip, the only hummer whose colored throat feathers form streaks against a white background, and, at only two and three-fourths inches long, the smallest bird in the ABA area. It first hovered and then lit on top of a bush about fifteen feet above us.

Early the next morning we drove to the end of the road in the highest mountains of the park and then walked in two miles to Bridalveil Campground through patches of snow two inches deep on the trail and two to three feet deep in the woods nearby. We got Mountain Quail near the start of the walk, and soon after we headed back, we sighted a beautiful male Williamson's Sapsucker. We heard Northern Pygmy Owl calling but couldn't find it, and we saw no sign of Black-backed Three-toed Woodpecker. But luck was with us when we stopped for a picnic lunch. A MacGillivray's Warbler hopped out of the brush across the road, and a Dusky Flycatcher sang and hunted above us the whole time. We then drove to Yosemite Village and found White-headed Woodpecker near the stables; its nest-hole was in a fencepost about four feet above the ground in the midst of all the activity connected with a major tourist attraction.

During the last few minutes of the twilight of May 14, I watched Rich do the impossible. Still in Yosemite Park, we had gone up above 6,000 feet after sundown to see what we could find in the way of owls. As soon as we left the car, a Flammulated Screech Owl, a migrant we had not expected to find, began to call up the slope from us, so close we could hear the little grace notes in its call. We stumbled up through patches of snow and chaparral in search of the little ventriloquist and finally became convinced that it was high up in a clump of three enormous Ponderosa Pines, each about twenty-four inches in diameter and 100 feet tall with branches extending down to the ground. The light was fading fast in the west and would be gone in fifteen minutes. Rich moved up the slope 100 feet east of the trees, searched them with his binoculars, found the owl about fifty feet up in the middle tree and perhaps four inches from the main trunk, and showed him to me. It was an incredible feat; the owl was only as large as my outstretched palm, and it was so dark that I could not see the ground clearly. When I asked him how he did it, Rich replied, "Well, I knew from experience that it was sitting close to the trunk, so I scanned all the trunks, and when I saw a stubby branch turn its head, I knew I had the owl." Almost immediately the little owl turned its head again, and we could detect not only this small movement but also its tiny ears. Considering how minute the owl was in proportion to all the branches of three huge trees, I am still amazed that I got to see it.

Our luck ran out May 15; I didn't add a single species because we had exhausted all possibilities in the preceding two days. We drove slowly back to San Francisco searching for shorebirds at every opportunity, but all the migrants I still needed had apparently passed through on the way north. Our trip list contained 140 species, including sixteen new ones that brought my total to 542.

I got to my motel in late afternoon, and my flight to Anchorage was not until late morning the next day, so I had plenty of time to bathe, eat, sleep, repack my luggage, think, and wonder about Alaska. I wondered especially about Attu. It was not only the westernmost part of the United States. It was also so far west that they had to put a big kink in the International Date Line just to keep it in time with the rest of us; if it were on the same latitude as Hawaii, it would be 1,500 miles west of it. To me Attu wasn't in North America, it was in Asia. Therefore many of its birds would be Asian birds, especially the accidentals. Would I be able to identify them?

The tour brochure described living conditions on Attu as primitive and suggested the kind of clothes to bring. Although it said that no one would be able to take a bath, I figured I could arrange one somehow. Was I bringing enough clothes of the right kind? Was I in good enough physical condition to endure fourteen days of camping while at the same time chasing birds under tough conditions?

12

SPRINGTIME ON ATTU

Can you imagine seeing a Boreal Owl nesting in someone's backyard only sixty feet from the back door, a Boreal Owl that would pop up to the nest-hole entrance, just like a trained monkey, every time you made a bird distress call with your lips? Two hours after I arrived in Anchorage, Alaska, in midafternoon on May 16, I saw such an unusual sight behind the home of Pat Abney and Donna Prator on the outskirts of the city. I even added two birds as I checked into the motel, a Rusty Blackbird in a tree across the street and a Northern Phalarope in a float-plane harbor nearby, and we got a Boreal Chickadee on the way back from seeing the owl. I hoped these were auguries of things to come.

I owed such good luck to Dr. David Sonneborn, an outstanding birder in Anchorage. I had met him, his wife Andy, and their children at Paul Sykes's home in Delray Beach, Florida, during the chase after Masked Duck on March 10, and he had followed my progress closely since then. When he heard about the owl nest, David called me in Jackson, arranged to pick up me and several others at the motel soon after we landed in Anchorage, and then took us to it. We owed perhaps an even greater debt to Andy; that evening she cooked us a splendid dinner, the last good meal we would have for a long time.

The Reeve Aleutian Airways plane to Attu on May 17 had all 59 seats filled, mostly with birders. The birders were divided into three groups: one headed by Larry Balch, one organized by Bird Bonanzas, and our nine-man party (Davis

Finch, our leader, had preceded us by a week). Our group was made up of Terry Hall from Barrow, Alaska, the coleader and Science Coordinator of the Naval Arctic Research Lab run by University of Alaska; Joe Burgiel, a physicist-turned-electrical-engineer with Bell Telephone Laboratories who hailed from Lebanon, New Jersey; Larry Peavler from Indianapolis, Indiana, a General Motors tool and die maker; Granville Smith, a retired Soil Conservation Service field biologist from Green Valley, Arizona; Macklin Smith, an English teacher at University of Michigan at Ann Arbor; Dr. Michael Greene, Sandy Hook, Kentucky; Dr. John Keenleyside, the Chief Radiologist at Queensway General Hospital in Toronto, Ontario; and Jon Dunn, professional birder from Encino, California.

All of them had life lists of over 650 and were much better birders than I, and most of them were twenty years younger as well. The members of the other groups seemed to be older, though, and included six women.

After stops at Adak and Shemya, other islands in the Aleutian chain, we landed at Attu at 3:00 P.M. Bering Time, five hours earlier than Central Time. In short order, we got a briefing from the commanding officer of the Coast Guard Station (total complement, twenty-two men) and moved our gear to what was to be our home for the next two weeks.

Our Attu home was a twenty-foot-by-twenty-foot Quonset hut built during World War II and abandoned soon thereafter. When we arrived our front yard was three feet deep in snow. There was no heat in the hut, and the steel sides brought the outside temperature inside without changing it. What warmth we got was from the cooking stoves and our own bodies. (The hut was a bit warmer after we borrowed a kerosene heater from Larry Balch, and it raised the inside temperature to about 50 degrees, but this wasn't until May 23.) There were no windows; you could get light by opening the only door if you didn't mind some wind or rain or both, and we had one Coleman gas lantern for use at night. There was, however, a sound wooden floor and a roof with only two leaks. Our kitchen consisted of two small Coleman gas stoves on a stack of wooden pallets in one corner, and the bedrolls and baggage of ten men lined three walls. Boxes of supplies covered about half the remaining space, leaving us about eight feet by ten feet in the center of the hut opposite the door for a living room and dining room.

Keeping warm was the major occupation, apart from birding. I slept in a bedroll on an air mattress with a down jacket as pillow and was very comfortable after I learned how to draw the top of it close around my head and neck. In place of pajamas, I wore underwear plus long winter underwear plus khaki shirt and trousers with a Balaclava helmet on my head and wool gloves on my hands. It was so warm in the bedroll that I often put a pair of damp socks near me and dried them overnight. Since I was tired after birding all day, I usually slept well in spite of the chorus of snores.

During the first few days we gradually worked out a division of labor for the daily chores. Terry Hall was chief cook and did most of the work of preparing the big evening meal. Joe Burgiel was usually first up in the morning and got the stoves and lantern filled and lit. Mack Smith did the dishes. The others assisted in these tasks but mainly handled the big job of hauling water. Even though there was no bathing, ten men used a lot of water. To avoid any chance of contamination, we drew drinking water from a stream of melting snow a quarter-mile above us and carried it in five-gallon collapsible plastic bags. In bad weather, with snow and ice underfoot, it was a hard, disagreeable job.

On Attu I learned to eat all my meals from a cup with a spoon or with my fingers. For breakfast I had a cup of Tang, a cup or two of instant oatmeal, several spoonsful of dried eggs from a cup, two cups of coffee with four lumps of sugar each, and one piece of pilot bread (like an unsalted cracker) three inches in diameter with peanut butter and jam. Lunch was usually a can of sardines eaten with the fingers, four individually wrapped slices of cheese, two small boxes of raisins, and one chocolate bar. Supper was the big meal of the day, almost always prepared from freeze-dried food, which was, I thought, delicious. I was especially fond of shrimp creole with rice, beef stroganoff with noodles, green peas, green beans, chicken with noodles, peaches, pears, and potatoes. The carrots were terrible. I wore so many clothes that I couldn't tell whether I was losing or gaining weight, and I wasn't sure about the nutritional value of my diet, but I never felt hungry.

Our toilet was a five-gallon plastic drum graced with a seat. It was located fifty yards away across the snow in another Quonset hut with a door that couldn't be closed. Within our first forty-eight hours on the island, it was filled to capacity. Everyone stood around looking at each other until, recognizing that I was probably the poorest birder in the group, I volunteered for the job of latrine orderly. The decision was both very popular and very profitable—the others were so glad to get out of the emptying and burying that they hardly let me do anything else.

Birding on Attu was concentrated in a winding strip between the mountains and the sea about eleven miles long and varying in width from a few hundred feet to a mile or so. A map of it appears on page 87. On the island during the spring of 1979 were four birding parties: a group of ten led by Davis Finch, sixteen by Larry Balch, four by Ben King, and four by Paul DuMont (a group that came out a week before the other three). By informal agreement each group worked a different part of the area each day in such a way that coverage was complete. Each leader carried a walkie-talkie radio, and all went on the air at thirty-minute intervals to report what had been seen. As soon as anyone spotted a rarity, he stayed with it and reported it on the next broadcast. Then all others converged on the spot. The two larger groups had bicycles, which were lifesavers since we usually traveled ten to fifteen miles a day.

On the day we arrived, although it was cloudy, forty degrees, and blowing twenty miles an hour, we climbed on bicycles brought by the tour groups and began birding.

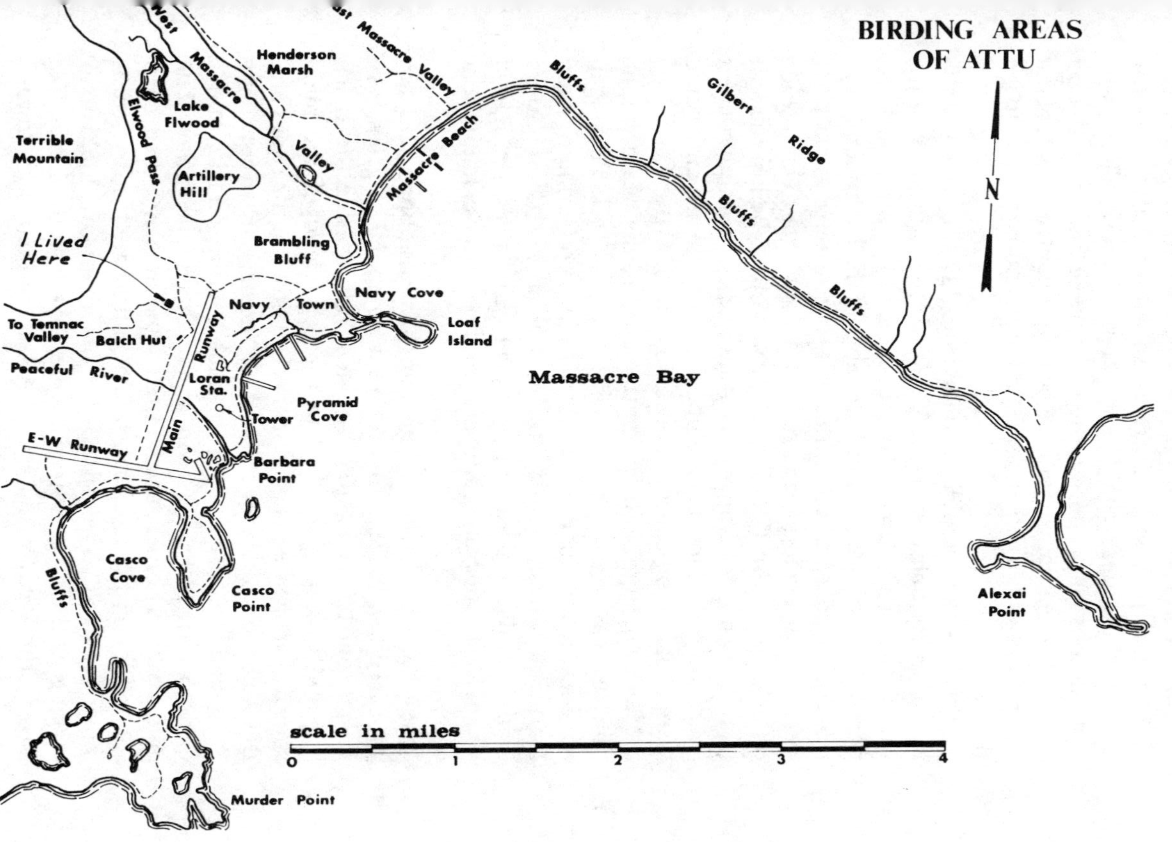
BIRDING AREAS OF ATTU
N
West
Massacre
Henderson Marsh
ast Massacre Valley
Valley
Lake Flwood
Elwood Pass
Terrible Mountain
Artillery Hill
Massacre Beach
Bluffs
Gilbert
Ridge
Bluffs
Bluffs
Brambling Bluff
I Lived Here
Navy Town
Navy Cove
Loaf Island
To Temnac Valley
Balch Hut
Peaceful River
Runway
Loran Sta.
Main
Tower
Pyramid Cove
Massacre Bay
E-W Runway
Barbara Point
Casco Cove
Casco Point
Bluffs
Alexai Point
scale in miles
0
1
2
3
4
Murder Point

Singing on top of a building about 200 yards away was a Rock Sandpiper, and a dozen or so Tufted Puffins were on an old dock near the Coast Guard Station. Those who preceded us had reported the presence of Smews, and after a two-hour search, we found a beautiful pair in a pond about two miles away. By then it was 9:30 P.M. and beginning to get dark.

May 18 was miserable. It rained steadily and blew twenty-five to thirty miles an hour. We spent the entire day in the hut, much of the time in our bedrolls to keep warm. I was bored, uncomfortable, and irritable; I had traveled more than 6,500 miles to see rare birds, not to stare out a rusty steel door at a cold driving rain. At least we got to know each other better. John Keenleyside turned out to be just the sort of fellow you need in such a situation; he has the greatest collection of humorous one-liners I've ever heard and would keep us laughing during the whole time on Attu.

May 19 brought a slight improvement in the weather. The rain decreased to a heavy drizzle. I got Rock Ptarmigan outside our hut door at breakfast, Red-faced Cormorant and Harlequin Duck early in the day near the Coast Guard Station, and, after walking well over eight miles, we sighted Wood Sandpiper along the airstrip. I was near exhaustion at bedtime.

May 20 was glorious. The rain finally stopped, the sun appeared, and the temperature rose to 50 degrees. We started out by seeing Red-throated Pipit outside the Balch hut and gradually worked to the south end of the main runway, where we got Rufous-necked Stint on the shore and Black-headed Gull over the bay. On the next broadcast, Jerry Rosenband reported a Greenshank (our first rarity and a Code 3 bird) at Henderson Marsh three miles away. The gold rush was on. You could tell something rare had been spotted; every human form visible on the bare landscape was moving as fast as possible. Out of breath, we took turns looking at the bird in Jerry's Questar telescope; it was like having the bird in my hand. As we worked back toward home, there was a Brambling on the bluffs, and I watched as Arnold Small, president of ABA, got number 700 on his life list. In late afternoon we found Bar-tailed Godwit in a small marsh among the ruined buildings of Navy Town. Almost simultaneously, someone called out, "Rustic Bunting by the old fuel tanks," and there they were—two brilliant males, a Code 4 species from Asia with striking black and white head patterns and rusty breast bands.

By 7:00 P.M. I had traveled more than ten miles and had eaten only two chocolate bars and four Granola bars, so I went to the hut for "lunch." After two cups of instant soup, I stretched out on my bedroll and slept an hour. About 9:00 P.M. several of the group returned and reported that Davis Finch had an Indian Tree Pipit (Code 3) near the Coast Guard Station. I was tempted to roll over and worry about it in the morning, but John Keenleyside booted me out. I raced down the hill and by 9:45 had it in the bag. Jon Dunn joined us, and we watched it until the light grew too dim at 10:30.

May 21 started slowly with Yellow-billed Loon and Yellow Wagtail at the south end of the big runway, Hoary Redpoll at the north end, and then nothing for hours. But about 6:00 P.M. Thede Tobish discovered Common Sandpiper (Code 4) near a sunken landing craft on the shore at Navy Town, and it allowed us to come close. Everyone on Attu had raced to see it after a day's hard work and was catching his breath when the broadcast reported, "Spotted Redshank on the big lake near Murder Point." Even though I was dead tired, I made the three-mile dash, two miles on bicycle and one on foot, in record time and added this Code 3 bird. Nobody minded that supper was late.

I will never forget May 22. At midmorning thirty of us were strung out in a line sweeping through Henderson Marsh when Ben King called, "Green Sandpiper flying right." This was a most exciting cry, for we all knew that it meant the first verified North American record for the species. Terry Savaloja, a distinguished young birder from Minnesota, had seen one on Attu in June 1978, but he was alone and verification requires three observers. The species is common in Europe and looks very much like our Solitary Sandpiper. We spent almost an hour looking at the bird through binoculars and telescopes and taking pictures of it and each other.

Then, moving slowly through the marsh, Larry Balch spotted Temminck's Stint (Code 3). About half an hour later, we studied a small flock of sandpipers feeding and, at one point, had both Temminck's and Long-toed Stints in the same telescope field. Later in the afternoon we saw two Aleutian Terns over Massacre Bay.

Ben King then turned in his second brilliant performance of the day; near the Balch hut about 8:30 P.M. he located a Pechora Pipit, a Code 6. It was very elusive and gave all thirty of us a difficult time as it walked through the grass or flew from one huge pile of rusting metal roadway strips to another, but eventually, we all saw it.

May 23 brought a south wind, low-hanging clouds, and a drizzle that gradually turned into a steady rain. At midmorning we saw King Eiders on Casco Bay and headed to Murder Point, hoping to see Laysan Albatross with telescopes from the hills. By the time we arrived, however, a strong wind was blowing into our faces, and rain and fog obscured everything. We were straggling home over about a mile of the runway, when suddenly everyone began to shout and point at an immature White-tailed Eagle wheeling over Peaceful River valley just west of us. This majestic Code 3 bird was a thrilling sight.

Jon Dunn produced the final find of the day. Standing outside the hut after supper, he saw a Peregrine Falcon and got all of us out in time to watch it. I was in high spirits. Prospects for the year certainly seemed bright. With our stay on Attu less than half over, we had seen nine rarities; by contrast, during the entire Attu portion of the 1978 Northeast Birding Tour, only ten such birds had been seen.

A steady south wind at ten miles per hour brought clouds and fog on May 24, but no new birds and no weekly plane.

This seemed like a bad sign, and we all hoped that this wouldn't happen on May 31, the day we were scheduled to fly back to Anchorage for a bath. This would also be the day that the variety and quantity of our food would drop off sharply.

On a day like the 24th, when all migrants had gone and only breeding birds were left, birding on Attu yielded a very small list. The common land birds were Snow Bunting and Lapland Longspur, and you could probably find Gray-crowned Rosy Finch and Snowy Owl. On the shore and sea the common birds were Common Eider, Red-faced and Pelagic Cormorants, Rock Sandpiper, and Glaucous-winged Gull. We walked and rode about ten miles and found little else.

May 25 was almost a repeat performance. With a gentle east wind and several periods of sunshine, the temperature climbed to 60 degrees, and birds were scarce again. We made the eight-mile trip out to Aleksai Point riding bikes when snow and road conditions permitted, walked several miles over the beaches and abandoned runways, returned the same eight miles, searched the beaches and ruined buildings at Navy Town, and wound up with another three miles along the main runway and the beach south of it. We traveled over twenty miles, half of it on foot, and all this physical exertion produced only one new species, Horned Puffin. Four other birding teams working all other accessible parts of the island had the same lack of success.

May 26 was much worse. It rained all day with a gentle south wind of ten to fifteen miles an hour. Nobody went birding. Although the rain decreased to a drizzle May 27, we found nothing in a six-mile trip to Murder Point. The only progress was the sighting of a pair of Parasitic Jaegers flying directly overhead about noon.

The same gentle, unproductive south wind held all day May 28, and a steady rain joined it to make matters worse. The Balch group lightened our spirits by inviting all birders over for lunch. It was good to eat slices of regular white bread again, and I also had a treat wholly unexpected on Attu: a cold can of beer. The gloom soon set in again, however, even though the rain ceased, for most of us had not seen a new bird since about noon May 23. Bored and discouraged, we got ready for bed early.

Soon after 9:00 P.M., we heard a distant shout, "Get on the radio." The only fully dressed man rushed outside with the radio; the rest of us began to throw on clothes in feverish haste, certain that any news at all would be exciting news. It was. Thede Tobish broadcast, "I've found a Siberian Rubythroat near the east end of the little runway. It was singing and hopping around the big pile of old barrels." The gold rush was on again, with birders converging from all directions on this Code 4 bird, a drab thing about five and one-half inches long with an incredibly brilliant red throat visible only when it faced you. Everyone got to the bird before 10:00 P.M. Because it showed up in spite of unfavorable conditions, the little straggler lifted the gloom immediately, and we joked and told stories until midnight.

There was good visibility, no rain, and no wind on May 29, and the ocean and bays were like glass. From the shore at Navy Town, with a Questar telescope, we got Kittlitz's Murrelet, a Code 1 bird that is nevertheless often hard to find. We spent late morning and early afternoon in a three-mile walking sweep of the marshes off Massacre Bay but turned up nothing exciting and very few birds of any kind. Things changed in a flash at 4:30 P.M. when Jeff Basham broadcast, "I've got an Eye-browed Thrush on the bluffs south of Kingfisher Creek," a spot three miles from us. All thirty-four birders got to the bird (Code 3), including two men who first heard about it when they were eight miles away on the road to Aleksai Point.

The next morning there was a twenty-five-mile wind and intermittent fog and drizzle, so we spent the morning looking out the door and talking about birds. The weather was too miserable to do otherwise. On the 1:30 P.M.

broadcast two birders reported a Mongolian Plover at Aleksai Point. I groaned. The thought of making that tough fifteen-mile round trip, the first half of it straight into the wind, made me want to stay by the stove. But I had come to Attu to see such birds, and Terry Hall agreed to go with me, so off we went. By the time we arrived, the drizzle had become a steady rain, the wind velocity had risen ten miles an hour, and the plover was gone. This was the seventh or eighth time I had chased and missed Mongolian Plover on Attu. I did get a consolation prize, however; on one of the old runways we flushed a Ruff, and I was glad to get this Code 2 bird out of the way.

May 31 was made torturous by frustration, boredom, and helplessness. The Coast Guard instructed us to have our baggage on the runway by 1:00 P.M. for the departure on Reeve Aleutian Airways. Everyone was eager to get back to the comforts of civilization, so we got up early, boxed and stored all the camping gear, treated the bicycles with WD-40, boxed all the food we could take with us, and assembled on the runway to watch the fog drift about in the still air. Then the rumor came from the Coast Guard station that the plane had left Anchorage two hours late and was supposed to arrive about 3:30. When this time came and went, we got a report that the plane was on the ground in Adak with mechanical trouble. Thirty minutes later, after we had become deeply worried about the mechanical trouble, we got a report that the plane was fifteen minutes out of Shemya, that Shemya was completely fogged in, and that it would have to circle in hopes of finding an opening. An hour and a half later the plane reportedly landed. Soon after 6:00 P.M. we were notified that the plane had left Shemya for Anchorage and that the next flight was June 4. I could have cried. I hated the prospect of going back to the Quonset hut and our living conditions on Attu. But more than that, I was worried that the migration had passed Attu, that the action was now taking place on St. Lawrence Island, and that, by being stuck on Attu and not there, I was missing for good several indispensable species. All thirty-four birders felt as I did.

We lugged our gear back to the hut and undid all the work of the morning. Then we divided the remaining food. My share consisted of fourteen assorted Granola bars, one pound of cheese made into twenty-four individually wrapped slices, two cans of sardines and one of kippered herring, six small boxes of raisins, three packets of hot cocoa mix, and one chocolate bar. There remained some undivided food: large amounts of powdered milk, instant oatmeal, coffee, and dry salami; moderate amounts of pilot bread and instant soup; and small amounts of peanut butter, jam, and mayonnaise. I wondered how long it would last. We could make it to the plane of June 4, but what if we had to wait until June 7 or June 11?

I became fifty-eight years old June 1 and was able to reach Virginia by phone (June 1 is her birthday too) to find out the situation at home and to report my status. It was wonderful to be in touch again and also the only rewarding event of the day. Our group made the Aleksai Point grind again and found nothing new. June 2 brought the best weather of the whole trip (blue sky, gentle south wind, and a temperature near 60 degrees), but no new birds; having little else to occupy us, we continued birding but got nothing more than exercise.

After spending the morning of June 3 unsuccessfully looking for albatrosses over the ocean off Murder Point, we walked a long way up Henderson Marsh and were heading home for supper when it began to rain. Near the bay John Keenleyside and I flushed five ducks, four Red-breasted Mergansers, and another that, as they flew by in poor light and at a distance, we decided was a female Greater Scaup. I didn't give the bird a second thought.

At 8:30 P.M. Mack Smith returned to the hut with news that he, Davis Finch, and Larry Peavler, who were following John and me, had spotted four Red-breasted Mergansers and a female Common Pochard, a Code 2 bird that all of us thought we had missed. I could have kicked myself. I had actually seen an essential bird but couldn't count it because I had missed an identification. The gold rush was on again, this time in the rain and with less than two hours of daylight remaining. We were on the hills above the marsh at 9:00, located a small and very distant flock of mergansers by 9:30, and had the female Common Pochard in all the telescopes at 10:05. It was the only bird I added during the four days of enforced delay.

On June 4, we once again packed up our gear and settled down on the runway to wait for the Reeve Airways plane. This time we were not disappointed. The drone of the plane as it came closer was one of the sweetest sounds I've ever heard. We climbed aboard, and I headed to Anchorage and my first bath in 18 days. I felt filthy, and the other thirty-odd birders were equally unwashed, so I wondered what impact we would have when we crowded into the warm cabin for the three-hour flight. The other thirty-nine passengers gave no sign that they noticed anything unusual.

In spite of the delayed departure from Attu, the trip was successful. I got thirty-nine new species, including eleven rarities, for a total of 581. One sighting was yet to be decided upon, however, that of a possible female Spot-billed Duck in a marsh next to the big runway a few hours after we arrived. All of us studied it with binoculars and telescopes, but no one got to view it as well as Davis Finch, who had examined it the day before in better light and at closer range, who had a better telescope, and who also made detailed notes on it. Davis was reasonably sure of the identification, but considering how rare the species is, he wanted to study the skins in the American Museum of Natural History before he made a final decision.

One of the striking things about my stay on Attu was the level of birding expertise of those who were with me. I have described Davis Finch's remarkable qualifications in Chapter 4. Ben King, the other birding professional who led a tour, has been wrapped up in birds since he started college in 1955. Beginning in 1962, he has traveled, studied, or led birding tours in Japan, Australia, New Guinea, Burma, Thailand, Malaya, India, Nepal, Ceylon, Iran, Afghanistan, Saudi Arabia, Borneo, and many parts of North America. Like some other birding pros, he had an unusual second career; to help finance his early studies and travels, he taught ballroom dancing in Kansas, California, Australia, and Thailand. He is undoubtedly one of the world's best birders, and I gather he's pretty remarkable as a dancer, too. Because of the Asian flavor of Attu birds, we found his book, *A Field Guide to the Birds of South-east Asia,* a great help. (The American edition is out of print, but you can find out how to get one by writing to Ben, c/o Bird Department, American Museum of Natural History, New York, New York 10024.) He is now writing a similar guide to the birds of India.

Two of the coleaders on Attu, Thede Tobish and Terry Hall, live in Alaska and have been birding there for years. Five of the eight members of ABA's 700 Club were present, and all other members of my tour group had life lists of more than 650 when they arrived. Birding with talent of this kind was a real thrill.

I was amazed at the physical stamina of those present. We traveled eight to fifteen miles a day, and although I stayed in good physical shape, I was very tired every night. And yet one tour group contained two men aged seventy-four and seventy-six and one woman aged seventy-one who had no bicycles and who walked every step of the way, and who also endured living conditions that reminded me of those I encountered in Europe during World War II. The other birders deserved medals for stamina, but those three septuagenarians deserved Distinguished Service Crosses.

Since very few birders will ever get to Attu, I have listed below all of the species I saw, in addition to those mentioned above:

Common Loon
Arctic Loon
Red-throated Loon
Red-necked Grebe
Horned Grebe
Snow Goose
Mallard
Common Pintail
Green-winged Teal
Eurasian Wigeon
Northern Shoveler
Greater Scaup
Tufted Duck
Common Goldeneye
Oldsquaw
Black Scoter
Common Merganser
Rough-legged Hawk
Sandhill Crane
Lesser Golden Plover
Whimbrel
Wandering Tattler
Ruddy Turnstone
Common Snipe
Red Knot
Dunlin
Pomarine Jaeger
Glaucous Gull
Herring Gull
Mew Gull
Black-legged Kittiwake
Arctic Tern
Thin-billed Murre
Pigeon Guillemot
Short-eared Owl
Northern Raven
Winter Wren
Water Pipit
Common Redpoll
Song Sparrow

13

SPRINGTIME AT GAMBELL

To one flying in from eighteen days on Attu, Anchorage looked like the most beautiful city on earth, and I enjoyed the fruits of civilization. I spent almost an hour in the shower; it was great just to feel warm water run over me again. Then a carload of us drove uptown to one of the many new restaurants and celebrated with a huge meal of real food cooked and served by someone else. I knew that accommodations at Gambell would be only slightly better than those on Attu, so I saw no reason to leave the restaurant and its bar before 1:00 A.M. on June 5. Who could go to sleep while the sun was still shining?

I regretted my carefree attitude when we had to get up three hours later and begin the fight to get on a plane to Gambell. To ordinary persons, Gambell is accessible only by plane; it is a tiny native village on the northern tip of St. Lawrence Island, 600 miles northwest of Anchorage, almost on the Arctic Circle, and only forty-six miles from Siberia. Our struggle illustrated once again that all the problems of a Big Year do not involve birds.

I was the first person at the Anchorage check-in counter and the last one to set foot on the Gambell airstrip. Because of a mixup in reservations (I understand that this is not uncommon in Alaska), our group was only on standby for the 7:40 A.M. flight to Nome, and when check-in began, we went through a torturous forty-five minutes as, one by one, all seats were filled and the plane took off without us. Bitterly disappointed and certain that we would miss several rarities, we tried some birding around Anchorage but had to quit when one member of our group got sick. When we finally reached Nome at 2:30 P.M., we found twelve of those from the earlier flight still waiting for a plane to Gambell, so we lined up for the second time of the day and finally took off at 6:30 P.M. The Aero Commander flew us over to Gambell at 4,500 feet in beautiful weather, affording us a good look at Siberia to the west of us and many groups of walruses below us, and touched down at 7:30. Because of another mixup, our checked baggage, including bed rolls and mattresses, was still in Anchorage. By this time we had not seen a new bird in two days, and there was more than enough gloom, irritation, and strain to go around. We had no idea how fast the situation would change.

Will Russell and Rich Stallcup met the plane and reported that, earlier in the day, they had sighted a Bluethroat (Code 2) and a Ringed Plover (Code 5). After two bowls of delicious hot canned beef stew to lift our spirits, we found the Bluethroat in a "boneyard" (see p. 101) and, only a short distance away, a White Wagtail (Code 2). While we were still there, we turned the telescope on the adjacent hillsides and picked up Crested Auklet. I also got a brilliant orange Ruff displaying before three Reeves about thirty yards away. Rich then took us over to the shore and finally found a male Spectacled Eider on the glassy sea about 150 yards out, so I bagged another hard-to-get Code 1. Our main target, Ringed Plover, eluded us for two more hours, but we finally saw not one but a pair in the telescope, and we even witnessed the first step in creating a new generation of Ringed Plovers. Such quick successes made all the foregoing hassle worthwhile, and I didn't much mind bedding down with nothing but a half-inch foam-rubber pad between me and the wood floor. When I turned in at 11:30 P.M., the sun was still above the horizon.

At Gambell our Attu group, less Jon Dunn and Terry Hall, joined another Northeast Birding group made up of: Tania

Bailey, of Berwyn, Pennsylvania, a consultant reading specialist; William J. Boyle, of Warren, New Jersey, an organic chemist with Allied Chemical Corporation; Paul and Francine Buckley, a husband-and-wife team of biologists with National Park Service who came from Carlisle, Massachusetts; James Cressman, a management analyst with the county government of North Las Vegas, Nevada, and his wife Marion; Robert Farris, a retired attorney and CPA from Tulsa, Oklahoma; Leonard Graf, a Traverse City, Michigan, civil engineer; Deloris Isted of Cushing, Oklahoma; Gary Lee, a psychiatrist from Tulsa, Oklahoma, and his wife Ellen, a dietitian; Bob Paxton of New York City, a professor of history at Columbia University; Fritz Scheider, a Syracuse, New York pediatrician; Martin Smith, a chemist, and his wife Linda, a registered nurse from Madison, Wisconsin.

All of them plus Will Russell and Rich Stallcup were quartered in a twenty-foot-by-twenty-foot room in the house of Tim Slwooko, six on double-decker bunks and eleven on folding cots. The room was furnished with oil heat and electric lights (three bulbs). As on Attu, members of this group were, I thought, much younger and much better birders than I, with Buckley, Paxton, and Scheider being near-professionals. This group plus ours plus others made a total of fifty birders at Gambell. We slept in the house next door at first but moved into this room when some of the others returned to Nome June 7.

The 400 natives at Gambell got part of their food from the birds and animals they killed, but most of it came in a four-engined, prop-jet cargo airplane that flew out from Anchorage every week or so and landed on the tiny airstrip even in weather that stopped the commercial Aero Commanders from Nome. The co-op grocery was small, clean, and modern and had a stock that was long on dried and canned foods but short on fresh vegetables and produce. Our menus were even more limited because Tim Slwooko displayed little imagination in planning meals. Breakfast was always Tang, toast, coffee, and as many fried eggs as you could get down.

Lunch was sandwiches, usually Spam but sometimes peanut butter and orange marmalade. Supper came from a can, either beef stew or some sort of meat and noodles, both of which I liked very much. We supplemented this fare with an occasional apple from the co-op store and our leftovers from Attu—instant soup, raisins, Granola bars, cheese, and candy bars. So far as cuisine was concerned, Gambell rated more stars than Attu.

There have been villages in this area for centuries, and all past residents left a residue of waste, which always included carcasses of whales and walruses. Twenty years or so ago, the residents of Gambell discovered that the artifacts and old ivory in the ancient sites could be sold for attractive prices, so they began digging into them in a haphazard manner, leaving holes two or three feet deep with mounds of soil piled next to them. At this point, there are three separate excavated areas containing two, three, and ten acres. The areas are littered with bones of all kinds, including some human ones, and are called, appropriately enough, "boneyards" by birders.

The birding area of Gambell is a flat gravel plain measuring three miles from north to south and one mile from east to west. On the north and west, it is bounded by the Bering Sea and on the east by a 600-foot hill with steep sides, and south of it lies the rest of St. Lawrence Island. The airstrip is about in the center along the sea. A mile-long lake lies between it and the hill; the village and the boneyards lie just north of the airstrip. Above the village the gravel extends perhaps a half-mile and forms what is called "the point." There is more action at the point than anywhere else on the island; every hour thousands of auklets, murres, puffins, gulls, and ducks pass by either singly or in lines of up to twenty birds. Migrating land birds usually occur singly and almost always show up in the boneyards, where the holes offer shelter from wind and where the old organic matter has allowed the growth of some small plants.

We started June 6 at the point, and, in less than two hours,

I added to my year list Least Auklet, Steller's Eider, Parakeet Auklet, Long-tailed Jaeger, and Emperor Goose (two flew directly overhead about fifty feet high). As we headed back for lunch, there was my first McKay's Bunting, feeding in the beach grass at the village edge.

After lunch, we were all sitting around and talking, half-listening to Will Russell on the 1:00 P.M. radio broadcast, when we heard him say, "Where is it?" Another chase was on. The target this time was a Terek Sandpiper (Code 4) at the south end of the lake about two miles away, and soon all fifty birders were heading along the airstrip on their way to the lake. I was the fourth to arrive and was hurrying to join the other three when they began to wave vigorously and point toward me. I stopped, and the bird flew directly over me and landed about fifty yards away. I could see its orange legs perfectly without binoculars.

The walk back to the village was joyous and leisurely, and it was after 5:00 P.M. when we assembled on the edge of the boneyard in preparation for a sweep or walk-through before supper. I heard Rich Stallcup shout, "There's a plover. Jim, get on that plover. It might be something." And it was really something, a Mongolian Plover, a bird I had chased all over Attu and missed. It was an especially welcome sight because I thought I had missed it for the year.

June 7 was calm with good visibility, and we spent much time at the point. For most of the time, a single Ancient Murrelet swam and fed in the smooth water about thirty-five yards off the shore. I did not expect to see this species before the Seward ferry and was glad to have a close and unhurried look at it. At 4:30 P.M. we got a report that a Dotterel had been seen on top of the hill, now shrouded in fog. Nevertheless, we struggled up the steep cliffs, coursed back and forth through fog so thick you could hardly see the persons on each side of you, then came down across a steep snow bank more than two feet deep. We found no Dotterel, and I got both boots full of snow.

After lunch on June 8 we were walking slowly down the

runway headed for the south end of the lake when Mack Smith, 100 yards ahead of us, started waving, running toward the telescope, and pointing out to sea. We soon discovered the cause of his excitement: two adult Ivory Gulls resting on and flying around passing ice floes—small, pure-white gulls easy to recognize even at great range, but a hard-to-get Code 1 species.

As a result of the four-day delay on Attu I had to change my itinerary, and the possibility of making a side trip to get Bristle-thighed Curlew made further alterations likely. After considering all probabilities, Finch, Russell, and Stallcup decided that I should remain at Gambell until the 11th, chase the curlew if it had been previously located, and reduce birding at Nome and McKinley Park, the reasoning being that Gambell offered the only chance for rarities. On June 9, this strategy paid off. In midafternoon Ben King's group found us an Arctic Warbler, and after supper all of us flushed a Northern Wheatear. And, as it turned out, other species that I had planned to get near Nome and McKinley could be found in the low forty-eight states.

Rain washed out all birding before noon on June 10 and gave me a long-awaited chance to spend two extra hours in bed. After a strong north wind stopped the rain at midday, we made an unsuccessful five-mile trek to the south end of the lake and back. But during the last mile, we noticed that, for the first time, the wind was westerly, a direction that might blow birds over from Siberia. That was the first sign that something extraordinary was about to happen, but I could not know that the stage was being set for the appearance of a bird that had caused more excitement in recent years than any other, that drew thousands to Newburyport, Massachusetts, several years ago, and that made the pages of *Time* magazine.

After supper we headed for the point, and I happened to be looking at Mack Smith as he moved up the last mound before the water's edge. Suddenly he looked as if he had stuck his finger in an electric socket. Pointing to the sea, he screamed, "Ross's Gull." Davis Finch was behind me with his rain pants around his knees; in his excitement, he made it to the top without pulling them up. Two immature Ross's Gulls, one of them as pink as an adult, were riding a twenty-mile-an-hour wind and feeding in the pounding surf less than fifty feet from us. They were soon joined by three others, and all five stayed in front of us, sometimes only twenty feet away, for more than an hour. They were beautiful. About an hour later, we spotted a Short-tailed Shearwater, the six hundredth species of the year.

After breakfast on June 11 Larry Peavler reported a Sabine's Gull at the point, and I went there to find it feeding near the water's edge, along with five Ross's Gulls and about 150 Black-legged Kittiwakes.

Many of the birds we saw at Gambell were blackened carcasses hanging from racks all over the village. They had been shot by the natives and dressed and were being cured by drying to be eaten later on. Although I have no objection to eating birds (we have chicken every Sunday), I doubted that, since I thought of them as creatures to be watched and studied, my stomach would be strong enough to handle one of these. I couldn't understand why these curing birds were so numerous, especially since the residents of Gambell seem well-supplied with food stamps. Some scientific collectors who have eaten the birds after they have skinned them told me that most birds taste about the same. One who ate the breasts of two eagles collected in Asia said that they were as large as softballs and tasty but tough.

Gunfire was a common sound in the village at all hours. Many youngsters seemed to enjoy using the birds for target practice; they certainly weren't hunting for food because anything they killed would drop into the sea where it couldn't be retrieved. And since they used 22-caliber rifles and the targets were moving twenty to thirty miles per hour, they probably didn't kill many. One young man did bag a very pink Ross's Gull, however; as we stood on the point watching all the gulls dive and feed, he came walking by with his family swinging the dead gull in his hand. Since the species is beautiful and extremely rare in the lower forty-eight states, many of the birders were horrified. If you live at Gambell or at Barrow on the north coast of Alaska, perhaps Ross's Gulls are as common as other gulls and just as good to eat.

Since very few birders will ever get to Gambell, I have listed below all the species I saw in addition to those mentioned above:

Yellow-billed Loon
Arctic Loon
Northern Fulmar
Pelagic Cormorant
Brant
Greater White-fronted Goose
Common Pintail
Green-winged Teal
Greater Scaup
Oldsquaw
Harlequin Duck
Common Eider
King Eider
Surf Scoter
Sandhill Crane
Lesser Golden Plover
Black-bellied Plover
Wood Sandpiper
Wandering Tattler
Ruddy Turnstone
Northern Phalarope
Red Phalarope
Western Sandpiper
Rufous-necked Stint
Baird's Sandpiper
Pectoral Sandpiper
Rock Sandpiper
Dunlin
Pomarine Jaeger
Parasitic Jaeger
Glaucous Gull
Glaucous-winged Gull
Herring Gull
Arctic Tern
Thin-billed Murre
Thick-billed Murre
Black Guillemot
Pigeon Guillemot
Horned Puffin
Tufted Puffin
Tree Swallow
Barn Swallow
Northern Raven
Gray-cheeked Thrush
Yellow Wagtail
Red-throated Pipit
Hoary Redpoll
Common Redpoll
Lapland Longspur
Snow Bunting

14

NOME, THE PRIBILOFS, AND THE SEWARD FERRY

My next trip was to have been to hunt for Bristle-thighed Curlew, but upon our return to Nome on June 12, we could not make the needed arrangements because the charter plane pilot's phone in St. Mary's (the town nearest the curlew habitat) was out of order. Most of the group then headed home, but Davis and I stayed in Nome to search for Gyrfalcon, and Mike and Cindy Greene (she had joined us at Gambell) came along with us. Nome has about 3,000 permanent residents and is ugly and covered with a thick layer of dark gray dust. Nevertheless, there were enough other tourists to fill up the two small hotels, and we were lucky to rent rooms in a private home. Davis and I shared ours with a stranger. This was, however, a minor drawback; the shower, after eight days without one, more than made up for the presence of an unknown person in our room.

Alaska was always full of surprises for me. On the plane from Gambell, Davis had said that we would rent a car from the Board of Trade in Nome, and I assumed that the city had an alert chamber of commerce that provided for the needs of all tourists. The Board of Trade turned out to be the biggest saloon in town with a 100-foot bar lined with drunks in midafternoon. I wondered where they got the name. The barkeeper was the car rental agent. The car was $55 per day plus gas, and I gave him a $100 bill. To make change he pulled out a roll of twenties bigger than a baseball and a roll of tens and fives even larger. He must have been carrying thousands of dollars. I decided that he qualified for his job by being the toughest character in a very tough place.

After supper in a very good Italian restaurant, we headed out the Kougarok road toward a Gyrfalcon nest site and, in a matter of minutes, began to see both Rock and Willow Ptarmigans along the roadside. The Gyrfalcon nest was located in what looked like a miniature orchestra shell about 200 feet up a rock cliff that in turn rose from the top of a small hill overlooking the valley of the Nome River. We found no birds in it, even though we climbed above the nest by coming up from behind it. On top of the hill we encountered a Northern Wheatear at very close range and a Lesser Golden Plover that gave us the old broken-wing act to decoy us away from its nest, and Arctic Warblers were singing everywhere in the thickets along the river.

When we returned to this spot the next morning, a Gyrfalcon was standing next to the nest. We moved slowly toward it up the hill, and it let us approach to within 100 yards before it flushed. It was immediately joined by another bird that we had not seen, and the two flew back and forth for a minute before vanishing over the hill. Residents of Jackson, Mississippi, rarely see one Gyrfalcon, much less two flying around the nest. Just before lunch we visited a colony of nesting Aleutian Terns twenty miles from Nome on the Council road and then caught the plane to Anchorage.

The weather thwarted us again on June 14. The Reeve flight to St. Paul in the Pribilof Islands stopped first at Cold Bay, and when we reached it at noon, we had to get off the plane and wait for the weather in St. Paul to improve enough to permit landings. The terminal was a Quonset hut with a waiting room that measured twenty-five feet by forty feet, and into it were jammed about 100 passengers waiting for the weather to improve at several other places. After six hours of trying to doze in uncomfortable positions, we flew back to Anchorage.

During the long wait at Cold Bay, I called home and ran

into something I should have been prepared for but wasn't. It was 7:00 P.M. in Jackson when my call came in, the most hectic time of the day. If ever six children are a burden, it's at the end of the day when supper is still simmering on the stove and everyone is hungry and tired. Virginia had had just about enough of being the stay-at-home parent, left with all the problems while the other was chasing a dream somewhere else for more than a month. Later in the year she would tell a reporter for *The Wall Street Journal,* "I would have sold him for a dime when he went off to Alaska and left me for weeks with the kids," and on this occasion I got the idea that she would have sold me for a nickel. Every man has had an unsatisfactory conversation with his wife at one time or another, but under normal conditions, both can keep talking until the problems are resolved. In this situation, though, it was impossible to talk the problem out. Our conversation was being carried on via satellite; therefore, only one person could speak at a time and could not begin speaking until one or two seconds after the other had finished. This feature would put a burden on even the easiest conversation. I didn't blame Virginia for feeling as she did, and I began to wonder whether my Big Year might really hurt my marriage.

The Alaska I had seen up to this point was beautiful at a distance, but ugly at close range. Attu was a scenic clump of mountains covered with snow, but the birding areas were a vast military junkyard that got started in the early days of World War II and was still being added to. Likewise, Gambell was pretty but had no satisfactory systems for disposing of trash or sewage, and I wondered how the residents could stand to live in it. Nome was better, but still very dirty and full of abandoned and unusable houses and equipment. Even the modern city of Anchorage was coated with a layer of grayish brown dust.

The village of St. Paul (population 500) and St. Paul Island, one of the four Pribilof Islands, were exceptions. The island of gently rolling plains and a few small hills was covered with a green carpet of knee-deep broad-leaved grass dotted with large patches of purple lupine flowers. The village houses scattered over a hillside were in need of paint, but they made a pleasing sight with their bright colors and white trim. The whole area was as neat as a small town in Mississippi.

Soon after the plane landed on June 15, we, about twenty-five birders who had been together at various times during the previous thirty days, went to the observation blind built for photographers by the natives at one of the fur seal beaches. About 1,400,000 fur seals breed on these islands, and the huge bull beachmasters had just arrived to stake out territories and await the females. From a hilltop observation post nearby, we looked down on a "bird" cliff, where hundreds of murres, auklets, puffins, and gulls were nesting on tiny ledges high above the water. Here we saw the first Red-legged Kittiwake, a common bird here but one found nowhere else in the ABA area, and therefore a prime drawing card for bird tours. (It was also at this "bird" cliff that the photograph was taken that appears on the jacket of this book.)

We were quartered in a tiny hotel with comfortable beds and a bathroom down the hall. I had just stretched out to doze for several minutes after lunch when someone shouted up the stairs, "There's a cuckoo in the graveyard!" Everyone dashed down the road toward the small plot surrounded by a white picket fence and filled with wooden crosses with two horizontal bars. After Martin and Linda Smith told us where they had discovered it, we swept the area and soon flushed the hawklike bird. It was noticeably larger than American cuckoos, barred underneath, and it seemed much darker to me. As though to defy identification, the bird was silent. But all of us got to observe it well several times, and there was much hurried study of field guides. The weight of all the evidence I saw and heard convinced me that the bird was a Common Cuckoo, a species that is found over most of

Europe and Asia and whose call is the familiar one of cuckoo clocks. Nevertheless, since we could not eliminate some doubt about the identification without either hearing it or catching it, I tallied it as "Cuculus species."

While we were stalking the cuckoo in the cemetery, we flushed a female Siberian Rubythroat and thus got to see two Code 4 birds simultaneously, a rare experience for any birder. Later in the afternoon we drove to Webster Lake and spotted a male Common Pochard in good light at close range for telescopes. Since I had picked up Alder Flycatcher near the motel while waiting for a car to the airport, June 15 was a very productive day. June 16 was a blank; most of it was spent getting back to Anchorage.

By this time Davis Finch had gone to lead another tour group, so I joined Will Russell, Rich Stallcup, and most of the birders who had lived at Tim Slwooko's house at Gambell. Will and Rich rented two large vans with plenty of windows, and we set out early June 17 on a leisurely drive to Seward, a small town about 125 miles south of Anchorage. We spent much of the day in the evergreen woods of Chugach National Forest. It was good to see trees big enough for lumber again; there are none more than about ten feet tall at Attu, Gambell, Nome, and the Pribilofs. At a campground near Hope, a tiny village about halfway to Seward, we found the nest of a pair of Northern Three-toed Woodpeckers about eight feet up the trunk of an aspen less than fifty feet from the parking lot and spent a long time watching and photographing both parents feeding the young in the hole. At Primrose Campground Bill Boyle found two young Boreal Owls, one of which let me approach to within a dozen feet, and a female Spruce Grouse and six chicks.

We boarded the *M. V. Tustumena,* a 293-foot ferry ship, at Seward in time for supper aboard and sailed at 7:45 P.M. for Kodiak, about 200 miles to the southwest. Once I pulled on enough clothes, I enjoyed the voyage down Resurrection Bay more than anything in Alaska so far. We stood on the second deck about forty feet back from the bow and constantly scanned everything around us. Snow-covered mountains, vertical rock cliffs, and one glacier rose from the water's edge, and birds were everywhere—murres, puffins, gulls, petrels, shearwaters, and auklets—sitting on the water or flying across the bow. Before I went to my stateroom at 10:30 P.M., I sighted Fork-tailed Storm Petrel and added it to my list.

Most of us were up again at 3:30 A.M. on June 18 so as to be observing when we passed through the deepest water of the voyage, the only time we could expect Scaled Petrel. There were no petrels, but we were compensated by brilliant sunshine, very smooth seas, and thousands of birds. We reached Kodiak, a fishing and port town and the prettiest one in Alaska, about 11:30 A.M. and had a pleasant three-hour stopover for lunch and shopping for gifts for the family. In midafternoon we sailed for Homer, 125 miles to the north, and I spent the afternoon and early evening in the bow, enjoying beautiful weather, marveling at magnificent scenery, and looking in vain for another new bird. Just before dark, we passed near a huge rock cliff that was almost covered with nesting kittiwakes; Will estimated that there were 10,000 of them. We docked at Homer near midnight, stumbled into a tiny hotel, and got up a few hours later to catch a 7:00 A.M. flight to Anchorage. I spent most of June 19 sound asleep on a long upholstered bench in the Anchorage air terminal.

My first Alaska trip was more productive than I had hoped for. In 1978 the tour group led by Finch, Russell, and Stallcup got thirteen rarities, whereas I got sixteen. I added sixty-six new species for the year, and when I boarded the plane home at 6:45 P.M. on June 19, tired, dirty, five pounds lighter at 152, and hungry to see my family, my total was 608. After flying all night and changing planes in Dallas, I found Virginia at the airport in Jackson with another surprise. She had lost twelve pounds. I had always thought she looked like a million dollars; now she looked like ten million.

15

FILLING IN THE GAPS

My homecoming was joyous. My wife still loved me; my kids still remembered me, even recognizing me under the ragged white whiskers I had sprouted during six weeks of not shaving; my forestry practice was winding up the most prosperous six months in its history; and there were messages of encouragement from birders all over the country who had been getting my newsletters. For three days I sat around and enjoyed all this. Even the thought of leaving so soon on the second trip to Big Bend National Park didn't seem too bad, because I would depart after breakfast one morning and return in time for supper the next day.

It wasn't to be that easy; the trip turned into a thirty-six-hour exercise in mental and physical strain. Soon after John Arvin and I met in Dallas on June 23, Texas International canceled our flight to Midland and rescheduled us on Braniff. This caused substantial overbooking; some passengers already standing in the aisle of the plane with us were sent back, and even after the door was closed, it was reopened, and still other passengers were removed and replaced. I didn't feel safe until we were airborne. This maneuver made us an hour late getting to the park, and although we looked closely at every flowering agave between the headquarters and the Basin, we found no hummingbirds.

To allow the maximum amount of time for birding, we had made reservations at the Cavalry Post Motel in Lajitas, forty miles west of park headquarters, but when we arrived at 9:30 P.M., we found that the manager had rented our room to someone else. This was a terrible blow, for in Big Bend country, motels are almost nonexistent

We drove back to the headquarters building where there were lights across the front of it, a water fountain, a men's room, and several low benches more than six feet long but only eighteen inches wide. I stretched out on one of them; John chose the concrete floor. Pain woke me every thirty minutes. At 1:00 A.M. I saw, crawling on the floor six feet from me and John, a tarantula that to my inexperienced eye looked as big as the palm of my hand and deadly as a rattlesnake. After ten minutes of watching it pounce on and eat insects attracted by the lights, I decided that its proximity was too much for me, woke John, told him about his new neighbor, and went to the car for the rest of the night. The car was a Firebird, a sporty little vehicle that my kids would love but that I needed a shoe horn to get into. I tried sleeping on the hood, the back seat, and the driver's seat without success and finally spent three hours dozing in the right front seat with my knees jammed against the dashboard. Although it was almost the shortest one of the year, the night seemed the longest so far.

After such an inauspicious beginning, things had to get better, and our luck turned the next morning. Peter E. Scott, a seasonal naturalist at the park and a transplanted North Carolinian doing graduate work in zoology at the University of Texas, led us about three-fourths of a mile up a canyon behind his apartment to the nest of our target bird, Lucifer Hummingbird. We found the nest on a short horizontal section of a long looping arm of ocotillo that was nearly invisible even with the female sitting on it. She flew off when we climbed up level with her but soon returned and settled down to her business only thirty feet away.

Next we walked the Window Trail from the campground to the hitching rail for horses, searching all flowering plants for hummingbirds and listening intently for Gray Vireo. We scored with hummingbirds, seeing Broad-tailed, Blue-throated, and several other Lucifers. Although we heard several Gray Vireos and saw one flying high up the canyon wall, we couldn't count it because it was too far away for a good look. The scenery was magnificent, especially where the canyon narrowed to a width of twenty feet at the bottom and rocky cliffs and slopes rose 1,500 feet on each side. The three hummingbirds raised my total to 611.

By now new birds were becoming hard to get. The Big Bend trip involved 2,000 miles of travel and two days of hard work but produced only three new ones. I had anticipated this, however; what I hadn't anticipated was *losing* one. Paul Sykes gave me the bad news in a telephone call June 25, and he hated the job because he lost one from his life list too.

The Canadian experts who showed me the Edmonton Chickadee and identified it in the field as a Siberian Chickadee later caught, banded, weighed, measured, and photographed it. After studying the data, they decided that the bird was actually a leucistic Black-capped Chickadee, one that, by a freak of nature, wound up much paler than all others. I removed the species from my total, reducing it to 610; I still had a chance to get it, since I would return to Alaska, where the species is Code 2.

Three days after my return from Texas, on June 27, Frances Wills and I drove down the Natchez Trace Parkway south of Jackson and picked up Mississippi Kite and Louisiana Waterthrush, two birds I had worried about since missing them during spring migration. Both leave early in the fall, and because it stops singing when nesting begins, the waterthrush can be very hard to find. I had already searched for both birds three times since returning from Alaska. The kite was easy; one flew over us on the road. I used a tape recorder to get the waterthrush to start singing and must have played it near the center of the territory; the bird reacted immediately, sang repeatedly and at very short intervals, and flew back and forth over our position.

Although it was only a small feat, I got a big thrill out of successfully stalking the waterthrush. The pressure was on. My business and birding schedule was full through late August with no time in waterthrush habitat, so, had I not seen it this time, I might have missed it for the year. The quarry was uncommon, inconspicuous, and silent at a time when ten or more associated species were abundant, very active, and singing with gusto. I had to get in the right spot and make the bird sing. I chose the spot by studying all my books on bird life histories and asking for advice from local experts. Then I borrowed a record of bird songs and transferred the waterthrush portion to my portable tape recorder. When I carried out my plan on the ground and the bird responded immediately, I felt like a World Series winner.

Hunts like this one had caused excitement and fascination up to this point of the year. The excitement would increase because the quarries were generally harder to find and would have to be stalked for a longer time. Except for the Monterey pelagic and Arizona trip, I didn't expect to add many new species at once; most remaining species would have to be hunted one at a time.

Thrills like this one made all the frustration worthwhile. No matter how tired or miserable I was, I always bounced back to above normal when I got a new bird, and the slightest chance to get another one kept me going well beyond what I thought was the limit of my endurance. Now I knew why men loved the hunt.

The day after the waterthrush hunt, Phoebe Snetsinger, Carmen Patterson, and Joe Greenberg met my plane in St. Louis at midmorning, and in less than ninety minutes, we had found a pair of Willow Flycatchers in the brushy area on the shoulder of a country road and a Eurasian Tree Sparrow on the shore of Creve Coeur Lake. Phobe's scouting the day before made it all so easy. We then drove to Augustus Busch Wildlife Area, which contained some beautiful stands of hardwood timber, and walked the trails hoping to get lucky with an American Woodcock. Not only did we miss it, but we also had to return to the airport early because of rain.

Larry Balch and Barbara Hickey met me in Chicago, and after stopping overnight in Grand Rapids, we joined the 11:00 A.M. tour from the U.S. Forest Service Ranger Station in Mio, Michigan. Our guide, a summer employee, brought back fond memories for me; a student at the forestry school at University of Michigan, she would graduate in 1980, thirty-eight years after I did. Since foot travel was prohibited through the young stands of jack pine where Kirtland's Warbler breeds, hearing a singing male from the road was more important than usual. In another demonstration of his skill as a birder, Larry located one before we even reached the regular stopping point. Although he was seventy-five yards away from us, the bird sang from the top branches of a small dead tree, and we saw him very well with the guide's telescope.

Always limited in numbers because of its tiny breeding area, Kirtland's Warbler was threatened with extinction first by the loss of its breeding habitat (all the young jack pines were growing into big trees) and later by the success of cowbirds in laying eggs in the warbler's nests. The Forest Service solved the first problem by changing its forest management practices and then reduced nest parasitism to a negligible level by trapping cowbirds, and we went to see how this is done on a large scale. The trap is a fine-mesh wire enclosure about twenty feet square and seven feet tall. In an attempt to get to food in the trap (mostly cracked grain not suitable for warblers and other insectivorous species), birds enter through holes in the wire just large enough to admit them but too small to allow them to fly back out. Eight or ten decoy cowbirds stay in the trap at all times as an additional lure. Over the course of a year many species, including several small hawks, were caught, and one Great Horned Owl pushed its way in through the door. A free lunch is an irresistible lure. We got my first Clay-colored Sparrow of the year near the trap.

At 8:00 A.M. on June 30 I met Jim Steffen at Woodland Dunes Nature Center between Two Rivers and Manitowoc, Wisconsin, to look for a pair of nesting Little Gulls discovered on the center's marsh by Jim and Tom Erdman. Since they weren't visible from the headquarters building, we paddled around in a canoe until we spotted one on a mud flat with several Bonaparte's Gulls. It let us approach within fifty feet while it preened and displayed its dark underwings; then it called several times and flew about 100 feet away. It and Ross's Gull are among the most beautiful birds. Jim then turned me over to Bernie Brouchoud, president of the center, and we found Least Flycatcher on another of its properties.

Woodland Dunes Nature Center is a nonprofit bird-banding station, wildlife research area, and wildflower sanctuary that is supported by private contributions. It owns over 500 acres of varied habitats, where more than 100 species breed, and its staff trapped and banded 1,425 birds of seventy-six species in 1978. It offers unique birding and may be unknown to many birders; for those interested in more information, its address is P.O. Box 763, Manitowoc, Wisconsin 54220.

At noon I flew from Green Bay to Duluth, picked up Kim Eckert at his home, and then drove sixty miles north to a small roadside tavern on a private holding deep inside Superior National Forest. The one 3.2 percent beer I drank wasn't the best in the world, but a tree overhanging the tiny parking lot contained a Black-backed Three-toed Woodpecker's nest, and we watched the female return several times to feed her young. Later we whiled away several hours searching for Connecticut Warblers and Whip-poor-wills and then drove down one of the most remote and least-traveled roads as twilight deepened. As we were getting out of our little car to listen for birds, I heard a noise as though a larger animal were walking through the woods, and when the sound was repeated I pointed my binoculars in the direction of it. Suddenly I was staring into the face of a full-grown bull moose, not more than fifty feet away. No one had to tell us to clear out, but fortunately, when we ran back to the car, the moose fled in the opposite direction. In a few moments, a Whip-poor-will sounded off close to us, and we found him sitting on a big rock twenty-five feet down the road.

Although we didn't get to bed until midnight the night before, July 1 began at 4:00 A.M. We made several stops to listen for birds active at night or at dawn but failed to score. By 7:00 A.M., however, Kim heard a Connecticut Warbler singing in a spruce bog fifty miles south of Duluth, and we found him in a tree top about 150 yards off the road. I was surprised at how far the song carried.

Hoping to win big by knocking off Baird's Sparrow quickly and then flying to a whirlwind tour in Wyoming, we drove like mad to a Nature Conservancy prairie in west Minnesota northeast of Fargo, North Dakota, and hit the ground running. But, to my disappointment, we missed; there were many Savannah and Grasshopper Sparrows, but no Baird's. I did get a surprise, however; I actually stepped on an Upland Sandpiper while walking slowly through the prairie grass over ankle deep. When the big bird flushed from underneath me, I froze and waved Kim over to help find the nest. My right foot was on top of the edge of it, only millimeters away from the nearest of four eggs. Missing the sparrow made it impossible to attempt the Wyoming trip (I had to be in Jackson early July 3 for a business meeting), so we headed for Aberdeen and got Franklin's Gull from the highway across Sand Lake National Wildlife Refuge in northeastern South Dakota. Early the next morning there were plenty of singing Baird's Sparrows on the Nature Conservancy's Ordway Prairie Reserve seven miles west of Leola, South Dakota, and I ended my first swing after Alaska with a total of 623 birds sighted.

I came away from the trip with renewed appreciation of Larry Balch's birding skills. Top birding pros must be experts in two fields: finding the birds in the field, and getting birders to the birds. All pros were so much better than I at finding and identifying birds that I was not qualified to judge performance in the first area, but I knew something about the second one because I had spent a lifetime getting foresters to the woods and arranging for their care and feeding while they were there. I saw no one better at birding logistics than Larry Balch. Not only did he make all the arrangements, he even handed me a typewritten script for the whole trip. My hat is off to him.

16

NONSTOP BIRDING IN ARIZONA AND WYOMING

The temperature was 109 degrees when I arrived in Tucson on July 7 to meet Kenn Kaufman for a fast-paced, meticulously planned run for the record. By design there was to be nonstop birding, meals on the run, and very little sleep. We would hardly even have time to talk to each other. To give you an idea of how fast the pace was, here are the sightings of July 7 in chronological order, with new species for the year marked by an asterisk:

7:29 P.M.	Mourning Dove, leaving Tucson airport
7:33	House Finch
7:36	White-necked Raven
9:37	Poorwill, in canyon near Sierra Vista
9:50	Whiskered Screech Owl*
9:58	Whip-poor-will

After only a few hours' sleep in Sierra Vista, we hit the road in high gear July 8, worked Carr and Ramsey Canyons early, reached the Chiricahuas by midafternoon, hunted owls by the light of the brightest full moon, and finally bedded down at Cave Creek Ranch. Here's how the day went:

5:00 A.M.	Barn Swallow, around Sierra Vista Motel
5:10	House Sparrow
5:11	Great-tailed Grackle
6:00	Cassin's Kingbird, driving toward Carr Canyon
6:05	Blue Grosbeak

l. to. r.: Paul Sykes, JV, Will Russell at strategy session In Jackson, Mississippi

l. to r.: Rich Stallcup, Kenn Kaufman, John Arvin, Larry Balch, Paul Sykes, Will Russell, Jane Werne, JV at strategy session in Jackson, Mississippi

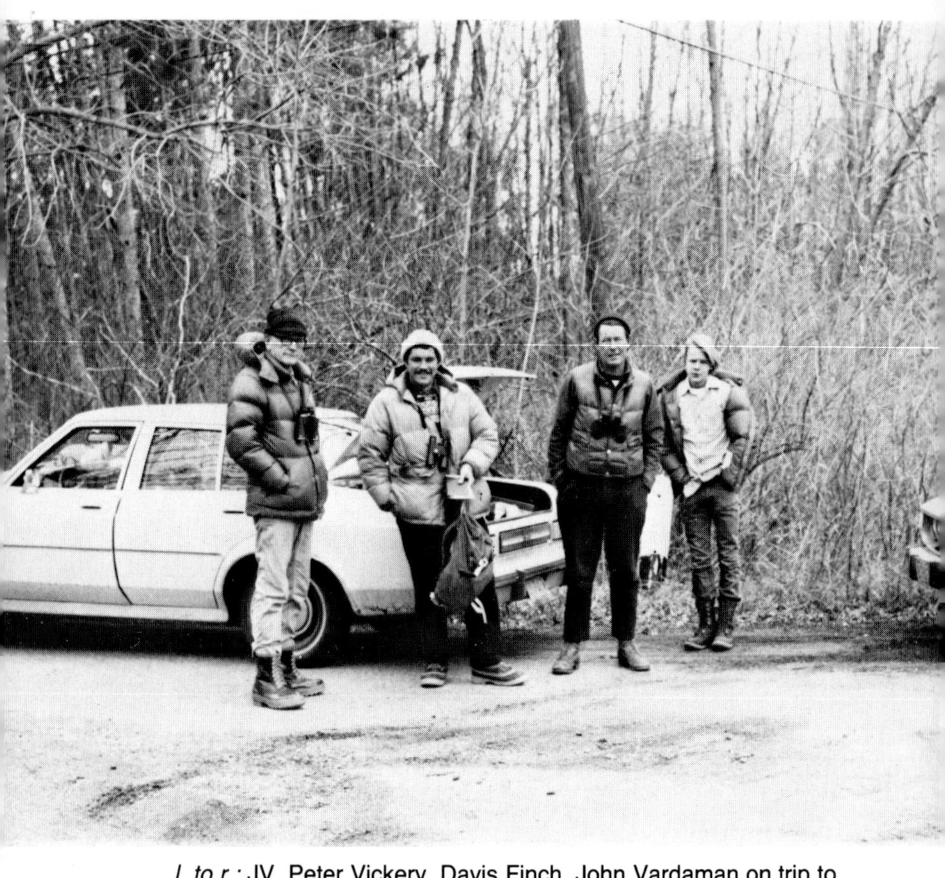

l. to r.: JV, Peter Vickery, Davis Finch, John Vardaman on trip to New England to see Great Gray Owl (Dennis J. Abbott III)

Dr. Ron Ryder and JV in the Colorado Rockies (Clait Braun)

David Vardaman and JV in the Colorado Rockies

Looking at Brown Noddys on the Dry Tortugas

l. to r.: David Wolf (looking through telescope), Rose Ann Rowlett (looking through binoculars)

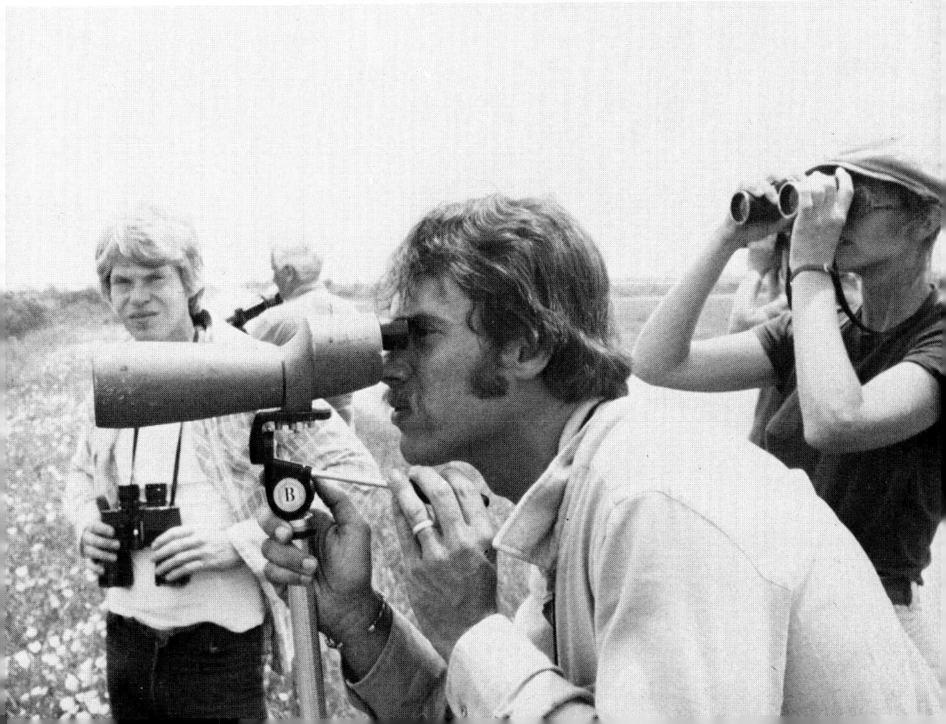

Rail-buggy in Anajuac National Wildlife Refuge in Texas

l. to r.: JV, Mike Greene, Benton Basham, Jon Dunn, leaving for Attu

l. to r.: Jon Dunn, JV, Ben King at the Attu Air Terminal

l. to r.: Thede Tobish, Lisa Oakley, Lt. Davis of the Coast Guard on Attu Island.

Paul Sykes with the Whitetail Eagle he carved on the Attu Island outhouse

l. to r.: Jon Dunn, Larry Balch, Jerry Maisel, Jerry Rosenband, on Attu in May (Larry Balch)

6:08	Curve-billed Thrasher
	Acorn Woodpecker
6:09	Gray-breasted Jay
6:14	Black-headed Grosbeak
6:23	Steller's Jay, driving up the mountain
6:33	Rufous-sided Towhee
6:39	American Robin
6:41	Common Flicker
6:45	Northern Goshawk*
	Brown Creeper
	Western Pewee
6:47	Coues's Flycatcher*
6:53	Eastern Bluebird, walking in Carr Canyon
	Bronzed Cowbird
6:56	White-breasted Nuthatch
7:03	Band-tailed Pigeon
7:04	Chipping Sparrow
	White-throated Swift
7:07	Canyon Wren
7:10	Solitary Vireo
7:11	Hermit Thrush
7:13	Western Flycatcher
7:18	Black-chinned Hummingbird
7:20	Anna's Hummingbird
7:25	Brown-throated Wren*
7:30	Lesser Goldfinch
7:32	Broad-tailed Hummingbird
7:33	Hairy Woodpecker
	Western Tanager
7:47	Mexican Junco
7:48	Indigo Bunting
7:53	Buff-breasted Flycatcher*
8:17	Rufous Hummingbird*
8:22	Hutton's Vireo
8:33	Bushtit
8:52	Olivaceous Flycatcher*
9:00	Broad-billed Hummingbird*
9:30	Brown-headed Cowbird
9:43	Blue-throated Hummingbird
10:17	Bridled Titmouse
11:02	American Kestrel,
	driving toward Ramsey Canyon
11:04	Northern Mockingbird
11:19	Violet-crowned Hummingbird*,
	at Ramsey Canyon feeders

11:39	Magnificent Hummingbird*
12:25 P.M.	Cooper's Hawk, driving toward Cave Creek Canyon
12:30	Eastern Meadowlark
12:47	Killdeer
	Cliff Swallow
12:49	Mexican Duck*
12:55	Lesser Scaup
2:00	White-winged Dove
	Turkey Vulture
2:59	Black-throated Sparrow
3:12	Western Kingbird
3:13	Loggerhead Shrike
3:30	Horned Lark
3:45	Swainson's Hawk
3:52	Cassin's Sparrow
4:00	Red-tailed Hawk
4:04	Brown Towhee
	Gambel's Quail
4:07	Summer Tanager
4:15	Bewick's Wren
5:07	Painted Redstart*, walking up Cave Creek Canyon trail
5:22	Hepatic Tanager
5:32	Sulphur-bellied Flycatcher
6:05	Brown-backed Woodpecker
7:48	Northern Pygmy Owl*, while eating supper from a can at the trail parking lot
7:50	Spotted Owl*

Before we turned in for the night, Kenn called in to the Arizona rare-bird network, as he did at least once a day during the period, and heard some exciting news: a White-eared Hummingbird was coming to a feeder in Summerhaven, a village in the Santa Catalina Mountains north of Tucson about three hours' travel away from us. This Code 3 bird was too good to pass up, so we set the alarm clock even earlier than planned. Here's what happened July 9:

6:22 A.M.	Scott's Oriole, in Cave Creek Canyon
6:40	Elegant Trogon*
6:50	Violet-green Swallow
7:31	Mexican Chickadee*, in the Chiricahuas

7:32	Red-breasted Nuthatch
7:40	Black-throated Gray Warbler
7:44	Virginia's Warbler*
8:30	Greater Roadrunner, driving toward Tucson

The house with the feeders in Summerhaven was set back about fifty feet from the narrow street, and there was no parking space in front of it, so we had to stand in the street. There wasn't one feeder, there were eight or ten of them—two or three under some big spruces in one corner of the yard, two on a small hardwood tree near the front door, and several more hanging at various points across the front porch. There wasn't one hummingbird either; there must have been fifty or 100 of them, sitting in trees, drinking from first one feeder and then another, or chasing each other in courtship or battle. They were like a swarm of bees near a hive. It took Kenn twenty minutes to find the one White-eared Hummingbird in this crowd and then almost ten more minutes to show it to me at 12:45 P.M. The prominent white stripe over the ear was unmistakable. We ran for the car and continued our chase in the forests south of town:

1:32 P.M.	Western Bluebird
1:40	Olive Warbler*
	Yellow-rumped Warbler
1:42	Pygmy Nuthatch
1:48	Grace's Warbler
2:05	Mountain Chickadee
2:45	Red-faced Warbler*
4:52	Northern Cardinal, driving toward Patagonia
5:15	Phainopepla
5:27	Gila Woodpecker
5:32	Say's Phoebe
5:26	Thick-billed Kingbird*
5:40	Rose-throated Becard*
	Rufous-crowned Sparrow
5:47	Lucy's Warbler*
6:01	Yellow-billed Cuckoo
6:02	Ladder-backed Woodpecker
6:05	Ash-throated Flycatcher
6:35	Verdin
6:47	Zone-tailed Hawk, east of Patagonia

That night, a situation arose that called for the kind of decision we were forced to make over and over again during the year. We had to be thirty miles west of Nogales the next morning to get Five-striped Sparrow, but there were two choices thereafter. On one hand, we could spend the afternoon looking for Montezuma Quail with almost 100 percent chance of success and then drive to Phoenix in time for some sleep and a dawn search for Gray Vireo sixty miles to the north. Or we could give up on the quail, travel east for three hours to Guadelupe Canyon, search it after dark for Buff-collared Nightjar, and then drive all night to the dawn rendezvous with the vireo. Kenn reported that he and several other birders had already failed to find the nightjar in several attempts earlier in the year. I decided that, in a try for 700 birds, sleep must be postponed and that a slim chance at a nightjar was better than a cinch at Montezuma Quail. We set the alarm for 4:30 A.M.

The next morning, after driving west of Nogales for more than an hour on an unpaved road so rough and crooked that the speed limit was often either ten or fifteen miles per hour, we had an encounter that reminded me of Charles Manson and his gang of female murderers. From the unpaved road, we turned down an even more primitive road that soon ended at the bottom of California Gulch, a hot, dry, rocky canyon. About 100 yards after we started walking, we came upon an old bus and two tents in which were camped seven humans, three or four dogs, a couple of cats, and a pet Red-winged Blackbird. The only man in the crowd was slim, dark-haired, and barefoot, seemed to be about thirty-five, and must not have bathed or combed his hair in a week. Three women were in the same state of cleanliness, but one was fully clothed, one was topless, and one was bottomless. One two-year-old child was completely naked. Another woman and a child remained in a tent. It was the strangest group I met all year, and after identifying the blackbird for them, we left quickly.

The pace of the day was much like that of July 8 and 9:

5:40 A.M.
Northern Raven, driving toward Nogales
6:45
Hooded Oriole*
7:22
Black Phoebe
Vermilion flycatcher
7:59
Rock Wren, walking in California Gulch
8:01
Lark Sparrow
8:08
Common Ground Dove
8:25
Five-striped Sparrow*
8:50
Black-tailed Gnatcatcher
9:55
Varied Bunting, returning to Patagonia
11:07
Black-bellied Whistling Duck
12:41 P.M.
Tropical Kingbird
Pyrrhuloxia
12:45
Inca Dove
1:33
Yellow-breasted Chat, walking in Patagonia-Sonoita Creek Sanctuary
1:37
Song Sparrow
1:40
Common Yellowthroat
1:41
Lazuli Bunting
1:42
Yellow Warbler
1:50
Gray Hawk*
2:18
Rough-winged Swallow, driving toward Guadelupe Canyon
4:56
Northern Beardless Flycatcher*, at canyon entrance
7:16
Bell's Vireo

7:58
Elf Owl
8:25
Common Screech Owl
9:40
Great Horned Owl
9:55
Buff-collared Nightjar*
10:37
Lesser Nighthawk, driving toward Phoenix

We found the nightjar by starting at the top of Guadelupe Canyon and playing a tape recording made by my old mentor, Ben B. Coffey, every quarter mile down. At the fifth stop Dr. John Hubbard and some friends from New Mexico drove up behind us to see what was producing the call, and at the ninth stop the real bird responded on my side of the car. We got another response near the canyon's entrance and examined both birds with a powerful flashlight. It was my fifteenth Code 2 bird of the year, and it convinced me that, with professional help, I could see the remaining eleven by year's end.

Kenn and I had not had a good night's sleep since July 6, so the drive to Phoenix and beyond seemed unending, and we had to switch places every hour. I learned, however, that for sleeping a Ford Fairmont beats a Firebird every time. Here's how the Arizona leg ended July 11 with my total at 655:

5:14 A.M.
Cactus Wren, 60 miles north of Phoenix
5:40
Gray Vireo*
5:48
Black-chinned Sparrow
5:50
Scrub Jay
6:19
Harris's Hawk
6:47
Wied's Crested Flycatcher

Abert's Towhee
7:02
Great Blue Heron
7:12
Lesser Black Hawk*
8:30
Red-winged Blackbird
8:35
Rock Dove
8:50
Starling (the 150th species of the trip), approaching Phoenix Airport

I was open-mouthed in wonder at the Arizona hummingbirds. We saw nine species and hundreds, maybe thousands, of individuals. During two hours in the wild woods at the head of Carr Canyon, we saw about fifty hummingbirds of six species working the bright red Penstemon flowers. Watching hummingbirds feed seemed to be the favorite outdoor sport of Arizona, and the results of such an interest were spectacular. At The Nature Conservancy's Ramsey Canyon Sanctuary, there were eighteen feeders close to several rows of chairs and benches, and I estimated that there were fifty hummingbirds in sight at all times, twenty on the feeders and thirty perched in nearby trees. Anyone from the eastern United States, where we have only the Ruby-throated Hummingbird, would be thrilled by such a sight and get an added charge when a Violet-crowned or a Magnificent came to feed only fifteen feet away.

I was surprised to discover that many of the country's great birding spots are in National Forests, since I have been accustomed to think of them mostly as timber producers. Among such places that I visited and enjoyed were the Kirtland's Warbler area in Michigan, Superior National Forest above Duluth, and, in Arizona, the Chirichuas, Carr Canyon, California Gulch, and the Santa Catalinas.

With my total of 655 birds, the record was within my reach, and this buoyed me up so much that I flew to Rock Springs, Wyoming, without thinking about how sleepy I was. Dr. Oliver K. Scott, my companion in Florida in May and the leading Wyoming birder, met my plane at 8:30 P.M., and we sped to the top of Rock Springs Uplift to try for Gray Flycatcher in the few minutes before dark. We missed. Since this was my last chance for the bird, we decided to sleep in the car among the junipers and under a full moon. I unrolled a foam pad and a bedroll on the roof of the Toyota Corolla and discovered that it was even better than a Fairmont. We got the flycatcher (#656) at 6:00 A.M. on July 12.

After a big breakfast, we headed for Grand Teton National Park where Trumpeter Swan was a permanent resident on Christian Pond. If I could get Ruffed Grouse near Jackson, the swan would give me 658 and break Scott Robinson's record of 657. Bad luck intervened. Heavy traffic and road construction delayed us so much that we couldn't even try for the grouse, but I saw the dependable Trumpeter Swan and tied Scott Robinson's record at noon on July 12, my one hundredth birding day of the year.

Sensing that victory was at hand, we drove rapidly to Chukar headquarters, a huge Bureau of Land Management area northwest of Thermopolis, and arrived with several hours of daylight left. Although we hunted until dark and were on the ground again at dawn on July 13, we saw nothing, not even a suspect. With this, two more fairly common birds, Montezuma Quail and Chukar, became minor problems.

Now that I had tied the previous record, the shape of the rest of the year became clearer, and so I considered in detail some of the unseen species. On the itinerary that had been set up by the Strategy Council in March, I felt sure I would reach 688 by seeing the following thirty-one birds:

Species	*Possible places of sighting*
Black-footed Albatross	Westport, Monterey
Cory's Shearwater	North Carolina, Florida
Pink-footed Shearwater	Westport, Monterey, southern California
Flesh-footed Shearwater	Westport, Monterey

Greater Shearwater	North Carolina, Maine
Buller's Shearwater	Westport, Monterey, southern California
Sooty Shearwater	Westport, Monterey, southern California
Leach's Storm Petrel	Westport, Monterey, Maine
Ashy Storm Petrel	Monterey, southern California
Black Storm Petrel	Monterey, southern California
Least Storm Petrel	Southern California
Red-billed Tropicbird	Southern California
White-tailed Tropicbird	North Carolina, Florida
California Condor	California
Ruffed Grouse	Many possibilities
Montezuma Quail	Texas, Arizona
American Woodcock	Many possibilities
Chukar	Many possibilities
Great Skua	Maine, Maryland
South Polar Skua	Westport, Monterey
Elegant Tern	Monterey, southern California
Xantus' Murrelet	Westport, Monterey, southern California
Craveri's Murrelet*	Southern California
Cassin's Auklet	Westport
Yellow-headed Parrot	California
Hawk Owl	Alaska
Saw-whet Owl	Many possibilities
Vaux's Swift	West Coast
Northwestern Crow	Vancouver, British Columbia
Crested Myna	Vancouver, British Columbia
Seaside Sparrow	East Coast

*Sometimes it's more comfortable to be ignorant of the future. In spite of strenuous efforts I would miss both tropicbirds and Craneri's Murrelet for the year.

Was it possible to get twelve more species of those still unaccounted for? After removing those species with codes higher than 4, since there was very little chance to see them, I drew up a list of others with the places where they might be seen and a guess about my chance of seeing them. There were thirty-two:

Species	*Code*	*Place To See*	*Chance to see*
Laysan Albatross	3	Alaska, West Coast	Fair
Scaled Petrel	4	Alaska	Poor
Blue-footed Booby	3	California	Good
Bean Goose	4	Alaska	Poor
Falcated Teal	4	Alaska	Poor
Garganey	3	Several places	Good
North American Jacana	4	Texas	Poor, may return to Maner Lake
Black-tailed Godwit	4	Alaska	Poor
Bristled-thighed Curlew	2	Hooper Bay, Alaska	Certain about July 31
Gray-tailed Tattler	2	Alaska	Good
Sharp-tailed Sandpiper	2	Vancouver, British Columbia	Good
Curlew Sandpiper	2	East Coast	Good
Spoonbill Sandpiper	3	Alaska	Fair
Broad-billed Sandpiper	4	Alaska	Poor
Slaty-backed Gull	2	Alaska	Good
White-winged Black Tern	4	East Coast	Good, if one returns to Delaware
Berylline Hummingbird	3	Arizona	Good
Fork-tailed Flycatcher	4	Anywhere	Poor
Bahama Swallow	4	Florida	Poor
Siberian Chickadee	2	Alaska	Certain somewhere in state
Rufous-backed Thrush	3	Mexican border	Good
Clay-colored Thrush	4	Mexican border	Good
Dusky Thrush	3	Alaska	Fair
Dusky Warbler	4	Alaska	Poor
Gray-spotted Flycatcher	4	Alaska	Poor
Yellow-green Vireo	3	Mexican border	Fair
Bananaquit	4	Florida	Poor
Stripe-headed Tanager	3	Florida	Fair
Hawfinch	4	Alaska	Poor
Eurasian Bullfinch	4	Alaska	Poor
Common Rosefinch	3	Alaska	Fair
White-collared Seedeater	4	Mexican border	Poor

With prospects like these, I was afraid to rely on getting the needed twelve by making the scheduled trip to Alaska later in the year and by chasing rarities whenever they appeared. Therefore, the only alternative seemed to be to schedule another trip to Alaska around July 31, this time in order to get Bristle-thighed Curlew and Whiskered Auklet.

17

BREAKING THE RECORD

Thirty-six hours after I returned from Wyoming, I hopped a plane for Key West, Florida, only this time I had Virginia and all six children with me. There would be some birding, but it was mainly time for our family vacation. Our first day, July 16, had some of both. I chartered the *We Five,* a twenty-nine-foot boat capable of speeds over forty miles per hour with Richard Farkas as captain, and we made the seventy-five-mile run west to the Dry Tortugas and back. This was the same boat we had used to go after Masked and Red-footed Boobies in May. We carried a picnic lunch, snacks, and cold drinks, and all the kids, including our six-year-old Sally, had a good time exploring the nooks and crannies of old Fort Jefferson, where Dr. Mudd was imprisoned after Lincoln's assassination.

Ben King, who had come down from New York, joined us to help with the birding. He wanted a White-tailed Tropicbird as badly as I did. There were no birds at Fort Jefferson except two Mourning Doves, one lost Canada Goose, about twenty dying Cattle Egrets, the usual terns and frigatebirds, and an adult Brown Booby on the old coaling dock; there were even fewer on the lighthouse key west of the fort—one Black-crowned Night Heron and several Cattle Egrets. There was nothing exciting over the water either, but at least the sea was like glass and nobody got seasick.

Larry Balch came down from Chicago that night. During the next three days, he, Ben, and I left at dawn aboard the

We Five and scoured an area that extended forty miles west, forty-five miles east, and thirty-five miles south of Key West. We did everything we could think of to find a tropicbird, including flying kites off the stern. We had no luck. Brown Noddies and Sooty, Bridled, Roseate, Little, Royal, and Black Terns were everywhere, and three Audubon's Shearwaters almost came aboard the boat. Hoping to find something rare, Richard gave full-speed chase to each petrel we spotted, but all were Wilson's Storm-petrels. Then Tropical Storm Claudette came near on July 20 and 21 and produced enough wind and rain to wipe out pelagic trips. I spent a few days playing with the family and then left Florida empty-handed, wondering whether I had missed this tropicbird for the year. And since I had already missed Chukar in Chukar headquarters and now missed White-tailed Tropicbird in tropicbird headquarters, I also wondered whether I really knew enough about the life histories of certain species.

I broke the record with American Woodcock in Chicago at about 11:30 A.M. on July 27 on CBS-TV. Larry Balch, Jerry Rosenband, Burleigh Hines (a CBS newsman), and a two-man camera crew met my plane at O'Hare Airport earlier that morning, and we headed directly for Lake Calumet, a heavily industrialized, smoky, smelly area on Chicago's south side. For six previous days a Curlew Sandpiper had drawn birders from all over the United States to a small drainage ditch there; its photograph, good enough for identification, had appeared on the front page of the Chicago *Tribune*. Larry had called me soon after I returned to Jackson, but I couldn't get away from my business until the morning of the 27th. Larry arranged the television coverage but failed to clear things with the bird; the rare and famous sandpiper was gone when we arrived at the ditch.

But no single bird was going to beat Balch. Several American Woodcocks had been spotted the day before feeding in the moist ground under an acre of small cottonwood trees alongside a railroad drainage ditch about a mile away, the only trees in sight. We drove toward them and parked nearby. Burleigh, Larry, Jerry, and I formed a line for a sweep through the area, and the TV crew, one carrying a thirty-five-pound shoulder camera and the other a forty-pound sound recorder (what a tough way to make a living!), moved through the woods close behind us. Less than sixty seconds after we started moving, the first woodcock jumped up ahead of Burleigh and me, and I broke the record on camera, as we discovered when we watched the 6:00 P.M. and 10:00 P.M. news on Channel 2 that night. Burleigh signed my sighting ledger along with Larry and Jerry and became my first witness among TV newsmen.

I was thrilled at breaking the record. I said on camera, "I was afraid I would never make it; anything could have happened at any moment since January 1 and blown my chances." I also never expected to break it in such an inhospitable habitat, but the woodcocks seemed perfectly happy.

Bruce McDonald, one of the leading birders of Vancouver, British Columbia, made getting my next three species easy. After flying to Seattle and driving through beautiful scenery to Vancouver, I picked him up at his home at 5:00 P.M. on July 28, and by 6:30, we had spotted Northwestern Crow, Crested Myna, and Vaux's Swift, a migrant I had missed in the spring. The crow and the myna are town birds and live only a few blocks from Bruce, the crows being found on chimneys like the jackdaws of Europe; the swifts are woods birds, and the ones we saw were flying over the dense forests of a mountainous park on the city's north edge. Since there was plenty of daylight left, we searched the sewage-sludge ponds on Iona Island, where Spoonbill Sandpiper appeared in 1978, and found my third Peregrine Falcon of the year and many common shorebirds.

At the start of the year I had given up the idea of seeing Whiskered Auklet because its total range is restricted to a small part of the Aleutian Islands centered on Adak and because access to Adak, a United States Naval Station, is in turn restricted by the Navy Department. Visitors must undergo a mild security check, and someone must arrange for them to stay in the Bachelor Officers' Quarters. Even getting on Adak is not enough; you also have to go by boat another forty miles east to Igitkin Pass in order to see the bird. At the time these obstacles seemed too formidable. Now, however, when I studied my decreasing possibilities and then missed the tropicbird, I decided to try to overcome them.

Larry Balch, the logistics wizard, did it for me somehow. Thede Tobish and I flew from Anchorage to Adak July 30 and by 1:00 P.M. were headed east in the *Molly B,* Chief Bob Packard's forty-foot converted aircraft rescue boat. It was cold—the 50-degree temperature was sharpened by the twenty-mile speed of the boat—but the sea was smooth and the scenery magnificent: one island east of Adak containing both a 5,700-foot peak and a steaming volcano. There were thousands of birds, mostly Least Auklets. Since they flushed far ahead of us and zipped along at thirty or more miles per hour, picking out Whiskered Auklets among the crowd was very difficult, but Thede finally found a single individual, then a flock of six, and just before we left, a flock of eleven that flew alongside us for a short while. One of the hardest-to-see Code 1 birds became #662 for the year.

Then began a string of bad luck long enough to make a grown man cry. We returned to Adak on the Pacific Ocean side and, though we looked hard, saw no trace of albatrosses. The next morning we searched Clam Lagoon and found thirty-nine Bald Eagles around its shore but no shorebirds other than twenty-five Ruddy Turnstones. Since the birds were scarce, I took five minutes out to examine carefully every tree in the Adak National Forest. On a hillside next to the road, there were eight or nine spruce trees that had finally struggled to heights of about eight feet. I guessed that they were perhaps thirty-five years old. The sign pointing to them with pride was almost as large as the whole forest. Even these trees were much larger than any I had found on Attu;

there someone had planted three spruces at the entrance to an old Army church and three more in a clump three miles away, and the tallest of them was under six feet. The nearest things to trees in the Aleutians and around Nome and Gambell were willows and alders that often grew prostrate on the ground like vines and rarely reached waist height.

We spent the morning of August 1 looking unsuccessfully for a Hawk Owl that had been reported near the Anchorage Airport and then flew to Kodiak that afternoon, in search of the Scaled Petrel. Although I had taken the ferry from Seward to Kodiak in June, I'd missed Scaled Petrel partly because the deep-water part of the trip took place mostly in darkness. I hoped to score this time by taking the ferry the opposite way, a fourteen-hour daylight passage.

The *M. V. Tustumena* sailed from Kodiak at 5:15 A.M. on August 2, on a glassy sea under a cloudless sky, ideal conditions for spotting and identifying birds from the bow. At 8:45 we encountered thousands of Short-tailed Shearwaters sitting or flying all around us, an experience that was repeated again and again during the next three hours. Soon there were small numbers of Fork-tailed Petrels and Sooty Shearwaters (#663) among them. There must have been more than 250,000 birds in these flocks, and our hopes were high.

But the beautiful weather struck us down. Because the weather was so clear, in itself a rarity in Alaska, the *Tustumena* was moving along ahead of schedule. Rather than arriving early, the captain decided to take the long way to Seward, turned off the regular deep-water route, and sailed through narrow passes between the hundreds of islands in the chain. This was the only "pelagic" trip I've ever taken on which I saw a Boreal Chickadee. Later one of the ship's officers told me that, in good weather, they followed this course only once every month or six weeks. The unexpected maneuver reduced my chances of seeing Scaled Petrel or other rare species by one-half or two-thirds, and we could only stand helplessly in the bow until failure became a certainty.

The next morning we flew from Anchorage to Bethel to catch the 2:00 P.M. plane to Hooper Bay, an Eskimo village on the west coast of Alaska near where Bristle-thighed Curlews congregate for several weeks before their fall migration to Tahiti. While we sat in the Bethel terminal, the weather at Hooper Bay worsened to fog and rain, zero ceiling, and forty-mile-per-hour winds, so airport officials postponed the flight, one hour at a time, until they finally canceled it at 5:20 P.M. There was only one flight to Hooper Bay on August 4 (and no assurance of improved weather) and no flights on August 5, so the door was slammed in our faces again. Trying to salvage something from the week, I called Larry Balch and learned that the two new Curlew Sandpipers that had showed up near Chicago after I left had also disappeared. Bitterly disappointed, and both physically and mentally exhausted, I flew home to lick my wounds.

On August 10, on the way to Bar Harbor, Maine, I did, however, see the biggest bird of the year. NASA's 747 with the space shuttle riding piggy-back landed on the runway next to ours in Atlanta, and it was so huge that I didn't see how they got it in the air. It was certainly the sensation of Atlanta that day as it flew over the airport, circled over the downtown district, and then landed.

The next day Will Russell, Rich Stallcup, Davis Finch, Cloe Mifsud, Peter Vickery, Larry Balch, and Barbara Hickey, all old friends and top birders, joined me on the *Bluenose* for a trip that has been a favorite among birders for many years. The *M. V. Bluenose,* a Canadian ship, is 339 feet long and sixty-five feet wide; carries 600 passengers and 150 cars between Bar Harbor, Maine, and Yarmouth, Nova Scotia; and contains a complete restaurant, a bar, and even a room full of slot machines. During the months it is in service, it sails from Bar Harbor at 8:00 A.M. and reaches Yarmouth (ninety-eight miles away) at 2:00 P.M., sails again at 3:30 P.M., and reaches Bar Harbor at 9:30 P.M. During the turnaround at Yarmouth, there is time to eat at one of the best seafood restaurants in Nova Scotia. Even more important, it is ideal for pelagic birding trips. Birders are allowed to stand on the bow; most of the trip occurs during daylight; the middle fifty-mile stretch is over deep water; and the ship is so large that its sailings are seldom canceled by bad weather.

Ours was a day of cloudy skies, gentle seas, and lots of shearwaters and petrels. I got three new birds, Greater Shearwater (#664) and Leach's Storm Petrel, which I'd anticipated seeing, and Cory's Shearwater, which I didn't expect to see until September 1 off Hatteras, North Carolina. Sooty Shearwater, Manx Shearwater, Wilson's Storm Petrel, Atlantic Puffin, and Northern Gannet completed our list of pelagic birds. The star of the show, Great Skua, did not appear, so Larry Balch, Barbara Hickey, and I repeated the trip August 12; all we got was steady rain, the species listed above, and no skua. Before breakfast that morning, however, Will Russell flushed a Ruffed Grouse (#667) for me just outside town.

I had planned to go home August 13, but Kenn Kaufman changed my mind that night when he called in the news that an Eared Trogon (a Code 6 bird) had shown up in Arizona. I hopped on the next available plane and arrived in Arizona eight hours later.

Getting from Bar Harbor to the upper part of Cave Creek Canyon in the southeastern corner of Arizona requires 2,500 miles of flying, 160 miles of driving, and five miles of walking. That was a lot of effort to miss a bird, but all part of any Big Year. The trogon had been discovered Saturday and was seen by perhaps fifty birders Sunday, but no one had seen it Monday. Kenn and I searched eight hours for it Tuesday and found Elegant Trogons, a Northern Pygmy Owl, Red-faced Warblers, and Painted Redstarts (plus other species), but no Eared Trogon. Certain that the bird had left, we gave up, drove to Paradise, Arizona (whoever named this town didn't share my view of it), and after combing a small area for one and a half hours, finally flushed a Montezuma Quail (# 668), thereby solving one of my small problems.

By the end of July, I had traveled over 100,000 miles; birded in twenty states, five Canadian provinces, and eight time zones; and spent 118 days at it.

18

GOOD AND BAD LUCK ON THE PACIFIC OCEAN

"Jim, there's a Curlew Sandpiper in Jamaica Bay Wildlife Refuge just off the end of the runway at Kennedy Airport here in New York. You probably can't find it except at high tide, and the next one is at 6:00 P.M., August 18." This good news from Bob Paxton got me on the first available plane for New York, for I remembered how delays had caused me to miss the same bird in Chicago and also Eared Trogon in Arizona. Less than forty-five minutes after my arrival I had an additional bonus: Bob and I found a Seaside Sparrow (#669) in the tall marsh grass around West Pond of the refuge.

The path into East Pond wound through grass or cane more than eight feet tall and was just wide enough for one person. When the last sharp crook brought us to the mud flat around the pond, we were almost within touching distance of about 100 Semipalmated Plovers. After looking them over carefully, we moved out of the cane to the water's edge and saw Tom Davis about 100 yards away, waving for us to hurry toward him. He had been watching the Curlew Sandpiper for thirty minutes. The bird (#670) was almost in full breeding plumage and allowed us to approach within fifteen yards. (Tom later told me that it stayed around for days and was seen by hundreds of other birders.)

On the way back to the car we encountered a large flock of Semipalmated Sandpipers that contained two birds stained orange with picric acid in the trapping program run by Dr. R. I. G. Morrison at James Bay, Canada. After catching the birds in nets near Hudson's Bay, Dr. Morrison stains them so that they will be conspicuous, puts bands of certain colors on each leg either above or below the knee, and then asks birders everywhere to report sightings of them and the colors and positions of the bands. In this way he hopes to learn more about the mysteries of bird migration. The orange showed up very well and gave us a thrill when we realized what we were seeing. The birds we saw had been captured only a few days earlier and had already traveled 800 miles; they were now feeding to store up fat for a nonstop journey of 2,700 miles to the east coast of South America. Tom noted the band positions and colors and said he would notify Dr. Morrison. The whole subject of bird migration and Dr. Morrison's work were treated in the August 1979 issue of *National Geographic.*

Jamaica Bay Wildlife Refuge was like no birding spot I had seen thus far. Not only is it within the city limits of one of the country's largest cities, it can also be reached by subway. Its fresh- and salt-water ponds and marshes and the thickets and young trees are full of birds at all seasons, but especially during migrations. Bob and Tom said that it is not unusual to find thirty species of shorebirds at East Pond.

Not long after I returned to Jackson from New York, Ann Biscan of Akron, Ohio, called to report that a Corn Crake (a Code 7 bird) had appeared on Lake Ontario forty miles west of Cleveland and had been seen two days running by many observers. While several of us from all over the country were making arrangements to fly there, local observers reported they couldn't find the bird on the third day, so we stayed home. Hurricane David arrived east of Miami around Labor Day and headed north up the coast; although we hoped that it would bring in some rare birds to help offset the damage it did, no one reported any finds.

Now the itinerary called for the first West Coast pelagic trips and hunts for a parrot and a condor. Jon Dunn and

Kimball Garrett, two young men who have almost finished a book on the birds of southern California, and Peter Peterson of Davenport, Iowa, met my plane in Los Angeles late in the afternoon of September 6, and we headed north a few miles to search for Yellow-headed Parrot. Los Angeles is full of parrots. They occur all over the residential areas and seem to be breeding, multiplying, and in general making themselves at home, but the only species on the ABA list—and therefore the only one I could count—was Yellow-headed. Although most parrots are big and brightly colored, they are almost impossible to find except at dawn and dusk when they make a lot of noise and fly around their roosts. So, as the sun went down, we drove around looking and listening for them while listening to the Rams-Broncos game on the radio. Three parrots flew by, all Lilac-crowned. When daylight began fading fast, I said, "Men, this is the two-minute warning; you had better find one fast." Almost immediately Kimball shouted, "Stop the car. There are two flying over." Number 671 was in the bag. A few minutes later Pete spotted two more out the back window, and we got even better looks at them.

Jon, Pete, and I left Los Angeles September 7 in time to arrive at 10:00 A.M. at Mt. Pinos, where we found clear skies but a fierce south wind. When an hour's watch produced nothing, we decided the wind was working against us, so we moved about ten miles north to another ridge top. We then split up and manned lookouts to the north, east, and south. For three hot, dry hours nothing happened. Then I saw, without a witness, a Red-breasted Sapsucker, a bird that might soon be classified as a separate species, on a tree near me; the bird landed, stayed twenty seconds, and then was gone.

Jon and Pete, as bored as I was, wandered over to my lookout, and in no time Jon spotted a speck above Mt. Pinos, perhaps ten miles—maybe only five miles—away. That speck came closer and soon became a distant but identifiable California Condor (#672). These majestic birds, heavy-bodied and with a ten-foot wingspread, sail along like space ships or hang-gliders without the man and can therefore be identified at very long range. So far as we know, there are only about thirty living California Condors, so the species may become extinct before I do. Someone told me that the United States Fish and Wildlife Service planned to catch two or three pairs and breed them artificially. If the program succeeds, I wonder where the huge products of it will find suitable habitat.

My first West Coast pelagic trip began at 5:30 A.M. on September 8 from San Diego. The boat was large (more than seventy feet long) and comfortable (food was served on board), the seas gentle, and the weather ideal. And Guy McCaskie, one of the most outstanding birders in the United States, was the leader. We sailed from San Diego to the south end of San Clemente Island and back, a total distance of about 125 miles. I added four species, Elegant Tern in the harbor, and Least Storm Petrel, Black Storm Petrel, and Pink-footed Shearwater at sea, bringing my total for the year to 676.

More important were the birds I missed: Red-billed Tropicbird, Craveri's Murrelet, and Xantus' Murrelet. Tropicbirds are always unpredictable, so missing this one was no surprise. Craveri's Murrelet was supposed to be certain, however, and those most familiar with San Diego pelagic trips in September told me they couldn't remember one without a Craveri's Murrelet. But missing Xantus's Murrelet was the result of a mistake in planning. The species is common off San Diego in spring but moves west and north after nesting and is almost never seen in fall. I repeated the trip September 9 with no better luck. Missing three species at this point was a severe blow, and I was not sure how to overcome it. I decided to try to get on board a special pelagic trip that was not on my original itinerary.

Twelve hours after I got off the boat in San Diego I stepped aboard the *Apollo,* a sixty-five-foot boat chartered by Terry Wahl, in Westport, Washington, a small seacoast town

120 miles southwest of Seattle. All I had had to do to make the connection was hop a jet to Seattle, rent a Pontiac Bonneville and drive two and a half hours to Westport, and sleep for four hours in the front seat until it was time for breakfast. This car was more comfortable for sleeping than any so far.

Most of those on board were on a Massachusetts Audubon Society tour led by Peter Vickery, an old friend, and Jim Lane, the engaging fellow whose books about where to find birds have added so much pleasure to the lives of many birders. Terry Wahl and his assistant, Bill Harrington-Tweit, an experienced young birder from Olympia, completed a team of four experts who didn't miss a thing. With their help I got to #680, adding to my list Buller's Shearwater, Cassin's Auklet, Black-footed Albatross, and South Polar Skua, all four of which at one time or another came to within a few yards of us.

For a birder who wanted to predict in advance what species he might see, this trip was the best I had seen during the year, and Terry deserved the credit. At half-hour intervals after we sailed, he and Bill met on the bow and recorded the species and numbers they had seen in the past half-hour. At the end of the day, Terry entered the totals of all species seen in a log of seventy or more similar trips off Westport since 1966, and then he reported the results of the thirty-four most recent trips. When I read his literature, I knew I would see Black-footed Albatross because they had never missed it and usually saw more than twenty-five. I also knew I would be lucky to see Flesh-footed Shearwater because they had missed it thirteen times, never saw more than five, and usually saw only one. So far as I know, no one else keeps such detailed reports of sightings for pelagic trips.

September 11 produced Chukar (#681) and a hard physical test. In response to pleas in my newsletter, the *Gold Sheet,* Phil Cheney had written me that Chukars were common in the high, dry country east of Wenatchee, Washington, and he arranged for Howard Oswood to guide me to the area.

After driving around and walking for almost two hours without seeing or hearing anything, Ossie and I walked to the rim of a canyon about 2,000 feet deep and perhaps a half-mile wide from the rim on one side to the rim on the other. We could hear Chukars calling far below. Since the birds are large and often call from the highest points on ridges and benches, we searched hard for them with binoculars with no luck and finally decided we would have to go down after them. I groaned. The canyon sides went down at an angle that was sometimes like a steep flight of stairs and sometimes perpendicular, and they were covered with loose rocks or scattered tiny bushes growing in handfuls of dirt among the rocks. Some of the distance going down or up would have to be covered on all fours. Nevertheless, the birds called repeatedly, and there seemed to be ten or fifteen, so I decided to go down after them until I reached an obstacle I couldn't get over. In forty-five minutes we had struggled down 1,500 feet and reached the top of a sheer cliff with the birds still down below us. Just as I was about to surrender, one Chukar and then another flew from under the cliff to the next ridge, and in a few minutes, two more flew across the bottom of the canyon. The climb back up took one and a half hours and seemed an eternity.

Jon Dunn and I joined David Sonneborn in Anchorage on September 12 and spent four hours in the late afternoon searching for a Hawk-owl in Westchester Lagoon, Potter's Marsh, and around the airport, a search I had made five times earlier in the year. We failed. The Hawk-owls that were continually reported around Anchorage must have seen me coming and promptly disappeared.

The next day I would fly to Attu for two weeks, needing a run of good luck in the worst way. The list of birds that had been missed for the year was much too long:

Species	*Reason for Missing*
Scaled Petrel	Good weather caused ferry to change course
Red-billed Tropicbird	None recorded this year
White-tailed Tropicbird	Couldn't find one on six trips
Blue-footed Booby	None recorded at Salton Sea this year
Slaty-backed Gull	None seen by my tour group to Alaska
White-winged Black Tern	None recorded where it could be chased
Xantus' Murrelet	Error in planning
Craveri's Murrelet	None recorded off San Diego this year
Berylline Hummingbird	None recorded where it could be chased
Eared Trogon	Did not reach locality in time
Yellow-green Vireo	None recorded where it could be chased
Bachman's Warbler	None recorded

Would I do well enough on Attu to get back in the game?

19

FALL BIRDING ON ATTU

My fall trip to Attu started out in an auspicious way.

On September 13, Thede Tobish and Lisa Oakley, who had gotten to Attu a week earlier, met Jon Dunn, Paul Sykes, and me on the runway and soon hustled us down to Navy Town to see a Garganey (# 682) they had spotted the day before. Although the bird was in eclipse plumage and therefore hardly beautiful, I could have kissed it because, earlier in the year, I had flown all the way to Los Angeles only to miss it. I was later to see the species almost every day. We birded until 9:00 P.M., the approximate time of sundown, without finding anything exciting.

Our accommodations for this trip were luxurious compared to those of the previous trip. We stayed at the Attu Balchon, so christened because it was the Quonset hut used by the Larry Balch tour group in the spring, to which had been added, thanks to a line connected to the generator at the Coast Guard station, electric lights and refrigerator. There were two stoves to keep it as warm as we desired and a concrete floor. We slept on mattresses six inches thick. There was even an outhouse about twenty yards away, so there was no need for me to be latrine orderly again. We had a great variety of canned food and brought fresh eggs, lettuce, and fruit on the plane with us. Best of all, the greatly improved living conditions allowed us to concentrate on the birds.

When we landed, the temperature was 50 degrees, the wind fifteen miles an hour, and the skies mostly cloudy.

Except for tiny patches remaining in mountain canyons, the snow had been replaced with a rank growth of plants, usually only knee-high but sometimes rising as high as a man's shoulder. This growth made it impossible to ride bicycles more than one-third the way to Aleksai Point, so we ended up walking a great deal more. At Anchorage, about 500 miles north of Attu, the birches were turning yellow and the mountain tundra red, but here everything was still green—a welcome change from the snow-covered landscape that had greeted us in May.

We left for the field on September 14 at 8:30 A.M., about as early as there was good light, and headed, mostly on foot, for Murder Point. Just before we reached it, we found an immature Gray-tailed Tattler (#683) that was kind enough to stand still while we studied it in detail at close range. After the long walk around the point and past two big ponds on it, we walked the beach from the south end of the big runway to Henderson Marsh and found no new birds. My tongue was hanging out and my feet hurt. Just before dark, Thede found a Siberian Ruby-throat, but by the time Paul Sykes reached him, the bird had disappeared.

Thick fog in the morning of September 15 developed into steady rain by midafternoon. We searched for the Rubythroat both early and late without success. The rest of the day we spent walking the beaches, and we found another Gray-tailed Tattler, Buff-breasted Sandpipers (the first I'd seen since April in Texas), Golden Plovers, and Dunlins. Although none of these was new for the year, they were new for the trip and clearly indicated that birds were migrating. We went to bed early, hoping that the rain was part of a storm that would bring more birds.

Sometime after we went to bed, a thirty-mile-an-hour southwest wind joined the rain, and the two continued all day long September 16. Birding was impossible, so I bathed and shaved. It took an hour and one and a half gallons of water, but it made me feel good, and there wasn't much better use of time. Since my goal of 700 species was beginning to seem distant, I hated to miss a single minute of birding on a place like Attu, but the other trips to Alaska had taught me that bad weather sometimes brought many new birds, and it was still early in our trip.

September 17 was a bit better. Although the wind continued all day, the rain let up enough at 11:00 AM. for us to go birding. We walked down to the runway and immediately jumped a Sharp-tailed Sandpiper (# 684). Much to my surprise, the strong wind seemed to keep the birds on the ground and make them tame, and we were often able to walk within twenty feet of species that usually flush at a distance of 100 feet. And so the wind, which before had hindered us, led to the greatest find of the trip.

After lunch we were walking along the beach near the Coast Guard Station, examining shorebirds one by one, when we came upon a tiny sandpiper feeding in the kelp. It was redder than most. We peered through the binoculars at it, identifying it at first as a Rufous-necked Stint. After we began a feather-by-feather description of it, however, we decided that it was a Little Stint, a Code 7 bird and only the second one ever recorded in the ABA area. Number 685 was a bird that no one had dreamed I would see. The rain began again and ran us in early, but we were a happy bunch.

Hoping that the bad weather had brought in a new crop of birds, we were out early on September 18 working the runways and the beaches from Casco Cove to Henderson Marsh. By the end of the afternoon, we had covered eight miles of rough walking without finding anything unusual, so we decided to make one final pass by the bluffs near Massacre Bay and then go home. Near the end of the bluffs, standing waist-deep in weeds, Paul Sykes shouted, "I've got a grasshopper warbler." Pinning down the identification was a maddening task. The bird would skulk in the heavy growth, then suddenly flush from beneath our feet, fly forty to fifty feet just over the top of the plants, drop out of sight, and continue to skulk so that we never knew where it would flush again. It was never visible to us for more than two or three seconds at a time, but each of us finally got a look at it when it lit nearby at the end of one short flight. It was a Middendorf's Grasshopper Warbler, a Code 6 bird and #686 for me. On the way home we flushed another Siberian Rubythroat, and Paul Sykes got 721 for his life list.

On September 19 we returned to the warbler's location, spent one and a half hours trying to catch it with a mist net, and found the task more maddening than that of identifying it. We flushed the bird a dozen or more times and even had it in the net twice. Once it crept under the net just three or four feet from me. Somehow, it escaped us every time. Giving up a job that might have taken forever, we walked among the old buildings around Massacre Bay and found two Bramblings, a species I had seen in the spring and one I was very familiar with from World War II days in Europe. Then we took the long hike to upper Henderson Marsh and over the saddle to our hut; the only rewarding sight was that of two Siberian Rubythroats, male and female, perched facing us on the same flowerhead. In late afternoon on a pond near the intersection of the two runways, we spotted a duck that, both sitting and flying, gave many indications of being a Baikal Teal. The prospect of getting another Code 7 bird excited us, but the light faded before we could get a good look.

Rain and twenty-five-mile-an-hour winds eliminated birding on the morning of September 20. We got a weather break after lunch and checked the teal prospect, but we failed once more to see enough for identification. When we checked again after the Reeve plane came and went, we couldn't find the bird.

Using a mist net, we caught a Middendorff's Grasshopper Warbler on September 21. The net is about twelve feet wide and four feet tall and is made of fine black threads almost like a hairnet. After tying the ends to sticks eight feet long, Paul Sykes held one end and I the other, and the others drove the bird into it. The net hangs loosely between the sticks, and the bird becomes entangled as soon as it hits. If you intend to make a specimen of it, as we did, you disentangle it and kill it by placing its breast in the palm of your hand and squeezing it under the wings, thereby collapsing the lungs and compressing the heart at the same time. Death is almost instantaneous.

The next step is to skin it, but this is a delicate job, one that we could not do in our situation on Attu. Special tools are very helpful, and proper drying of the skin takes several days. Therefore, we froze the bird and delivered it to Dan Gibson at the University of Alaska Museum in Fairbanks later. It was only the third specimen ever taken in North America.

After more sightings and study, we decided that the Baikal Teal prospect was actually a Garganey in unusual plumage.

By then, we had walked more than twelve miles, and my feet weren't the only ones dragging.

That night there was a frost, and ice was glazed on the puddles on the morning of the 22nd, and all mountain peaks within sight had fresh snow. Up until noon we had the first cloudless day I had seen in the Aleutians. It was like the fine fall days at home.

The good weather did nothing for our birding, however; I saw no new birds, and we added only Barn Swallow and Emperor Goose to our trip list. Four days without a new bird were discouraging when I needed a fruitful stay at Attu so badly.

Steady rain and twenty-mile-an-hour winds began before dawn of September 23, so I bathed and shaved again for lack of anything better to do. (If nothing else, this fall trip was certainly a cleaner one than the May trip.) The rain continued all day, and the wind increased to thirty-five miles an hour at times, so birding was impossible.

Paul Sykes, a champion at birding, demonstrated that he was also a champion at remodeling. The object of his attentions was our outhouse. He added a new roof, a new floor, and a latch on the door, but his crowning glory was the hole in the front door usually fashioned in the shape of a half-moon. Paul cut his in the shape of a flying White-tailed Eagle, part of the logo for the Balch tour group, and then made it into a window by putting a piece of Plexiglass behind it. I was latrine orderly for fourteen persons in the spring, but my creative accomplishments were nothing compared to his.

The rest of us had nothing so tangible to show for the day. We spent it reading, sleeping, eating, and talking about birds or national and world problems, anything to pass the time until the weather improved.

Before this year, I thought Alaska was a place to enjoy the great outdoors; now I know it's the place to enjoy the great indoors. The reason is the weather; it can become beastly on short notice, anywhere, anytime, and make outdoor activity unpleasant or impossible. On this day no one left the hut for more than a few minutes at a time. By 10 o'clock at night there were wind gusts of almost 100 miles an hour, and sometime during the night the anemometer and part of the roof blew off the Coast Guard Station. About 11:30 A.M. on September 24, the wind dropped to twenty-five miles an hour, and it was raining only a third of the time, so we went birding for six hours but found nothing new.

Since we were in the final seventy-two hours of our stay and hadn't found a new bird in ages, we were in the field early on September 25, but we struck out again. With so little time remaining here and with our luck so poor when I needed it to be so good, I began to lose hope of reaching 700. Paul Sykes hiked over to Temnac Bay searching for White-tailed Eagle but had no better luck than we did.

On September 26, we spent another long, unsuccessful day combing Navy Town and the bluffs halfway to Aleksai Point. The only unusual sighting was a flock of three Yellow-billed Loons swimming in full sunlight on smooth Massacre Bay only 100 yards from us. To relieve the boredom, we attended the nightly movie at the Coast Guard Station and then walked home under a cloudless, moonless sky, marveling at the brilliance of the stars.

During the spring when there were thirty-four birders and only twenty-two Coast Guard men, we were not allowed into the warmth and comfort of the Station because we might have interfered with the important work that goes on there. Now that there were only five of us, Lt. Davis, the commandant, was able to be much more hospitable. He sometimes came to our hut to visit after supper, and he allowed us to come into the Station at night to attend the movie and buy beer at the bar. Since we brought whiskey and wine with us, we seldom patronized the bar, but the movies helped kill time when the weather was bad. Otherwise we had little contact with these men. We were chasing birds in the field in other parts of the island; they were busy with the Loran equipment inside the station.

It began to blow and rain before dawn on September 27 and continued with few letups until late afternoon. Fortunately, the weather didn't prevent the Reeve plane from landing, and we flew back to Anchorage. Since we were almost in Asia at what is usually the peak of the fall migration, it was hard to believe that we had not seen a new species for nine days. We saw a total of sixty-one species, but except for the five new ones mentioned above, our list was similar to that of the spring trip.

I left Attu discouraged. It wasn't that I had traveled 13,000 miles and spent two weeks to get a very few birds. I knew from the beginning that, at this point in the year, I would be traveling long distances and working hard to add one species at a time. It was that, of the fifteen possibilities listed in Chapter 16, only four showed up (we never dreamed that we would see Little Stint). Being optimistic by nature, I had thought we would see seven or eight new ones and had hoped for nine or ten. Instead of being above 690, I was still fourteen long steps from my goal.

In spite of my discouragement, I could say nothing but good about Thede Tobish. Even for a twenty-five-year-old, his physical stamina was enormous, and he must have walked fifty miles around the contours of the steep bluffs, trying to flush passerines from the rank growth. His identification of birds in the field was usually instantaneous, but always very careful, and since many of the birds were strange to birders from outside Alaska, he saved us a lot of time. Finally, he was a good cook.

We were the first birding party ever to study the fall migration on Attu, and what we found may eventually change our occurrence codes. We saw five grasshopper warblers and nine rubythroats and encountered both species for five consecutive days. Although our limited observations were not enough to reveal the true occurrence of these species, they indicated that both may be Code 1 on Attu in the fall instead of Code 6 (warbler) and Code 4 (rubythroat).

Collecting the tiny warbler September 21 was my first experience at this since I had helped shoot some sandpipers below Memphis in 1937. During the year, I learned a lot about why collecting is useful, how it is done, and what impact it probably has on the bird populations. Specimens, which are usually skins of birds, are essential for the correct classification of birds into species and particularly for the investigation of hybridization, such as I described earlier among the orioles. They are also essential for anyone preparing field guides; most of the birds Audubon used as models were shot by him, and no one can get the colors exactly right unless he has the bird in hand. All collectors must have permits from both federal and state agencies, and these permits are issued only after thorough investigation to be sure that the purpose of the collecting is valid and that the collector is qualified for the job.

There are roughly 4,000,000 bird skins in collections in the United States and Canada. More than 900,000 are in the American Museum of Natural History in New York, where they are stored in trays in dark, cool cabinets to preserve them as nearly as possible in their original condition. The trays are periodically fumigated to eliminate the chance for damage by insects. Dr. Lanyon told me that some of the skins were more than 100 years old, and I watched Ben King work with those of some skuas more than fifty years old.

The number of birds collected for scientific purposes each year is estimated to be only a few thousand, probably not many more than are killed by the natives at Gambell. On the other hand, in 1978, hunters shot 1,951,000 geese and 15,146,000 ducks in programs that are carefully regulated by the U.S. Fish and Wildlife Service, and the numbers of birds killed on the roads by vehicles may be larger than those killed by hunters. Even all these losses added together is insignificant compared to the total number of living birds; the total number of breeding birds in the United States alone has been estimated to be between five and six billion. You can see that collections for scientific studies have little effect on bird numbers.

The Attu trip was my last scheduled long absence from home, and I was just getting reacquainted with my family over supper on October 1 when the phone rang at 7:00 P.M. It was Larry Balch reporting a Scarlet-headed Oriole (a Code 5 species from Mexico) coming to a feeder in Tucson, Arizona. In a flurry of phone calls, I made plane reservations, arranged to meet Larry Peavler in Dallas both to guide me to the bird and to serve as my witness, and arrived at the airport at 8:10 P.M. Larry didn't make our date because his flight out of Indianapolis was canceled by bad weather, but Bob Farris of Tulsa came up behind me in the Dallas airport on his way to see and photograph the same bird. By 2:00 A.M. on October 2 we were bedded down in the front and back seats of a Ford LTD II outside a twenty-four-hour pancake house in the middle of Tucson, worrying about how to introduce ourselves over the phone at 7:00 A.M. to total strangers and win permission to observe the feeder.

We needn't have worried; these strangers turned out to be Gale and Sally Monson, two of the most gracious birders I met all year. They welcomed us into their home in spite of the early hour and installed us before a one-way window eight feet away from a sugar-water feeder. The male oriole was taking a bath while we were asking directions to the house and did not return during our visit, but a female came repeatedly to the feeder and once to the bath. Bob got his picture, and I got #687 and was back in Jackson twenty hours after I left. It was nice to be a winner again.

Eric Tull called October 3 and gave me the details about why they had changed their minds about the Edmonton "Siberian Chickadee," the bird I had seen March 7 and then removed from my count on June 25. After I saw the bird, they caught it, photographed it in great detail, banded it, and released it. Then Terry Thormin took the photos to Godfrey at the National Museum, and the two of them compared the photos to the skins there. They quickly noticed these differences:

1. The Edmonton bird was much paler than all others.
2. The Edmonton bird showed an obvious contrast between a dark cap and a pale back, whereas the others were quite uniform above.
3. The Edmonton bird had three outer rectrices edged with white, whereas the others had only two edged with white.
4. The flanks of the Edmonton bird were much paler.

These facts led them to believe that my bird was actually a leucistic (partially albino) Blackcapped Chickadee.

20

HIGH COUNT, LOW SPIRITS

I had squeezed in an extra Terry Wahl pelagic trip on my way to Alaska in September but didn't get all the birds I needed. My original itinerary had called for a trip from Westport, Washington, in early October, so I hopped a plane for Seattle and then on October 7 became both a loser (seasickness) and a big winner.

The first victory came only an hour from port. Dennis Paulson, an environmental consultant, coauthor of a bird-finding guide, and outstanding birder from Seattle, was standing in the bow with me, Terry, and three or four others when he pointed ahead and shouted, "Xantus' Murrelets flying left about 1:30!" There they were, two little beauties zipping along at the rapid rate common to alcids, crossing the bow at a range of perhaps fifty yards, and I got #688 by seeing a bird I was sure I had missed for the year. Since the big swells were slick at the time and allowed us to see small birds on the water at a great distance, we hoped to see more, but the wind picked up, and there were no more sightings. Only six or seven of the thirty-one persons on board saw them. By sheer luck I happened to be in the bow when they flew by; soon thereafter, I was called to the rail to say goodbye to my breakfast and then had to spend the rest of the trip in the stern where there was no crowd.

Fishing trawlers are sometimes numerous off Westport, and on his pelagic trips Terry searches for one that has attracted seabirds because this is where Flesh-footed Shearwaters often show up. In late morning as we approached the first one, he called me to the bow to see an amazing sight.

Both the air and the water around the trawler's stern were full of birds, 2,000 or more gulls and shearwaters swimming or flying about like Chimney Swifts going to roost or bees around a hive. The birds were so thick that my binocular field always contained eight or ten. Just about the time I wondered how anyone could pick out a single bird and show it to someone else, someone said, "There's a Flesh-footed in the middle of that group of gulls." I could see fifteen or twenty groups of gulls. Then someone else found one and tried in vain to tell us where it was. But the birds weren't going anywhere, and as the captain slowly worked our boat through the swarm, Terry was soon able to show me one flying away. A few minutes later, we came upon one sitting on the water no more than twenty yards away, and all of us saw plainly its pink bill with black tip. Standing beside me at the time was Wayne Weber of Vancouver, British Columbia, who had just finished four years as a doctoral student at Mississippi State University; he was my witness for #689. I flew back to Jackson in high spirits; I had expected the shearwater, but the murrelet was a surprising bonus!

I said in Chapter 18 that Terry publishes a list of the numbers of each species seen on each Westport trip and thereby gives each birder a way to calculate his chances of seeing the species he most wants to see. To illustrate what I mean, here are the lists for three trips; I was on the September 10th and October 7th trips, but not on the one in between:

Species	*September 10*	*September 23*	*October 7*
Common Loon	1	1	7
Arctic Loon			6
Red-throated Loon		1	
Loon species	25		3
Western Grebe		1	8
Black-footed Albatross	13	37	12
Fulmar			5
Pink-footed Shearwater	61	184	25
Flesh-footed Shearwater		2	3
Buller's Shearwater	4	33	24
Sooty Shearwater	1117	1746	1282

Short-tailed Shearwater		1	
Fork-tailed Storm Petrel	6		
Double-crested Cormorant		21	120
Brandt's Cormorant			20
Pelagic Cormorant		2	40
White-winged Scoter	1	4	23
Surf Scoter		7	14
Water Pipit		1	
Pectoral Sandpiper	8	2	
Duck species	8		260
Northern Shoveler	19		10
Common Pintail	13		70
Dowitcher species			40
Red Phalarope	74		23
Northern Phalarope	8		
Pomarine Jaeger	17	8	4
Parasitic Jaeger	15	7	1
Long-tailed Jaeger	4		
South Polar Skua	4	2	5
Glaucous-winged Gull	66	149	41
Western Gull	255	149	66
Herring Gull		1	44
Thayer's Gull			11
California Gull	194	1879	1438
Ring-billed Gull			1
Mew Gull			2
Bonaparte's Gull	810		
Heerman's Gull	10	6	50
Black-legged Kittiwake	2	2	105
Sabine's Gull	9	27	8
Arctic Tern	213		
Common Tern	100		
Thin-billed Murre	66	93	193
Marbled Murrelet		1	
Xantus' Murrelet			2
Cassin's Auklet	39	12	233
Rhinoceros Auklet	44	17	80
Tufted Puffin	2	1	1

On October 13 Nat Whitney of Rapid City, South Dakota, joined me in San Francisco, and we drove to Monterey for two scheduled pelagic trips, one on October 13th and one on the 14th. Both were organized by Debi Love, whose labors of love provide a unique birding resource; were led by Rich

Stallcup; and attracted many top birders. On one or both trips were three of the top four listers, Paul Sykes, Paul DuMont, and Larry Balch; at least four authors of bird books, Alan Baldridge, Jon Dunn, Kimball Garrett, and Don Roberson; and the dean of the San Diego group, Guy McCaskie. These experts made sure that we didn't miss anything. The weather was good and the seas gentle, but my only new bird was Ashy Storm Petrel (#690). Craveri's Murrelet, one that I needed badly and that could have appeared on these two trips, was nowhere to be seen. I guessed that I had missed it for good; no expert on the trip could suggest where I could go to get one. Except for the petrel just mentioned, our trip list was similar to those of other West Coast pelagic trips already described.

Near the end of the October 13th trip, while we were cruising near shore at Moss Landing, we encountered a lone frigatebird sailing and turning to avoid some gulls. Since the bird—an adult male—was all black and since they were able to see brown patches on its upper wings, Rich Stallcup and Alan Baldridge tentatively identified it as a Great Frigatebird, *Fregata minor,* a wide-ranging species never before seen in the ABA area. The common bird on our coasts is Magnificent Frigatebird, *Fregata magnificens.* Although I watched the bird from below for fifteen minutes, I never saw the wing patches, known as alar bars, so I couldn't have counted it even if it had turned out to be a Great Frigatebird. This incident demonstrated for me four important things about birding:

1. How cautious experts like Rich and Alan are about claiming new records.
2. How much misinformation remains in bird reference books.
3. What problems professional ornithologists must contend with.
4. How much more knowledge we need about many birds.

Within days after seeing the bird, Rich studied more than twenty-five reference books, all of which mentioned the alar bar as diagnostic of *minor.* He also examined frigatebird skins in the California Academy of Sciences museum. There were five or six skins of *minor,* all showing the alar bar, and eight skins of *magnificens,* none showing the alar bar. Although all this evidence tended to confirm the identification, Rich was still not satisfied because the number of skins was too small and because he also knew that a mistake in one reference work can sometimes be repeated in later ones, so he wrote out a long description of the bird he saw and sent it along with some poor photographs to Dr. Ralph Schreiber, Curator of Ornithology, Los Angeles County Museum of Natural History.

Drawing on the knowledge he gained in extensive studies of frigatebirds of the central Pacific, Ralph solved the problem for us in a long letter to Rich, part of which is quoted below:

> I wish that I could offer some help. No doubt it was a frigatebird. Unfortunately, based on my experience both in the field with three species and an examination of essentially all specimens held in most museums of all species of *Fregata,* [I have to conclude that] it is impossible to identify them in the field (and probably many specimens in the hand for that matter). The major problem is the extreme variability of all species, coupled with *Fregata minor* being excessively variable and with at least two undescribed subspecies. . . .
>
> Unfortunately, most if not all of the field guides and supposedly scientific works on these species are misleading. The point you mention, the alar bar, is highly variable in amount and even presence or absence in various species, and especially in males. It *is* found in *magnificens* in both the Galapagos and Florida and simply cannot be used to separate these species where they overlap, which may be anywhere in the oceans.
>
> In answer to your questions, there is no question in my mind that *minor* wanders extensively in the Pacific Ocean as well as the Atlantic. What we need are some specimens, and fewer guesses and photographs that don't show anything. I also am afraid that my examination of specimens will not hold the alar bar as a 'good character.' Size is impossible [to use as a determining factor in identification here] and likewise so is shape.

> I am not saying that this bird was not *minor.* I just do not believe they can positively or with any certainty be identified in the field in areas where both species overlap, especially males and juveniles.

After the October 14th trip I drove home with Rich Stallcup for a hurried supper, a dash to the woods near Point Reyes, and another example of his remarkable way with owls. It was pitch dark and cloudy. After giving several owl calls with his voice, he got a reply close at hand. Suddenly he switched on his flashlight, picked up a Saw-whet Owl *in flight,* and showed me #691. When I asked how he spotted the owl, he said, "The sky is a tiny bit lighter than the tree, and I saw the bird silhouetted against it." I'm still amazed.

Inevitably, anyone working on a Big Year gets a season ticket on an emotional rollercoaster. His hopes soar to great heights when he gets news that a rarity has showed up, but he sinks into deep despair when, for one reason or another, he misses the bird. I got a double ride on the rollercoaster in mid-October.

When I reached my office early on October 20, there was a message from Frank Haas on my "Call Collect, Ask for Birdman" recorder that the New Jersey Rare Bird Alert was reporting a Barnacle Goose at Brigantine National Wildlife Refuge north of Atlantic City. Frank lives in a Philadelphia suburb, is superintendent of Ridley Creek State Park, and is a real expert on birds of the Philadelphia area. He said he would investigate the report and call me back about supper-time.

Barnacle Goose, a Code 7 bird, breeds in Greenland, winters in southern Europe and northern Africa, and, on the rare occasions when it comes to North America, usually shows up on our northeastern coast. On the other hand, the species is raised in captivity at several locations on Long Island, and since escapees can't be counted, I called Dick Ryan in New Jersey for a judgment on the probable status of the Brigantine bird. He dampened my hopes a bit by telling me that Long Island breeders did not band or pinion their birds, that conditions under which the birds were kept made unreported escapes a good possibility, and that wildness or tamness of the birds' behavior in the field was not a reliable indicator of whether they were escapees. In addition, he noted that certain knowledge was impossible but that he would be skeptical about the wildness of first-year birds, and that such a bird could be identified by the fuzzy demarcation between the two colors on the head. Even with the doubts that this raised in my mind, I decided to chase the bird, since I had few chances at the remaining nine birds, and to count it if it were an adult. I made my plane reservations. Frank Haas shot me down at dusk, even before I was to leave. He called to report that the bird had not been seen for almost a week and volunteered to search for it the next day.

His call of October 21 contained bad news and good news. The bad was that the goose had not been seen again and that the report on it might have been the result of a misidentification. The good news was that he had seen a Black-tailed Godwit, a Code 5 bird, about an hour earlier at Tinicum National Environmental Center, a 700-acre refuge one mile from the Philadelphia Airport. This looked like an ideal chase setup: a large bird in a small area of habitat, a recent sighting, and a very accessible location. My hopes soared. I took off at 2:30 A.M. on October 22 and was on the ground by 8:00 A.M.

There was a large and distinguished crowd ahead of me. Standing in a group at the best observation point were Thompson Marsh of Denver, whose list was the third largest in the ABA; Larry Peavler of Indianapolis, whose list stood at 697; Bob Farris of Tulsa, who had photographed more than 550 species in the ABA area; Stuart Keith of New Jersey, whose world list is the largest; and Johnny Miller, who grew up near Tinicum and is considered the leading birder of the area. Before the day was over, more than fifty birders came to the refuge and other nearby tidal flats. All of us were disappointed; although we stayed until dark, the bird never showed up. Farris, Peavler, and I had a farewell drink together at the airport, and it was my saddest cocktail party in a long time.

Sadness changed to joy October 26. The day before, while I was in Boston on the way to Nova Scotia, Larry Balch had called Virginia, and she in turn called me to report that the godwit had been seen again at Tinicum. After a half-dozen phone calls to change my plans, I arrived at Philadelphia at 8:25 A.M. and joined Johnny Miller to search for #692. In less than an hour, we had it in sight, first while it was flying so we could see its big wingstripe and light underwings and then as it sat on the tidal flats. Since I had given up on the bird twice, once in Alaska and again after the first Tinicum trip, you can imagine how tickled I was.

An unexpected plus of the trip was the chance to go birding with John C. Miller. He is the size of a pro-football lineman, a ramp boss for Northwest Orient Airlines (the man in charge of the platoon that airline passengers see out the window), and the only person I know who spent his first five years of birding *without binoculars of any kind.* To overcome such a disadvantage, he had to learn birds by habitat, habits, flight characteristics, shapes, and calls, and he has no equal on his home grounds.

In order to get Great Skua, which I'd missed in four trips already, Larry Balch and I decided to take trips on the *Marine Atlantica* and the *Marine Nautica,* twin 361-foot ferry ships that make the 100-mile, six-hour run between North Sydney, Nova Scotia, and Port aux Basques, Newfoundland, twice each day. Surely we would see Great Skua by making this journey during daylight on October 27 and 28.

We were wrong. By standing on the steel decks of these ships for a total of twelve hours (six hours each way), we discovered only that the scenery is beautiful, that, of the nine time zones in the ABA area, eight are one hour apart and one—the Newfoundland Time Zone—is only one half-hour from the Atlantic Time Zone, and that the bird population in this area is sparse in comparison to that of the Pacific Coast. Here's our list for the two days, broken down into half-hour periods so you can see why boredom was something to contend with:

Half-hour beginning October 27	Common Loon	Loon species	N. Fulmar	Gr. Shearwater	N. Gannet	Canada Goose	W-w. Scoter	Pom. Jaeger	Iceland Gull	Gr. B-b. Gull	Herring Gull	B-1. Kittiwake	Sabine's Gull	Murre species	Dovekie	alcid species	Swallow species	Am. Robin	Wh.-thr. Sparrow	Passerine specie
11:00 A.M		2								3	7									
11:30					4															
12:00 P.M.			1	6									1							
12:30			4	1								2								
1:00								1			3									
1:30											4									
2:00											4									
2:30										1	7									
3:00										1	7	1					1	1	2	7
3:30						4														
4:00			1								6	6								
4:30			1								2	1								
5:00																				
October 28																				
11:00 A.M.	1											23								1
11:30			10	16							2	1	1	2	2					
12:00 P.M.			22	4							1									
12:30																				
1:00			3						1	2			3							
1:30																				
2:00			1									2	1							1
2:30*			8	1					1	75	22	5								
3:00					4															
3:30										1			1							
4:00					14				1	2	1	4								1
4:30							5		2											

*Passed fishing boat at 2:55 with estimated 300 gulls behind it.

Jacob Sonneborn, the five-year-old son of David and Andy Sonneborn, preserved my chance to make 700 by insisting that his father take him to the Anchorage city dump on a rainy Sunday. On every fall day a thousand or so gulls feed at the dump, and David, a longtime admirer of gulls, examined the sitting birds carefully. One of them stuck out like a sore thumb: a Slaty-backed Gull, the Asian counterpart of Great Black-backed Gull, a resident of the coasts of China and northeast Asia, and a rare spring and very rare fall visitor to Alaska. David's call about the bird set me on fire; here was a chance to get a bird given up for lost. He and I were at the dump soon after sunrise of November 2 and found no trace of our quarry. So, figuring that the bird might have switched dumps, we raced for the dump at Elmendorf Air Force Base, drove the car close to the middle of a flock of 500 or more gulls, and soon found # 693 struggling for his share of the garbage and totally unaware of how different he looked. Thank you very much, Jacob.

At this point I would have gone all the way to Anchorage to get one bird, but since I still needed Hawk Owl, I now tacked on a trip to Fairbanks, less than an hour's flight from Anchorage, where Hawk Owl should be a cinch. My plane didn't leave until midafternoon, so David and I drove a long way up the McKinley highway and back but found very few birds in four hours. Our total list included one Pine Grosbeak, eight or ten finches that looked like redpolls, two Gray Jays, eight or ten Black-billed Magpies, and a dozen or so Northern Ravens. The scenery was impressive, though; Mississippians rarely get to see snow-covered mountains. When my plane landed in Fairbanks at 5:00 P.M., it was cold, dark, and snowing.

Dan Gibson, a tall, bearded assistant at the University of Alaska Museum who probably knows more about Alaskan birds than any living man, spent the first two hours of November 3 searching for Hawk Owls with me in two areas close to Fairbanks where they had been seen hunting several days earlier. Finding nothing, we picked up Jennifer Jolis, headed down the Parks Highway toward Anchorage, and passed one of the most memorable hours of the year. The road climbed quickly into low hills, occasionally rising above the clouds. The cold air had turned the moisture from the clouds into a heavy coating of frost, and the whole countryside sparkled and shone whenever the sun hit it.

While I was still in a trance induced by the scenery, Jennifer suddenly called out, "Stop! We just passed something in a tree by the side of the road." After a quick U-turn and a short drive back, Dan stopped the car by a Ruffed Grouse eating buds about ten feet up in a birch tree perhaps twenty feet off the road. I had never been so close to a Ruffed Grouse.

Less than five minutes later we found a Hawk Owl (#694) teed up on a forty-foot spruce tree about sixty feet off the road. It was ridiculously easy to spot; you could have seen it a half-mile away. With our mission accomplished, we headed home. Ten minutes later a Northern Goshawk, only the second one I'd seen in my life, flew directly over us. In driving around Fairbanks, we encountered redpolls, Northern Ravens, and Gray Jays, and the Black-capped Chickadees and Downy Woodpecker at Dan's feeders made a total of eight species for the day. (I watched these feeders like a hawk; there was one chance in a million that a Siberian Chickadee would come to one of them.)

The Hawk Owl was the last species I could depend on getting. Great Skua was certainly somewhere out in the Atlantic, but no one knew exactly where, and I had already chased it for 600 miles in boats. All the other eligible species had returned to their winter homes and were therefore almost impossible to see; their appearance in the ABA area would be strictly accidental. I was forced to admit that, although it was almost two months to the end of the year, 694 might very well be my final count.

This was a grim prospect for employees of Vardaman & Co. Throughout the year, the *Gold Sheet* had been going to people associated with magazines, newspapers, and television networks, but apparently my adventures had aroused no interest. And since one of the purposes of my Big Year was to create interest in and increase revenue for my firm, this was a serious problem.

A producer for the "Today" show had called in late spring but then decided to do nothing until I had broken the record; when I talked to him after seeing the Woodcock, I discovered that his interest had vanished. There had been three stories about the project in the Jackson papers, one story in each of two papers far south of the timbered part of Florida, and the TV report in Chicago, where there was no timber at all. On the other hand, I had been away from the office more than 50 percent of the time during 1979, and my expenses had risen to $40,000, well over the original budget. Those who were paying the bills began to wonder whether they had made such a good deal after all. I was completely in sympathy with them. They didn't say anything to me, but they didn't have to; I had worked with them so long that I soaked up their feelings by osmosis.

There was a similar atmosphere at home. To the outside world, I seemed to be near my goal with plenty of time left, but Virginia knew how desperate the situation was because I kept her fully informed. In fact, I had done such a good job of informing her that she was sick and tired of the whole thing.

With so few of the desired results achieved and with no ideas about how to improve matters, I reached the bottom of the emotional rollercoaster at the very time when so many thought I was doing so well.

21

ALMOST A PHOTO FINISH

In early October, while they were on a National Marine Fisheries Service ship, Gary Friedricksen and Bob Pittman saw four species that most birders would give an arm to see: Craveri's Murrelet, Red-billed Tropicbird, Red-tailed Tropicbird, and Cook's Petrel. The news of these sightings didn't reach Rich Stallcup for almost five weeks, but when he heard, he didn't waste another minute in arranging (with help from Debi Love) for a boat to search the area again and then had no trouble filling it when nearly every birder he called jumped at the chance to go along. Thirty-eight birders, including me, sailed from Morro Bay, California, aboard the sixty-foot *Princess* at 10:00 P.M., November 16, on the first birders' pelagic trip to Davidson Seamount, an underwater mountain that rises over 6,000 feet from the floor of the Pacific about 120 miles northwest of Morro Bay. There's little danger of hitting it; its peak is still 4,400 feet below the surface.

When I woke up at 6:15 A.M. on November 17 in my tiny bunk in the forward hold, I asked someone coming down the stairs whether it was daylight on deck, and he said that it barely was. I decided to doze another fifteen minutes. Five minutes later, there were screams from above, "Cook's Petrel, Cook's Petrel, Cook's Petrel!" All twenty of us still in bed tried to get up narrow stairs at the same time, and by the time I finally made it, the bird had flown by. I could have kicked myself. I had come 2,500 miles to see the species and then missed it because I got lazy for a moment. To make matters worse, I got seasick an hour later and stayed that way all day.

I was destined to be a winner, however, for two more Cook's Petrels showed up about 9:00 A.M., and four more individuals came by at different times before noon. One passed only fifty yards off the starboard side and we all got a good look at it. This was #695 and another first verified North American record. There is some doubtful evidence that Cook's Petrel had occurred in the ABA area at an earlier time. One died in the San Diego Zoo many years ago, and its skin is preserved in a local museum. The tag on it states that the bird arrived in San Diego on a ship from Alaska. Since petrels are almost impossible to keep alive in captivity, most experts think that the tag information is incorrect and that the bird was actually picked up off Mexico, near the northern limit of its range. It breeds in New Zealand, and then wanders widely over the Pacific Ocean.

We also saw another bird that later proved to be a first North American sighting. When the bird first came into view, everyone thought it was another Cook's Petrel. As it came closer, however, Rich Stallcup, Guy McCaskie, and Jon Dunn noticed that it had a dark cap and white forehead, and they pointed this out to me and several others. This feature made it something other than a Cook's Petrel, but no one could be sure what it was. During the days thereafter, Rich went to the museum at the California Academy of Sciences in San Francisco and studied skins of four petrels collected between November 14 and 19, 1914, about 550 to 650 miles due west of Morro Bay, and Guy and Jon conducted their own investigations. After more conferences, these men, perhaps the best field ornithologists on the West Coast, determined that the bird was a Stejneger's Petrel, and Rich called to report that we had another first North American record.

The next problem for me was whether to count it. Without doubt I had seen the bird and its identifying marks, but I certainly didn't identify it at the time. I discussed what to do with Larry Balch and Jim Tucker, ABA's Executive Director. Larry said he would count it. Jim said that ABA had decided how to handle this common problem long ago. Here, in my words, is what he reported: If you have definitely seen a bird and its diagnostic marks but can't identify it until you discuss it with others who saw it then or at other times or study skins or photographs of it or books about it, you can count it when it has been identified. Jim had done this with birds on his list and thought most other birders had done the same. Considering all this, I decided to count Stejneger's Petrel as #696. Now all I needed to know was how to pronounce it.

Although we identified no more new species, we were jubilant at our great success; you can bet there will be more trips to the same area. The two rare petrels may occur there regularly, but no one knew because no birders ever went there. He's our trip list:

Arctic Loon
Black-footed Albatross
Northern Fulmar
Pink-footed Shearwater
Buller's Shearwater
Sooty Shearwater
Short-tailed Shearwater
Cook's Petrel
Stejneger's Petrel
Ashy Storm Petrel
Leach's Storm Petrel
Brant
Red Phalarope
Pomarine Jaeger
South Polar Skua
Glaucous-winged Gull
Western Gull
Herring Gull
Thayer's Gull
California Gull
Bonaparte's Gull
Xantus' Murrelet
Cassin's Auklet
Rhinoceros Auklet

In late November, with time running out and the species I hadn't seen few and far between, I decided to appeal for help from the general public. Perhaps somewhere in the great tropical garden of Miami, someone knew the location of a Blue-gray Tanager. The bird, supposedly an established introduction there, is so distinctively colored that anyone could recognize it, and the last one seen had been coming regularly to a feeder at a trailer park. After making arrangements with Harvey Abrams and Jane Behr of the Tropical Audubon Society there, I ran the following ad for a week in the classified sections of all the Miami papers:

> $100 REWARD
>
> For information leading to the first sighting of WILD Blue-gray Tanager in this area. Bird 6″ long, blue-gray with blue wings & tail. NO CREST. Eats fruit, nectar, insects. May be coming to feeder. Sighting needed for national birding project. Call Tropical Audubon, (305) 666-5111, for information.

The newspapers loved the story. Reporters called Jane constantly. *The Miami News* got an artist to sketch the bird and ran the sketch and a story about the project across the top of the front page November 20. The item was picked up by the wire services and popped up in newspapers everywhere.

Unfortunately, though, the bird popped up nowhere. Besides several calls asking for information, the only results were a report of six or seven birds that turned out to be Scrub Jays and a letter that suggested I take my problem to a psychic medium who was then appearing at a motel in Miami.

The first indication that the project was generating some national interest came in a telephone call on November 20 from Urban C. Lehner, a reporter at the Washington, D.C., bureau of *The Wall Street Journal.* Urb, who usually covers labor matters, is also a birder, and his story about Rich Rowlett's February pelagic trip had appeared opposite the *Journal's* editorial page in March. I had called him then and put him on the mailing list for *Gold Sheets.* Now he said that he wanted to go with me on the next chase so he could then do a profile of me for the front page. I warned him that chase calls could come at any moment and jotted down all his phone numbers.

Robert Northshield, producer of the CBS-TV network show "Sunday Morning" with Charles Kuralt, called me at the office at 9:00 A.M. on Saturday, December 1, to say that he planned to do a segment on me for a future program. He said he was a birder, was especially interested in photographing birds, and had been following my progress all year long. He also wanted to send a camera crew on my next chase. After giving him the same warning I gave Urb, I jotted down his phone numbers. Neither of us dreamed how soon I would need them.

"Please go up to San Ygnacio and look around for a White-collared Seedeater. If you find one, run to the nearest phone, call me, and then stay with the bird until I can get there." These few words from me to John Arvin on November 29 caused the greatest chase of the year, first of all because Virginia went with me, and second because it became my first media event. John called me at 11:00 A.M. on December 1, just two hours after I'd spoken to "Shad" Northshield. I immediately called Northshield, who was amazed at the sudden response, and Urb Lehner. By 9:00 P.M. Virginia and I were in Laredo, Texas, with John, Urb, and David Dick, Pat O'Dell, and Arnie Jensen (a CBS-TV News team from Dallas). They filmed me at every step, leaving the plane, entering the terminal, renting the car, checking into the motel, even greeting John, and the bright light attracted much attention. When a woman asked, "What famous person is causing all this?" and Pat, the cameraman, pointed at me and said, "That man right there," I realized that my birding had taken on a new dimension.

Early the next morning all of us except David (who had to rush back to San Antonio to cover an appearance by the Shah of Iran) drove through San Ygnacio and turned toward the Rio Grande on a bumpy dirt road a mile south of town. We began a slow search of a strip about fifty yards wide along the river. The ground was very irregular and covered with a tangle of grasses, cane, bushes, and small trees; I found it tough going and still don't see how the camera crew made it with such a heavy load of equipment. After an hour or so John, about ten yards ahead of me, said softly, "Come up here. I've got one." I moved quietly toward the bird, but it disappeared before I made it. We worked back and forth for another forty-five minutes. Suddenly, about fifteen yards ahead of me, a female White-collared Seedeater jumped up on a bush and paused long enough for me to get a good look. I was soon able to show her to John and Urb, and #697 was in the bag.

Then I watched some camera work that still amazes me. Pat was filming the bird while we were studying it, and when we finished, he and Arnie somehow worked their way through the tangles to a point closer to the bird without flushing it and got some better shots. We reviewed the film after we returned to the motel and had no trouble identifying the bird.

The Wall Street Journal story ran December 10 and gave me a taste of what it must be like to be a celebrity. I got calls from many friends and clients, ten or fifteen newspapers, two magazines, two networks, one publisher, an Indiana man named Vardaman who wanted to explore possible kinship, and a talk-show host at a radio station in Sarasota, Florida, who put me on the air live at 6:45 one Saturday morning. Some unusual calls came *collect* because the story contained my frequent plea, "CALL COLLECT 601-354-3123, ASK FOR BIRDMAN." A man in North Carolina reported that Passenger Pigeons were not extinct, that he and his wife saw some on vacation in Haiti, and that he was sure about the identification because he looked up the bird in a book after he got home. Two men, from California, I think, called to tell me at great length that they were pulling for me all the way, that I shouldn't get discouraged about ruffling the feathers of other birders, and that I should "Go, man, go."

Urb later told me that, when he received my call about the

chase, he was getting his new home in Washington ready for occupancy and had a plasterer there with him. After getting the details from me, he dropped everything and began his own flurry of calls, to his editor for approval of the trip, to the airlines for reservations, to associates and other persons he had planned to work with Monday, and so on. After this was over and he was packing, the plasterer looked at him very carefully and then asked, "Is a seedeater really a bird?" When Urb said it was, the plasterer replied, "I'm glad of that. When I heard your side of all those phone calls, I decided you were an agent for the CIA and that you were using a code name for something bad that had happened on the Mexican border."

On December 12 Elmer Aldrich of Sacramento, California, called to report that a Red-crested Pochard had been discovered on a small pond in the middle of Sacramento. Not being familiar with the species, I called Dick Ryan again. He said that it was perhaps the most common foreign bird raised in captivity here, that it frequently escaped, that several of them were flying around New York almost all the time, and that the chances of the Sacramento bird's being wild were almost zero. Hope was born and then died in less than ten minutes.

I got #698 about suppertime on December 12 when Davis Finch called from New York to say that he was now positive of the identification of Spot-billed Duck for the bird we all saw on Attu May 17. (I mentioned this possibility in Chapter 12.) Davis is perhaps the most careful observer I watched all year long, and he saw this bird under better conditions than did anyone else. To show you how these real pros handle a difficult problem in identification, I have quoted his report:

> Here is the description of the Attu Spot-billed Duck from my diary of 16 May 1979:
>
> The day was clear, sunny, mild, and still. In the late afternoon, Thede, Jerry, and I went birding, and Thede soon found a funny duck: a Mallard type, but unmistakably a

darker bird, fully as dark as a Black Duck; bill dark brownish, almost black, with dark nail and a ghost image, in a pale indeterminate shade, of a subterminal band across maxilla; minutely orangish at gape or commissure; interramal area bright orange; face dull brown with a very clearly defined transocular line, thicker before the eye and narrowing very slightly anteriorly; crown dark, almost black, as was transocular line; an ill-defined pale patch behind base of mandible; neck and upper breast about the same, medium-light brown; back feathers with very dark, brownish-black centers, fairly obvious *buffy* edges; feathers of sides below folded wings blackish brown like Black Duck with *orange* edges. The paler breast was faintly lined darker; below it the bird was abruptly darker, almost blackish; the under tail coverts even darker. Tail was dark centrally with dirty white outer 4-5 rectrices which, when folded, looked to be barred with gray-brown. Legs orange; speculum blue-violet with white forward and rear borders. Wing linings white like Mallard. In flight the back and belly looked very dark, almost black.

The bill looked smaller to me proportionately than a Mallard's, shorter, I guess. When the bird looked directly at me, I was struck by the effect of the convergence of the transocular lines at the base of the upper mandible, and the dark cap reminded me of a female Masked Duck. This plus the pale spot behind the lower mandible *gave the bird a wholly unfamiliar look.* I really felt I had never seen this bird before. A male Mallard later approached it, and the two flew off together, the dark female type being decidedly smaller than the male but perhaps no smaller than the average female Mallard. Some observers (Thede Tobish, Jerry Rosenband) saw a faint, dark, moustachial mark. Paul DuMont, Robert Ake, Howard Langridge, Bill Blakeslee [also saw the bird].

Other details—upper tail coverts looked blackish to tip.

At American Museum of Natural History December 12, I examined 19 examples of *Anas poecilorhynca zonorhynca* (the Japanese race of Spot-billed Duck), mostly from Japan, and compared them with my description. Only minor problems: absence of white tertials (but these can clearly—demonstrably—be lost by wear) and the dullness of the bill spot. These are very easy to live with when everything else so strongly indicates Spot-billed Duck.

Great Skua is such a large and distinctly marked bird that many of us have long thought that it could be spotted from an airplane. Since I'd already made several trips in search of it by boat, I decided to test this theory by chartering an airplane. Larry Balch, Kevin D. Powers, and I took to the skies from Boston on December 13, accompanied by David Dick (reporter), Garfield Arthur (cameraman), and Norman White (sound man), all of CBS News. The plane was a twin Beech AT-11 owned by Aero-Marine Surveys, Inc. of Groton, Connecticut, containing the computers and Loran equipment needed for precise navigation, and, like an old bomber, equipped with a glass nose big enough for two observers. The pilot, John Rutledge and copilot, Paul Gilman, had been flying scientists researching marine mammals and birds for months; Kevin Powers, a wildlife biologist and Project Director—Seabirds, Manomet Bird Observatory, Manomet, Massachusetts, came along because he had been studying skuas for years, and he brought a chart with all November sightings plotted on it. In other words, the search team was as good as we could make it.

When we reached the search area off the island of Nantucket, Kevin and I got in the nose, and Larry moved to the copilot's seat. Even though our altitude was 500 feet and our ground speed 120 miles per hour, we had no trouble spotting and identifying Northern Gannets, Herring Gulls including immatures, and Great Black-backed Gulls, and we felt sure that we could spot a skua if it showed up. We spent hours flying over a square of Atlantic Ocean about fifty miles on a side with its northwest corner about thirty-five miles south of Nantucket and found only thirteen fishing boats with flocks of seabirds around them. There was no sign of Great Skua. To the 600 miles of fruitless boat search for it, I had to add 500 miles of fruitless air search. Would I ever see the bird?

The experience did teach me something about searching for seabirds in a plane. The need for safety makes it essential to use a plane with two engines, and none of those available can fly under 100 miles per hour. A good observer can spot a big bird like a skua or an albatross under these conditions, but even when sitting in a bomber-type nose, he probably couldn't show it to another observer or find it again once the plane had passed it. Therefore, a plan I had been saving as a last-ditch measure was worthless. I had hoped to find Laysan Albatross in an airplane search off the West Coast, but what good would it do to find one if I couldn't show it to a witness? One more possibility went down the drain.

Wally George of Fort Lauderdale, Florida, found a Stripe-headed Tanager on the West Palm Beach Christmas Bird Count about 9:30 A.M. on December 15 and called me soon after lunch. After a series of phone calls, Paul Sykes picked up Larry Peavler, Bob Farris, and me at the airport soon after 9:00 A.M. the next day and drove us to the location of the find. We arrived less than thirty minutes later at an impenetrable thicket of Brazilian Pepper and native shrubs shaded by a few scattered pine and casuarina trees, alongside a powerline right of way. The bird is usually hard to see but has a loud, distinctive call note that can be heard fifty or more yards away, a call that had attracted Wally's attention in the first place.

Barbara and Al Lieberman met us on the ground with glum faces. They had been there since dawn and had neither seen nor heard the bird. We stayed until 1:30 P.M. but had equally bad luck. Although Wally and his teammate had watched the bird for more than ten minutes, it must have moved on after they left. The Liebermans revived our spirits by leaving us their lunch: two sandwiches, one hard-boiled egg, several stalks of celery, and two six-ounce cans of apricot nectar. Bob Farris divided this into four parts, and Larry, Paul, and I got to select our portions before he did. But even the sandwiches couldn't make up for the disappointment we all felt.

On December 17, at my request, Victor Emanuel braved a wind-chill factor of zero degrees to search Maner Lake near Houston, Texas, in a boat for a North American Jacana, but he found no sign of it. I called Elaine Cook, a friend of Kenn Kaufman, in Tucson that night to see whether there was any news; there was none. There were no calls on the "Birdman" hotline on December 18 or 19. Eric Tull in Edmonton reported on December 20 that there had been no Bewick's Swans in Saskatchewan this fall and that everything up there was now frozen solid.

Then Paul Sykes called with the worst kind of news: Dan Gibson had finally compared our "Little Stint" from Attu with other specimens in the University of Alaska Museum and decided that it was actually a Rufous-necked Stint. Since the bird was in juvenile plumage, we had recognized it as a very difficult identification problem, but we thought we had solved it correctly. Extreme caution had prompted us to send it to Dan, an outstanding authority on Alaskan birds. Although we asked him to double-check with skins in the American Museum of Natural History, I had no doubt that he was correct. With sinking spirits, I removed Little Stint from my count and fell back to 697. How could I find three more birds in the remaining eleven days?

Dan Gibson called later in the day and reported that the temperature in Fairbanks was 30 degrees below zero with no Siberian Chickadees. I also talked to John Sarvis, manager of Izembek National Wildlife Refuge at Cold Bay, Alaska, about a rumored Steller's Sea Eagle; he said they had not seen one for over a year, would be doing a Christmas Bird Count in a few days, and would call me if they found something.

At noon on December 21 Bernie Brouchoud reported that three Egyptian Geese had appeared at Manitowoc, Wisconsin, but a quick check with my advisors convinced me that these were surely escapees and not countable. There were no calls on December 22 or 23, the days when Christmas Bird Counts were taking place at many points, and hope began to die. Dr. Staub of Houston, Texas called Christmas Eve just to be sure I had seen Masked Duck (I had), and Joel Ruiz, operator of Hawaii Campground in San Ygnacio, Texas (512-765-5182), called Christmas night to say that White-collared Seedeater had been seen on his land that morning. There were no bird calls on the 26th, 27th, or 28th, and failure to reach 700 became more and more likely. We had a little excitement December 28 when NBC-TV sent a crew to Jackson to interview Virginia and the children for the "Prime Time" show with Tom Snyder.

My last chance to add another bird on a scheduled trip was Rich Rowlett's Christmas Bird Count aboard the sixty-five-foot *Miss Ocean City* on the Atlantic Ocean, from the shore to a point about sixty miles east of Ocean City, Maryland. Rich is a thirty-two-year old Missouri native who first became interested in birds when he observed the 1961 Bohemian Waxwing invasion of northwest Missouri while studying zoology there under Dr. David Easterla. He is a professional birder now working on a cetacean and turtle survey from Nova Scotia to Cape Hatteras under a grant from the University of Rhode Island.

Since the boat was due to leave at 6:30 A.M. on December 29, Rich invited me, as well as others, to come up the night before and stay at his apartment. This gave me a chance to learn the hardships some birders will put up with in order to see birds. There were only five single beds or sofas in the apartment, but ten men and one woman slept there, the unlucky bedless six stretching out on the floor in bedrolls with nothing except the carpet between them and the concrete floor of the building. They were to endure two consecutive nights of this. In spite of it, all were in great good spirits and stayed up half the night looking at slides of birds and swapping tales, like the one about the four Florida birders who wanted to see a Rufous-capped Warbler that showed up in Big Bend National Park several years ago. At the time a national car-rental firm was offering an unlimited-mileage special, so they rented a car in St. Petersburg, Florida; drove 1,300 miles nonstop to Brownsville, Texas, detouring to see a Mexican Crow; continued another 650 west to Big Bend and saw the Warbler. They returned nonstop to St. Petersburg. When the check-in agent noticed that they had driven more than 4,000 miles in less than six full days, she could hardly believe it.

A crowd of birders gathered at the dock before dawn on December 29 only to learn that the trip had to be postponed for twenty-four hours because of strong winds that were causing ten- to fifteen-foot seas in the count area. The only noteworthy event that morning was the filming by the same NBC-TV crew of other birders and me on the boat during a thirty-minute test run. The film was not shown that night and may never appear.

The next morning was clear, cold, and not quite so windy, and we sailed at 6:30. The birders had come from everywhere: sixteen from Maryland; five from Pennsylvania; four from Delaware, Ontario, and Ohio; three from Virginia and New York; two each from New Jersey, District of Columbia, Illinois, Texas, and California; and one each from West Virginia, Florida, Mississippi, Minnesota, and Alaska. Many top birders mentioned earlier were there: Ben King, Larry Balch, Barbara Hickey, Paul Sykes, Terry Savaloja, Jon Dunn, Guy McCaskie, and Thede Tobish. The others came from all occupations: four lawyers, four reporters, four teachers, two physicists, a computer programmer, a doctor, an immunologist, an officer in the U.S. Corps of Engineers, a historian, a railroad car inspector, a Wall Street banker, an administrator for a medical college, and a construction company executive.

By the time we reached the foreign fishing fleet—vessels from Russia, Japan, and other countries—around noon, the seas were five to six feet, and the motion was beginning to test the effectiveness of the anti-seasickness pill I had taken at dawn. There were gulls everywhere. Rich decided to "chum" heavily to attract them to our boat, and in no time there were several hundred following us. Soon a cry rang out, "There's a skua way, way back!" Fifty of us crowded toward the stern, and I was in the back row. Someone's head was always blocking my view, and I must have been the last one to find the big brown bird. There was no need to hurry.

The bird, a Great Skua at last and # 698, gradually overtook us and passed about 150 yards off the port side, and we later saw five more. Our total list for the day included:

Northern Gannet	Scoter species
Black-legged Kittiwake	Surf Scoter
Herring Gull	Bonaparte's Gull
Great Black-backed Gull	Ring-billed Gull
Common Loon	Manx Shearwater
Red-throated Loon	Great Skua
	Large alcid species

Our sighting of the Great Skua caused a celebration on board. After all, Larry Balch and I had spent countless hours and days hunting for the species. The bird was #700 for both Ben King and Jon Dunn, so the 700 Club gained two more distinguished members. I was more excited than anyone, for this sighting set the stage for a near-miraculous finish for my Big Year.

When bad weather had postponed our trip on December 29, I had called Virginia and learned that another Stripe-headed Tanager had been found on December 28, this time on Upper Matecumbe Key about an hour's drive south of Miami. If it stayed around and if I saw both Great Skua and Yellow-nosed Albatross, a rarity seen near Ocean City during December, I could get 700. At 4:00 P.M. Virginia called again and reported a fantastic find: a Golden-crowned Warbler, a Mexican bird that would be a first North American record, had been seen that day in Steve Benn's back yard in Brownsville, Texas. The magic 700 was once again within my grasp.

We spent the next six hours on the telephone. The phone of the Florida birder nearest the tanager was out of order. We called several others. All were tied up December 30 or 31 on Christmas Bird Counts, so there was no one either to "baby-sit" the bird or to be my witness. Damn! Paul Sykes then said that these tanagers usually stayed in a small area for a while, and Larry Balch and Guy McCaskie agreed to go along to witness it, provided we also tried for the warbler in Texas.

Since the Benns promised to keep track of the warbler on December 30, the next problem was to charter a jet to get from Miami to Brownsville before dark on December 31. The fee would be $6,000 to $7,000, and we spent most of Saturday night trying to arrange it. Can you imagine the reaction of the charter companies to a call late at night from someone who wanted to arrange an expensive charter to, of all things, go see a bird? I wasn't about to call a total stranger. My next-door neighbor owned a charter service, but he turned out to be out of town. An old friend owned a jet, but there was no answer at her phone. Virginia agreed to try to solve this problem while we were on the boat Sunday.

After we spotted the last skua about 1:00 P.M., another problem arose. Under ordinary conditions, we were five hours' run from the dock, but we had a head wind that might delay us for thirty minutes. A delay of this length would prevent us from making the flight from Baltimore to Miami. We pounded into the wind for an hour, long enough for me to get seasick again, and then, fortunately, the wind died. We docked at 6:05 P.M. I jumped from the boat to the dock, dashed for a phone, and called Virginia; she had nailed down a plane for $7,500. Hot dog! Larry dashed for another phone and called the Benns. The warbler was gone! A team of observers had searched for it all day and found no trace. Damn! The last chance for 700 died right there.

Should I try for 699? The tanager had not been seen after December 28 because no one had looked for it, and since Balch and McCaskie wouldn't be going to Miami now, I might not find a witness even if I found the bird. In addition, 699 would still be one short of the magic number, and $7,500 was a lot of money to blow chasing a ghost. I decided to quit, made the plane in Baltimore by breaking all speed records, and arrived home dead tired at 2:15 A.M. December 31.

After I woke up at about noon, I spent several hours thinking back over the most unusual year of my life. I was disappointed in not reaching 700 under the counting rules adopted in the beginning, but I had learned during the year that many things we didn't know much about could change the way these rules would be applied. On one hand, were the Whooper Swans at Toronto really wild birds or escapees? On the other hand, shouldn't I have counted Canary-winged Parakeet? Wasn't the Antillean Nighthawk we saw in Florida in May, with its completely different call, actually a separate species? Isn't the same thing true of the Tropical Kingbird in Arizona and the Red-breasted Sapsucker in California? I finally decided that the answers to these questions didn't matter to me. I had set a goal that really challenged me, had given the try for it the best I had in me, and had enjoyed almost every minute of it. That was enough.

Later when I went downstairs to mix a before-dinner drink, the doorbell rang, and there were Tom and Frances Barber, who live across the street, handing me a bottle of Wild Turkey bourbon whiskey with a tiny plastic bird wired to the cap. Tom said that the plastic bird was 699 and the bourbon was 700, and that he and Frances wanted to be the first to congratulate me on reaching my goal. It was a wonderful end to a wonderful year.

But there was to be an intriguing postscript. In response to our request Dan Gibson sent the mysterious little sandpiper from Attu to the American Museum of Natural History so as to be doubly sure of the identification. We had no doubts about Dan's expertise in identification, but the number of specimens available for comparison in New York was far larger than the number in Fairbanks, and I have already emphasized the importance of specimens. Dr. Eugene Eisenmann, one of our leading taxonomists, examined our bird and concluded January 29 that it was actually a Little Stint. At Dan Gibson's request, Dr. Eisenmann sent the specimen to the National Museum of Natural History in Washington, D.C., for a further check. At present it seems, however, that we had been right in the first place, so my final total was 699.

What would have happened if I had known this at 6:00

P.M. December 30? Even though we knew that the warbler had not been seen that day, Balch and Sykes thought that there was a good chance that it was still in the area. No one knew the status of the tanager, but we had already decided that, if the warbler was a sure thing, searching for the tanager on a cold trail was worth the investment of time and money. Although the cost was high and nothing was certain, there seemed to be two chances to get to 700, and we had to hit on only one. Would I, a seasoned poker player with a 50-50 chance to win big, have made the trip under these conditions? I think so.

What would have happened if I had made the trip? So far as we know, the tanager was never seen again. Barbara and Al Lieberman looked for it December 30 and missed. With two expert birders and me in the party, we might have found it the next morning simply because, there being three of us, we could have covered more ground. There is no doubt, however, about the warbler. It showed up again on December 31 (a fact we could have learned by calling from the Miami airport), was around all day long, and was seen by many people. It was still there January 6 when Sykes, Balch, and others flew down to see it, and John Arvin saw it January 28. It would have been the magic number 700 for me.

The answer to the question, "Is 700 possible?" must, then, be "Yes."

22

COSTS, RESULTS, AND FUTURE PLANS

When the Big Year was over, it was time to count the costs. The biggest one was the irreplaceable commodity, time. I spent 159 days either actually birding or undertaking major traveling, such as the plane and car trip from Bar Harbor, Maine, to Cave Creek Canyon, Arizona. In many cases, I left home or the office early to catch a plane to the next day's birding spot. I didn't keep exact records of this, but I estimate that the total amounted to eleven days. Therefore, in terms of time, the cost of my Big Year was 170 days.

In relationship to my travel in an ordinary year, the distances I covered in 1979 were huge. Here is the breakdown of miles by means of travel:

Plane	137,145
Car	20,305
Boat	3,337
Bicycle	160
Foot	385
	161,332

I was such a familiar figure at the local office of Delta Air Lines that they elected me a Flying Colonel of the Delta Fleet, an office that entitles me to buy my tickets for the same price paid by everyone else. I got seasick four times, a record for me—one that I didn't try to set. All the bicycle travel and 260 miles of the foot travel were on Attu. My trips took me to twenty-three states, six Canadian provinces, and nine time zones. Much of the travel was to and from Alaska, a round trip of about 10,000 miles, on four separate occasions. Except for the May–June and September trips to Alaska, I never checked baggage. I was afraid some of it would get lost in the shuffle and wanted to save time that would ordinarily be spent in baggage lines. I learned that you can wear the same clothes several days running without losing all your friends and that telescopes, tripods, cameras, and field guides are unnecessary 90 percent of the time.

Mrs. Bobbye Davis, our bookkeeper, reported the following money costs for the Big Year:

Guide fees		$10,157.12
Air fares and air charter fees		9,966.87
Gold Sheet newsletter:		
Typesetting and printing	$6,000.00	
Postage	2,616.00	8,616.00
Car rentals and gas		4,694.49
Lodging		3,534.73
Strategy Council meeting		2,628.29
Food		2,537.97
Boat rentals and pelagic trips		889.00
Telephone		887.54
Miscellaneous items		595.37
Total		$44,507.38

Of the guide fees, $4,200 was for the spring tour of Alaska. Without doubt much of this was for airfares, food, car rentals, and ferry fares, but I didn't ask for a breakdown. Most of the Strategy Council cost was for air fares for the members. Not included in these figures were the small costs incurred during the planning stages of 1977 and 1978, but these probably did not exceed a total of $1,500. We missed our original estimate of $35,000 because we failed to consider the cost of the *Gold Sheet,* yet the *Gold Sheet* was a major factor in the success of the project. Cost per bird came to $63.67.

When it was all over, what were the results of the Big

Year? First of all, I saw 699 species of birds, one short of my goal, but far more than many persons thought I would see and far, far more than I thought my life list would ever be. (My final list for the year appears in Appendix C.)

Could I have done anything different to increase my total? I'm not sure. One or two pelagic trips from San Diego in the spring or one that went farther out in the fall might have produced Craveri's Murrelet or a tropicbird. More time spent in Alaska waiting for the weather to improve at Hooper Bay might have produced Bristle-thighed Curlew, and since I was already in Alaska, I might have taken the Kodiak-Seward ferry trip again and found Scaled Petrel. I might even have done this without spending more time or money. Better planning would have enabled me to find Chukar, Northern Gannet, Ruffed Grouse, Hawk Owl, and Saw-whet Owl in less time, and knowing more about how to find Great Skua might have saved me four days and several thousand dollars. But two anecdotes will give you an idea of how difficult adding another species can be.

Trying to find a Siberian Chickadee in Alaska, Larry Balch, Jerry Rosenband, Thede Tobish, Arnold Small, and Doug Krause decided in the spring of 1979 to charter a single-engine float plane in Fort Yukon and to fly from one small lake to another, searching the surrounding woods at each place. When it came time to leave one lake, Lake Vettatrin, it became apparent that the lake was too small to function as a runway. Their only hope of getting out, the pilot said, would be a U-turn take-off. They roared across the lake toward one shore, made a tight U-turn on the water just in time, roared back toward the first shore, finally lifted off, and cleared the trees along the water's edge by no more than twelve inches. Larry Balch remembered thinking that the trees looked small and pliable and hoping that they might let them crash gently. But in spite of risking their lives, they didn't find a single chickadee.

Because of earlier work, at least we know where to find Bristle-thighed Curlew. The species spends most of the year in Tahiti, Hawaii, and the South Pacific but nests in western Alaska. Herbert Brandt and Henry Conover found curlews in abundance at Hooper Bay August 1, 1924, on their way back to their southern home, and twenty-odd years later Henry Kyllingstad, at that time a schoolteacher in St. Marys, observed them passing northward toward nesting sites in late May. Finally Kyllingstad, Arthur A. Allen, and Allen's son found two nests June 12, 1948, on a mountaintop near a lake they named Curlew Lake. Larry Balch and Barbara Hickey found the third nest June 11 thirty years later in the same locality. All five of these persons had to get to Curlew Lake, twenty-five miles north of St. Marys, and then climb a 1,100-foot mountain to the nests.

But knowing where to find a species is only half the battle; getting to the site is the other. In June 1979, Balch and his group got to Curlew Lake on the second day after leaving Nome and searched unsuccessfully for the curlew until worsening weather ran them out. They returned to St. Marys and waited three more days for the weather to improve. On the sixth day of the try, they finally saw six curlews.

In situations like these, I'm not sure that doing things differently would have produced more species.

So far as my publicity for my forestry firm was concerned, the results of my Big Year exceeded our expectations by a wide margin. Its logo appeared on CBS-TV, and it was mentioned in *The Wall Street Journal, Time,* and many newspapers, some as far away as the *Asahi Evening News* in Japan. More important than this, however, the year proved that the company had a vitality of its own, that it could do without me for half a year. In fact, since 1979 was a record year for it in every way, the company might decide to do without me altogether. And, if this proves to be a popular book, it will get all its money back.

Another result seemed to be ruffled feathers among some birding leaders. Stuart Keith, a transplanted Englishman who has the largest world list, was asked by the *Wall Street*

Journal reporter what he thought of my project and was quoted as saying, "He isn't a birder, he's a businessman. The whole thing leaves a very sour taste in my mouth." When the reporter told him of my plans for a World Big Year, Keith's comment was, "That idea turns me off even more than I'm turned off by his current venture." In an interview with a reporter for *Time,* Les Line, editor of *Audubon* magazine, complained that my project "has more to do with sport than with nature or the beauty of birds. It's not an appreciation of nature—it's a game." Line likened my pursuit to "counting out-of-state license plates."

I encountered no sentiments like these in face-to-face meetings during the year, but I may have been too busy to notice them. I certainly would have ignored them. I was playing my game, and they were playing theirs; I didn't object to or criticize theirs or care what they thought about mine.

In addition to its economic benefits, publicity about the project generated many warm, touching, human, humorous responses. My father died when I was five, and I have always been curious about what kind of person he was. After they saw news items about me, one of his cousins in Florida and one of his college friends wrote me with some stories about him. A classmate at forestry school who had dropped out of forestry called me as he passed through Jackson. A college fraternity brother who had not seen me for forty years wrote me from his United Nations post in Kenya. Alvaro Chaves, a total stranger from San Jose, Costa Rica, called to invite me to come to his country if I tried a World Big Year and offered to help me find birds there. I was a guest on many radio talk shows, where the host interviews you in a telephone call during the program, but I was very surprised when one call came from Radio Station 3UZ in Melbourne, Australia. The Brooks Bird Club of Wheeling, West Virginia, elected me an Associate Member and sent me a warm letter of thanks. Roger Tory Peterson, whose great field guides appeared about the time I started birding and have helped me all these years, took time out from revising his Eastern Guide to write me a long, encouraging letter.

In the beginning I worried about what my absences chasing birds would do to my children. At first, when I called home from time to time and one of them answered the phone, he or she would say, "Where are you?" or "How are you feeling?" or "We miss you," or "When are you coming home?" By the middle of the year, however, the first words after the child recognized my voice were always, "What's your count?" At that point, I knew they were caught up in the chase and would survive my travels. They made tears come to my eyes Christmas morning when they gave me a huge leather-bound scrapbook with its title embossed in gold letters, "Jim Vardaman, 1979, The Big Year."

The most important effect of the Big Year was on my marriage. There were other unhappy incidents besides the telephone call from Cold Bay. When the Cook's Petrels were discovered off Morro Bay, I pulled out and left Virginia to entertain some of my old friends for the weekend, and when I returned tired and needing sleep, I was unpardonably rude to one of her friends. At this point she would have sold me for a penny, and I probably would have been overpriced.

These incidents and the long separations during the year caused me to think hard about my relationship with her. I discovered that, all my life, I have needed to love a woman and be loved in return, that without such a relationship I am completely miserable and incapable of any substantial accomplishment. Neither business nor birds nor cards (I played poker for a living for two years) was enough; I had to love and be loved. And, of all the women I had known and chased during my first fifty-eight years, Virginia was the only one who even came close to being the answer for me. The Big Year produced a much sharper and deeper realization of how precious she is to me. And what effect did it have on Virginia's feelings? You'll have to ask her about that.

Toward year-end many persons asked what my birding plans for 1980 were. You can understand why my first answer was always, "None. I'm going to spend next year being with my family as much as possible. I may go after enough species to make ABA's 700 Club, but I won't be in a hurry about it. My family will come first."

I usually add that I will definitely start planning a World Big Year. You can do this without leaving home, and much of the fun of doing anything is planning it. I can't wait to start learning where to find all 9,000 species of the world and how to identify them. I'll get a big bang out of chasing them in my imagination. But because of the distances and the complexities involved, planning a World Big Year will take some years, and executing the plan will take 365 days and probably cost $700,000 even at present prices. Therefore, I couldn't make the try before 1985, and I'll be glad to turn the plan over to someone else if I can't carry it out.

Is 5,000 possible?

APPENDIX A

DIRECTORY OF ABA BIRDS

In the chart on the following pages, the numbers indicate the likelihood that each ABA species will occur in certain geographical regions in each of the four seasons. The likelihood code is:

1 Can be found in at least one pre-selected day within the given season and locality.

2 Present within the given season and locality, but may not be found on any one pre-selected day. Category includes very scarce residents, scarce migrants, reclusive species, etc.

Species with the remaining code numbers have not been recorded in the ABA area in each of the last 10 years, and the code number indicates the probability of occurring in any one year.

3 90%-60% chance of occurring

4 59%-30% chance of occurring

5 29%-10% chance of occurring

6 less than 10% chance of occurring

7 No realistic chance of occurring

The chart is intended as an aid to finding birds quickly and surely. It is not intended to show the total distribution of each species. Therefore, only the highest code numbers for each species are entered.

The "Occurrence Class" number just to the right of the species name reflects the bird's North American status according to the code above and is useful for a quick review.

The seasons begin on these dates: Spring March 1, Summer June 1, Fall September 1, and Winter December 1..

Asterisks (*) indicate that the species occurs near one of the large geographical regions or in a tiny part of it.

Species	Occ. Class	Alaska				Westport Pelagic				Monterey Pelagic				San Diego Pelagic			
		S	S	F	W	S	S	F	W	S	S	F	W	S	S	F	W
Common Loon	1	1	1	1	1	1			1	1		1	1	1		1	1
Yellow-billed Loon	1	1	1	1	1												
Arctic Loon	1	1	1	1	1	1		1	1	1		1	1	1		1	1
Red-throated Loon	1	1	1	1	1	1		1	1	1		1	1	1		1	1
Red-necked Grebe	1	1	1	1	1												
Horned Grebe	1	1	1	1	1	1		1	1	1		1	1	1		1	1
Eared Grebe	1					1		1	1	1		1	1	1		1	1
Least Grebe	1																
Western Grebe	1									1		1	1	1		1	1
Pied-billed Grebe	1																
Wandering Albatross	7						7	7			7	7					
Short-tailed Albatross	7		7	7													
Black-footed Albatross	1						1	1			1	1					
Laysan Albatross	3		3			6		6	6	6		6	6				
Shy Albatross	7						7	7			7	7					
Yellow-nosed Albatross	6																
Cape Petrel	7										7	7					
Northern Fulmar	1	1	1	1	1	1		1	1	1		1	1				
Cory's Shearwater	1																
Pink-footed Shearwater	1					1	1	1		1	1	1			1	1	
Flesh-footed Shearwater	2						2	2			2	2					
Greater Shearwater	1																
Buller's Shearwater	1						1	1			1	1					
Sooty Shearwater	1		1			1	1	1		1	1	1		1	1	1	1
Short-tailed Shearwater	1		1						1				1				
Manx Shearwater	1													1		1	1
Little Shearwater	7																
Audubon's Shearwater	1																
Streaked Shearwater	6										6	6					
Black-capped Petrel	3																
Scaled Petrel	4	4	4														
South Trinidad Petrel	7																
White-faced Storm Petrel	6																
Fork-tailed Storm Petrel	1	1	1			1	1	1				1	1				
Leach's Storm Petrel	1					1	1	1						1	1	1	
Ashy Storm Petrel	1						1	1			1	1					
Band-rumped Storm Petrel	7														7	7	
Galapagos Storm Petrel	7										7	7					
Black Storm Petrel	1										1	1			1	1	
Least Storm Petrel	1														1	1	
Wilson's Storm Petrel	1																
British Storm Petrel	7																
Red-billed Tropicbird	2														2	2	
White-tailed Tropicbird	2																
American White Pelican	1																
Brown Pelican	1									1	1	1	1	1	1	1	1
Masked Booby	3																
Blue-footed Booby	3																
Brown Booby	1																
Red-footed Booby	6																
Northern Gannet	1																
Great Cormorant	1																
Double-crested Cormorant	1	1	1	1	1												
Olivaceous Cormorant	1																
Brandt's Cormorant	1					1	1	1	1	1	1	1	1	1	1	1	1
Pelagic Cormorant	1	1	1	1	1	1	1	1	1	1	1	1	1				1
Red-faced Cormorant	1	1	1	1	1												
American Anhinga	1																
Magnificent Frigatebird	1																
Lesser Frigatebird	7																
Great Blue Heron	1								1								
Green Heron	1								1								

Species	Occ. Class	California				Colorado				Arizona				Texas			
		S	S	F	W	S	S	F	W	S	S	F	W	S	S	F	W
Common Loon	1	1		1	1	1		1		1		1	1	1		1	1
Yellow-billed Loon	1																
Arctic Loon	1	1		1	1												
Red-throated Loon	1	1		1	1												
Red-necked Grebe	1																
Horned Grebe	1	1	1	1	1									1		1	1
Eared Grebe	1	1	1	1	1	1	1	1	1	1		1	1	1		1	1
Least Grebe	1													1	1	1	1
Western Grebe	1	1	1	1	1					1	1	1	1				
Pied-billed Grebe	1	1	1	1	1	1	1	1		1		1	1	1	1	1	1
Wandering Albatross	7																
Short-tailed Albatross	7																
Black-footed Albatross	1																
Laysan Albatross	3																
Shy Albatross	7																
Yellow-nosed Albatross	6																
Cape Petrel	7																
Northern Fulmar	1																
Cory's Shearwater	1																
Pink-footed Shearwater	1																
Flesh-footed Shearwater	2																
Greater Shearwater	1																
Buller's Shearwater	1																
Sooty Shearwater	1	1	1	1	1												
Short-tailed Shearwater	1																
Manx Shearwater	1																
Little Shearwater	7																
Audubon's Shearwater	1																
Streaked Shearwater	6																
Black-capped Petrel	3																
Scaled Petrel	4																
South Trinidad Petrel	7																
White-faced Storm Petrel	6																
Fork-tailed Storm Petrel	1																
Leach's Storm Petrel	1																
Ashy Storm Petrel	1																
Band-rumped Storm Petrel	7																
Galapagos Storm Petrel	7																
Black Storm Petrel	1																
Least Storm Petrel	1																
Wilson's Storm Petrel	1																
British Storm Petrel	7																
Red-billed Tropicbird	2																
White-tailed Tropicbird	2																
American White Pelican	1	1	1	1	1	1	1	1						1	1	1	1
Brown Pelican	1	1	1	1	1									1	1	1	1
Masked Booby	3																
Blue-footed Booby	3		3	3													
Brown Booby	1																
Red-footed Booby	6																
Northern Gannet	1																
Great Cormorant	1																
Double-crested Cormorant	1	1	1	1	1	1	1	1		1	1	1	1	1	1	1	1
Olivaceous Cormorant	1													1	1	1	1
Brandt's Cormorant	1	1	1	1	1												
Pelagic Cormorant	1	1	1	1	1												
Red-faced Cormorant	1																
American Anhinga	1													1	1	1	1
Magnificent Frigatebird	1														1	1	
Lesser Frigatebird	7																
Great Blue Heron	1	1	1	1	1	1	1	1	1	1	1	1	1	1	1	1	1
Green Heron	1	1	1	1	1	1	1	1	1	1	1	1	1	1	1	1	1

Species	Occ. Class	Great Lakes				Mississippi				South Florida				New England			
		S	S	F	W	S	S	F	W	S	S	F	W	S	S	F	W
Common Loon	1	1		1	1	1		1	1	1		1	1	1	1	1	1
Yellow-billed Loon	1																
Arctic Loon	1																
Red-throated Loon	1													1		1	1
Red-necked Grebe	1	1		1										1		1	1
Horned Grebe	1	1		1		1		1	1					1		1	1
Eared Grebe	1																
Least Grebe	1																
Western Grebe	1																
Pied-billed Grebe	1	1	1	1		1	1	1	1	1	1	1	1	1	1	1	1
Wandering Albatross	7																
Short-tailed Albatross	7																
Black-footed Albatross	1																
Laysan Albatross	3																
Shy Albatross	7																
Yellow-nosed Albatross	6																
Cape Petrel	7																
Northern Fulmar	1																
Cory's Shearwater	1																
Pink-footed Shearwater	1																
Flesh-footed Shearwater	2																
Greater Shearwater	1																
Buller's Shearwater	1																
Sooty Shearwater	1																
Short-tailed Shearwater	1																
Manx Shearwater	1																
Little Shearwater	7																
Audubon's Shearwater	1																
Streaked Shearwater	6																
Black-capped Petrel	3																
Scaled Petrel	4																
South Trinidad Petrel	7																
White-faced Storm Petrel	6																
Fork-tailed Storm Petrel	1																
Leach's Storm Petrel	1																
Ashy Storm Petrel	1																
Band-rumped Storm Petrel	7																
Galapagos Storm Petrel	7																
Black Storm Petrel	1																
Least Storm Petrel	1																
Wilson's Storm Petrel	1																
British Storm Petrel	7																
Red-billed Tropicbird	2																
White-tailed Tropicbird	2									2	2						
American White Pelican	1					1		1		1		1	1				
Brown Pelican	1					1	1	1	1	1	1	1	1				
Masked Booby	3									3	3						
Blue-footed Booby	3																
Brown Booby	1									1	1						
Red-footed Booby	6										6						
Northern Gannet	1													1		1	
Great Cormorant	1													1		1	1
Double-crested Cormorant	1	1	1	1		1	1	1	1	1	1	1	1	1	1	1	
Olivaceous Cormorant	1																
Brandt's Cormorant	1																
Pelagic Cormorant	1																
Red-faced Cormorant	1																
American Anhinga	1					1	1	1	1	1	1	1	1				
Magnificent Frigatebird	1						1			1	1	1	1				
Lesser Frigatebird	7																
Great Blue Heron	1	1	1	1	1	1	1	1	1	1	1	1	1	1	1	1	1
Green Heron	1	1	1	1	1	1	1	1	1	1	1	1	1	1	1	1	1

Species	Occ. Class	Maine Pelagic				N. Carolina Pelagic				Florida Pelagic			
		S	S	F	W	S	S	F	W	S	S	F	W
Common Loon	1	1	1	1	1	1		1	1	1		1	1
Yellow-billed Loon	1												
Arctic Loon	1												
Red-throated Loon	1					1		1	1				
Red-necked Grebe	1												
Horned Grebe	1					1		1	1				
Eared Grebe	1												
Least Grebe	1												
Western Grebe	1												
Pied-billed Grebe	1					1		1	1				
Wandering Albatross	7												
Short-tailed Albatross	7												
Black-footed Albatross	1												
Laysan Albatross	3												
Shy Albatross	7												
Yellow-nosed Albatross	6		6	6			6	6	6				
Cape Petrel	7												
Northern Fulmar	1	1		1	1								
Cory's Shearwater	1						1	1			1	1	
Pink-footed Shearwater	1												
Flesh-footed Shearwater	2												
Greater Shearwater	1		1	1									
Buller's Shearwater	1												
Sooty Shearwater	1	1	1				1	1					
Short-tailed Shearwater	1												
Manx Shearwater	1												
Little Shearwater	7		7	7			7	7					
Audubon's Shearwater	1						1	1		1	1	1	
Streaked Shearwater	6												
Black-capped Petrel	3							5		3	3		
Scaled Petrel	4												
South Trinidad Petrel	7						7	7					
White-faced Storm Petrel	6						6	6					
Fork-tailed Storm Petrel	1												
Leach's Storm Petrel	1												
Ashy Storm Petrel	1												
Band-rumped Storm Petrel	7						7	7			7	7	
Galapagos Storm Petrel	7												
Black Storm Petrel	1												
Least Storm Petrel	1												
Wilson's Storm Petrel	1	1	1	1		1	1	1		1	1	1	
British Storm Petrel	7												
Red-billed Tropicbird	2												
White-tailed Tropicbird	2									5	5	5	
American White Pelican	1												
Brown Pelican	1					1	1	1		1	1	1	1
Masked Booby	3												
Blue-footed Booby	3												
Brown Booby	1												
Red-footed Booby	6												
Northern Gannet	1	1	1	1	1	1		1	1	1		1	1
Great Cormorant	1				1								
Double-crested Cormorant	1	1	1	1		1		1	1	1		1	1
Olivaceous Cormorant	1												
Brandt's Cormorant	1												
Pelagic Cormorant	1												
Red-faced Cormorant	1												
American Anhinga	1												
Magnificent Frigatebird	1												
Lesser Frigatebird	7												
Great Blue Heron	1					1	1	1	1				
Green Heron	1												

Species	Class	S	S	F	W	S	S	F	W	S	S	F	W	S	S	F	W	S	S	F	W	S	S	F	W	S	S	F	W	S	S	F	W	S	S	F	W	S	S	F	W	S	S	F	W	S	S	F	W	S	S	F	W	S	S	F	W	S	S	F	W
Great Egret	1																	1	1	1	1	1	1	1		1	1	1	1	1	1	1	1	1	1	1		1	1	1	1	1	1	1	1	1	1	1						1	1	1	1				
Snowy Egret	1																	1	1	1	1	1	1	1		1	1	1	1	1	1	1	1					1	1	1	1	1	1	1	1	1	1	1						1	1	1	1				
Little Egret	7																																																												
Chinese Egret	7		7																																																										
Louisiana Heron	1																													1	1	1	1					1	1	1	1	1	1	1	1									1	1	1	1				
Black-crowned Night Heron	1					1	1	1	1									1	1	1	1	1	1	1		1	1	1	1	1	1	1	1	1	1	1		1	1	1	1	1	1	1	1	1	1	1	1					1	1	1	1				
Yellow-crowned Night Heron	1																													1	1	1	1					1	1	1	1	1	1	1										1	1	1					
Least Bittern	1																	1	1	1		1	1			1	1	1		1	1	1		1	1			1	1	1		1	1	1	1	1	1							1	1	1					
American Bittern	1					1	1	1	1									1	1	1	1	1	1	1					1	1	1	1	1	1	1	1		1	1	1	1	1		1	1	1	1	1						1		1	1				
Wood Stork	1																		1												1	1										1	1	1	1																
Glossy Ibis	1																																									1	1	1	1	1	1							1	1	1	1				
White-faced Ibis	1																	1	1	1	1	1	1							1	1	1	1																												
White Ibis	1																													1	1	1	1					1	1	1	1	1	1	1	1									1	1	1					
Roseate Spoonbill	1																													1	1	1	1									1	1	1	1																
American Flamingo	1																																									1	1	1	1																
Mute Swan	1																																													1	1	1	1												
Whooper Swan	2	3		3	3																																																								
Bewick's Swan	6																				6																																								
Whistling Swan	1	1	1	1					1									1	1	1	1	1	1											1	1																			1		1	1				
Trumpeter Swan	1	1	1	1	1																	1	1*	1	1																																				
Canada Goose	1	1	1	1	1				1									1	1	1	1	1	1	1	1	1		1	1	1		1	1	1	1	1	1	1		1	1					1	1	1	1					1	1	1	1				
Brant	1	1	1	1	1				1				1				1	1		1	1																									1		1	1					1		1	1				
Barnacle Goose	7																																															7													
Emperor Goose	1	1	1	1	1																																																								
Greater White-fr. Goose	1	1	1	1					1				1					1		1	1									1		1	1																												
Bean Goose	3	3																																																											
Snow Goose	1	1	1	1					1				1				1	1		1	1	1		1		1		1	1	1		1	1	1		1		1		1	1					1		1						1		1	1				
Ross's Goose	1																	1		1	1									1		1	1																												
Black-bell. Whist. Duck	1																										1			1	1	1	1																												
Fulvous Whistling Duck	1																	1	1											1	1	1										1		1	1																
Mallard	1	1	1	1	1	1	1	1	1	1	1	1	1	1			1	1	1	1	1	1	1	1	1	1	1	1	1	1	1	1	1	1	1	1	1	1	1	1	1	1		1	1	1	1	1	1				1	1	1	1	1	1			1
Mexican Duck	1																									1	1	1	1	1	1	1																													
American Black Duck	1																																	1	1	1	1	1		1	1					1	1	1	1	1	1	1	1	1		1	1	1			1
Mottled Duck	1																													1	1	1	1									1	1	1	1																
Spot-billed Duck	7	7		7	7																																																								
Gadwall	1	1	1	1	1	1			1	1	1	1	1	1			1	1	1	1	1	1	1	1	1	1		1	1	1	1	1	1	1	1	1		1		1	1	1		1	1	1		1	1					1	1	1	1				
Common Pintail	1	1	1	1	1	1	1	1	1	1	1	1	1	1			1	1	1	1	1	1		1	1	1		1	1	1		1	1	1		1	1	1		1	1	1		1	1	1		1	1					1		1	1				
White-cheeked Pintail	5																																											5	5																
Falcated Teal	4	4		4																																																									
Green-winged Teal	1	1	1	1	1	1	1	1	1	1	1	1	1	1			1	1	1	1	1	1	1	1	1	1		1	1	1	1	1	1	1	1	1	1	1		1	1	1		1	1	1	1	1	1					1	1	1	1				
Baikal Teal	7	7		7																																																									
Blue-winged Teal	1					1			1	1				1						1	1	1	1	1		1				1	1	1	1	1	1	1		1	1	1		1		1	1	1	1	1						1	1	1	1	1			1
Cinnamon Teal	1										1				1			1	1	1	1	1	1	1		1	1	1		1		1	1																												
Garganey	3	3		3																																																									
Eurasian Wigeon	1	1		1	1													1		1	1																									1		1	1												
American Wigeon	1	1	1	1	1				1									1	1	1	1	1	1	1	1	1		1	1	1		1	1	1	1	1		1		1	1	1			1	1		1	1					1	1	1	1				
Northern Shoveler	1	1	1	1	1	1			1	1	1	1	1	1			1	1	1	1	1	1	1	1	1	1		1	1	1		1	1	1	1	1		1		1	1	1		1	1	1		1	1					1	1	1	1	1			1
Wood Duck	1																													1	1	1	1	1	1	1		1	1	1	1	1	1	1	1	1	1	1													
Redhead	1								1				1				1	1	1	1	1	1	1	1	1	1	1	1	1	1		1	1	1		1		1		1	1					1		1	1					1		1	1				
Common Pochard	2	2		4	4																																																								
Ring-necked Duck	1								1				1				1	1		1	1	1	1	1	1	1	1	1	1	1		1	1	1		1		1		1	1	1		1	1	1	1	1						1		1	1	1			1
Canvasback	1	1	1	1					1				1				1	1	1	1	1	1	1	1	1	1		1	1	1		1	1	1		1		1		1	1					1		1	1					1		1	1				
Greater Scaup	1	1	1	1	1				1				1				1	1		1	1	1		1	1				1					1		1	1									1		1	1				1								
Lesser Scaup	1	1	1	1	1	1			1	1			1	1			1	1		1	1	1	1	1	1	1		1	1	1		1	1	1		1		1		1	1	1		1	1	1		1						1		1	1	1			1
Tufted Duck	1	1		1	1																																																								
Common Goldeneye	1	1	1	1	1	1			1	1			1	1			1	1	1	1	1	1	1	1	1	1		1	1	1		1	1	1		1	1	1		1	1					1		1	1	1	1	1	1	1		1	1	1			1
Barrow's Goldeneye	1	1	1	1	1	1	1	1	1									1		1	1	1	1	1	1				1																	1		1	1	1											
Bufflehead	1	1	1	1	1				1				1				1	1		1	1	1	1	1	1	1		1	1	1		1	1	1		1	1	1		1	1	1		1	1	1		1	1	1			1	1		1	1	1			1
Oldsquaw	1	1	1	1	1	1			1	1			1					1		1	1																									1		1	1	1			1								
Harlequin Duck	1	1	1	1	1	1	1	1	1	1	1	1	1					1		1	1																									1		1	1	1											
Steller's Eider	1	1	1	1	1																																																								
Common Eider	1	1	1	1	1																																									1		1	1	1	1	1	1								
King Eider	1	1	1	1	1				1																																					1		1	1	1											
Spectacled Eider	1	1	1	1																																																									
White-winged Scoter	1	1	1	1	1	1		1	1	1		1	1	1			1	1		1	1													1		1	1									1		1	1	1			1	1		1	1				

Species	Occ. Class	Alaska				Westport Pelagic				Monterey Pelagic				San Diego Pelagic				California				Colorado				Arizona				Texas				Great Lakes				Mississippi				South Florida				New England				Maine Pelagic				N. Carolina Pelagic				Florida Pelagic			
		S	S	F	W	S	S	F	W	S	S	F	W	S	S	F	W	S	S	F	W	S	S	F	W	S	S	F	W	S	S	F	W	S	S	F	W	S	S	F	W	S	S	F	W	S	S	F	W	S	S	F	W	S	S	F	W	S	S	F	W
Surf Scoter	1	1	1	1		1		1	1	1		1	1	1			1	1	1	1	1													1		1	1									1		1	1	1				1		1	1				
Ruddy Duck	1					1			1	1			1	1			1	1	1	1	1						1																			1		1	1	1				1		1	1				
Black Scoter	1	1	1	1	1	1			1	1			1					1		1	1	1	1	1	1	1		1	1	1		1	1	1		1	1	1		1	1	1		1	1	1		1	1	1				1		1	1				
Masked Duck	2																													2	2	2	2											3	3																
Hooded Merganser	1								1									1	1	1	1									1		1	1	1		1	1	1		1						1		1	1					1		1	1				
Smew	2	2	5	2	2																																																								
Common Merganser	1	1	1	1	1				1									1	1	1	1	1	1	1	1	1		1	1	1		1	1	1		1	1	1		1	1					1		1	1					1		1	1				
Red-breasted Merganser	1	1	1	1	1	1			1	1		1	1	1			1	1	1	1	1	1	1	1	1	1		1		1	1	1	1	1		1		1		1	1	1		1	1	1		1	1	1			1	1		1	1	1			1
Turkey Vulture	1																	1	1	1	1	1	1	1		1	1	1	1	1	1	1	1	1	1	1		1	1	1	1	1	1	1	1	1	1	1													
Black Vulture	1																									1		1	1	1	1	1	1					1	1	1	1	1	1	1	1																
California Condor	2																	2*	2	2	2																																								
White-tailed Kite	1																	1	1	1	1									1	1	1	1																												
Swallow-tailed Kite	1																																									1	1	1																	
Hook-billed Kite	3																													3	4*	5	5																												
Mississippi Kite	1																									1	1			1	1	1						1	1	1																					
Snail Kite	1																																									1	1	1	1																
Northern Goshawk	1																									1	1							1	1	1										1	1	1													
Sharp-shinned Hawk	1	1	1	1														1	1	1	1	1	1	1	1	1	1	1	1	1	1	1	1	1	1	1		1		1	1	1		1	1	1	1	1													
Cooper's Hawk	1																	1	1	1	1	1	1	1	1	1	1	1	1	1	1	1	1	1	1	1	1	1	1	1	1	1		1	1																
Red-tailed Hawk	1	1	1	1														1	1	1	1	1	1	1	1	1	1	1	1	1	1	1	1	1	1	1	1	1	1	1	1	1	1	1	1	1	1	1	1												
Red-shouldered Hawk	1																	1	1	1	1									1	1	1	1	1	1	1	1	1	1	1	1	1	1	1	1	1	1	1	1					1		1	1				
Broad-winged Hawk	1																													1		1		1	1	1		1	1	1						1	1	1													
Swainson's Hawk	1																	1	1	1		1	1	1		1	1	1		1	1	1																													
Zone-tailed Hawk	1																									1	1			1	1																														
White-tailed Hawk	1																													1	1	1	1																												
Short-tailed Hawk	1																																									1	1	1	1																
Rough-legged Hawk	1	1	1	1																	1	1		1	1					1		1	1	1		1	1																								
Ferruginous Hawk	1																	1		1	1	1	1	1		1		1	1	1		1	1																												
Gray Hawk	1																									1	1	1																																	
Harris's Hawk	1																									1	1	1	1	1	1	1	1																												
Lesser Black Hawk	1																									1	1	1		1	1	1																													
Golden Eagle	1	1	1	1	1													1	1	1	1	1	1	1	1	1	1	1	1	1	1	1	1			1																									
White-tailed Eagle	3	3	3																																																										
Bald Eagle	1	1	1	1	1													1	1	1	1	1	1	1	1									1	1	1	1	1	1	1	1	1	1	1	1	1	1	1	1												
Steller's Sea Eagle	7	7		7	7																																																								
Northern Harrier	1	1	1	1														1		1	1	1		1	1	1		1	1	1		1	1	1	1	1		1		1	1	1		1	1																
Osprey	1																	1	1	1		1	1	1						1	1	1	1	1	1	1		1	1	1		1	1	1	1																
Crested Caracara	1																									2	2	2	2	1	1	1	1																												
Gyrfalcon	1	1	1	1	1																																																								
Prairie Falcon	1																	1	1	1	1	1	1	1	1	1	1	1	1	1	1	1	1																												
Peregrine Falcon	1	1	1	1	1													1	1	1	1															1								1	1			1													
Aplomado Falcon	7																									7	7			7	7																														
Merlin	1	1	1	1														1		1	1				1							1	1			1								1	1			1													
Eurasian Kestrel	7			7																																																									
American Kestrel	1	1	1	1														1	1	1	1	1	1	1	1	1	1	1	1	1	1	1	1	1	1	1	1	1	1	1	1	1		1	1	1	1	1	1												
Plain Chachalaca	1																													1	1	1	1																												
Blue Grouse	1																	1	1			1	1			2	2																																		
Spruce Grouse	1	1	1	1																														1	1	1	1									1	1	1	1												
Ruffed Grouse	1																	1	1	1	1													1	1	1	1									1	1	1	1												
Willow Ptarmigan	1	1	1	1	1																																																								
Rock Ptarmigan	1	1	1	1	1																																																								
White-tailed Ptarmigan	1	1	1	1	1																	1	1	1	1																																				
Greater Prairie Chicken	1																													1	1			1	1	1	1																								
Lesser Prairie Chicken	1																													1	1																														
Sharp-tailed Grouse	1																																	1	1	1	1																								
Sage Grouse	1																	1	1	1	1	1	1	1	1																																				
Common Bobwhite	1																													1	1	1	1	1	1	1	1	1	1	1	1	1	1	1	1																
Scaled Quail	1																					1	1	1	1	1	1	1	1	1	1	1	1																												
California Quail	1																	1	1	1	1																																								
Gambel's Quail	1																	1	1	1	1					1	1	1	1	1	1	1	1																												
Mountain Quail	1																	1	1	1																																									
Montezuma Quail	1																									2	1	2	2	1	1	1	1																												
Ring-necked Pheasant	1																	1	1	1	1	1	1	1	1					1	1	1	1	1	1	1	1									1	1	1	1												
Chukar	1																	1	1	1	1																																								

Species	Occ. Class	Alaska				Westport Pelagic				Monterey Pelagic				San Diego Pelagic				California				Colorado				Arizona				Texas				Great Lakes				Mississippi				South Florida				New England				Maine Pelagic				N. Carolina Pelagic				Florida Pelagic			
		S	S	F	W	S	S	F	W	S	S	F	W	S	S	F	W	S	S	F	W	S	S	F	W	S	S	F	W	S	S	F	W	S	S	F	W	S	S	F	W	S	S	F	W	S	S	F	W	S	S	F	W	S	S	F	W	S	S	F	W
Black Francolin	1																													1	1*																														
Wild Turkey	1																									2	2	2	2	1	1	1	1					1	1	1	1	1	1	1	1																
Common Crane	7	7																				6*		7																																					
Whooping Crane	1																													1*		1	1																												
Sandhill Crane	1	1	1	1														1		1	1	1		1	1	1		1	1	1		1	1	1	1	1		1	1	1	1	1	1	1	1																
Limpkin	1																																									1	1	1	1																
King Rail	1																													1	1	1	1					1	1	1	1	1	1	1	1																
Clapper Rail	1																	1	1	1	1					1	1	1		1	1	1	1					1	1	1	1	1	1	1	1	1	1	1													
Virginia Rail	1																	1	1	1	1	1	1	1	1	1		1	1	1		1	1	1	1	1		1		1	1	1		1	1	1	1	1													
Spotted Rail	7																																																												
Sora	1																	1		1	1	1	1	1	1	1		1	1	1		1	1	1	1	1		1		1	1	1		1	1	1	1	1													
Yellow Rail	1																													1		1	1	1	1																								
Black Rail	1																	1	1							1	1	2	2	1	1																														
Corn Crake	7																																																												
Paint-billed Crake	7																																																												
Purple Gallinule	1																													1	1	1						1	1	1		1	1	1	1																
Common Gallinule	1																	1	1	1	1	1	1	1	1	1	1	1	1	1	1	1	1	1	1	1		1	1	1	1	1	1	1	1	1	1	1													
European Coot	7																																																												
American Coot	1					1	1	1	1	1	1	1	1	1	1	1	1	1	1	1	1	1	1	1	1	1	1	1	1	1	1	1	1	1	1	1		1	1	1	1	1	1	1	1	1	1	1	1					1	1	1	1				
Caribbean Coot	1																																												1																
North American Jacana	4																									4	4	4	4																																
American Oystercatcher	1																													1	1	1										1	1	1	1																
Black Oystercatcher	1					1	1	1	1	1	1	1	1	1	1	1	1	1	1	1	1																																								
Black-necked Stilt	1																	1	1	1	1					1	1	1		1	1	1										1	1	1	1																
American Avocet	1																	1			1	1	1			1	1			1		1	1									1			1																
Double-strioed Thick-knee	7																													7		7																													
Northern Lapwing	7																																															7	7												
Ringed Plover	5	5	5	5																																																									
Semipalmated Plover	1	1	1	1														1		1	1	1		1		1		1		1		1	1	1		1		1		1	1	1		1	1	1		1													
Little Ringed Plover	7		7																																																										
Wilson's Plover	1																													1	1	1	1					1	1	1	1	1	1	1	1																
Killdeer	1	1	1															1	1	1	1	1	1	1	1	1	1	1	1	1	1	1	1	1	1	1	1	1	1	1	1	1	1	1	1	1	1	1	1												
Piping Plover	1																													1		1	1	1		1	1	1		1	1	1		1	1	1	1	1	1												
Snowy Plover	1																	1	1	1	1	1	1	1						1	1	1	1					1	1	1	1	1	1	1	1																
Mongolian Plover	3	3	3	3																																																									
Mountain Plover	1																	1		1	1	1	1	1		2		2	2	1		1	1																												
Greater Golden Plover	5																																																												
Lesser Golden Plover	1	1	1	1																		1		1						1		1		1	1	1		1		1						1	1	1													
Black-bellied Plover	1	1	1	1														1	1	1	1	1		1						1	1	1	1	1	1	1	1	1		1	1	1	1	1	1	1	1	1	1												
Dotterel	5	5	5	5																																																									
Black-tailed Godwit	5	5	5																																											5		5													
Hudsonian Godwit	1	1	1																											1				1		1												1													
Bar-tailed Godwit	1	1	1																																																										
Marbled Godwit	1																	1	1	1	1	1	1	1						1	1	1									1	1		1	1			1													
Eskimo Curlew	7																													7																															
Whimbrel	1	1	1															1		1	1									1		1	1	1	1	1		1		1		1		1	1	1	1	1													
Bristle-thighed Curlew	2	2	2																																																									
Eurasian Curlew	7																																															7	7												
Far Eastern Curlew	6	7	6																																																										
Long-billed Curlew	1																	1	1	1	1	1	1	1						1	1	1	1									1		1	1																
Upland Sandpiper	1																					1	1							1	1	1		1	1	1		1	1	1						1	1	1													
Spotted Redshank	3	4	3	3																																																									
Marsh Sandpiper	7	7	7	7																																																									
Greenshank	3	3	3	3																																																									
Greater Yellowlegs	1	1	1	1														1	1	1	1	1	1	1	1	1	1	1	1	1	1	1	1	1	1	1		1	1	1	1	1	1	1	1	1	1	1	1												
Lesser Yellowlegs	1	1	1															1	1	1	1	1	1	1		1	1	1		1	1	1	1	1	1	1		1	1	1	1	1	1	1	1	1	1	1													
Solitary Sandpiper	1	1	1																			1	1	1			1	1		1	1	1		1	1	1		1	1	1		1	1	1		1	1	1													
Wood Sandpiper	1	1	1																																																										
Willet	1																	1	1	1	1	1	1	1			1			1	1	1	1					1	1	1	1	1	1	1	1		1	1													
Terek Sandpiper	5	5	5																																																										
Common Sandpiper	3	3	3	4																																																									
Spotted Sandpiper	1	1	1															1	1	1	1	1	1	1		1	1	1	1	1	1	1	1	1	1	1		1	1	1	1	1	1	1	1	1	1	1													
Gray-tailed Tattler	2	2	2	2																																																									
Wandering Tattler	1	1	1	1														1		1	1																																								
Ruddy Turnstone	1	1	1	1														1	1	1	1	1	1	1						1	1	1	1	1	1	1		1	1	1	1	1		1	1	1	1	1													

Species	Occ. Class	Alaska				Westport Pelagic				Monterey Pelagic				San Diego Pelagic				California			
		S	S	F	W	S	S	F	W	S	S	F	W	S	S	F	W	S	S	F	W
Black Turnstone	1	1	1	1				1				1						1	1	1	1
Wilson's Phalarope	1																	1	1	1	
Northern Phalarope	1	1	1			1	1	1		1		1						1	1	1	1
Red Phalarope	1	1	1	1		1	1	1		1		1		1		1		1	1	1	
European Woodcock	7																				
American Woodcock	1																				
Common Snipe	1	1	1	1														1	1	1	1
European Jacksnipe	7	7	7	7																	
Short-billed Dowitcher	1	1	1															1	1	1	1
Long-billed Dowitcher	1	1	1	1														1	1	1	1
Surfbird	1	1	1	1														1		1	1
Great Knot	5	5	5																		
Red Knot	1	1	1	1														1		1	1
Sanderling	1	1	1	1														1	1	1	1
Semipalmated Sandpiper	1	1	1																		
Western Sandpiper	1	1	1	1														1	1	1	1
Rufous-necked Stint	2	2	2																		
Little Stint	7	7	7																		
Temminck's Stint	3	3	3																		
Long-toed Stint	2	2	2																		
Least Sandpiper	1	1	1															1	1	1	1
White-rumped Sandpiper	1																				
Baird's Sandpiper	1	1	1																1	1	
Pectoral Sandpiper	1	1	1	1																	
Sharp-tailed Sandpiper	2	5	2	2																	
Purple Sandpiper	1																				
Rock Sandpiper	1	1	1	1	1													1		1	1
Dunlin	1	1	1	1														1	1	1	1
Curlew Sandpiper	2	6	6																		
Spoonbill Sandpiper	6	6	6																		
Broad-billed Sandpiper	5		5	5																	
Stilt Sandpiper	1																				
Buff-breasted Sandpiper	1	1	1																		
Ruff	2	2	2	2																	
Pomarine Jaeger	1	1	1	1														1	1	1	1
Parasitic Jaeger	1	1	1	1														1	1	1	
Long-tailed Jaeger	1	1	1																	1	
Great Skua	2																				
South Polar Skua	2		6				2	2			2	2									
Glaucous Gull	1	1	1	1	1																
Iceland Gull	1																				
Glaucous-winged Gull	1	1	1	1	1	1	1	1	1	1	1	1	1	1		1	1	1	1	1	1
Great Black-backed Gull	1																				
Slaty-backed Gull	2	2	3	2	2																
Western Gull	1					1	1	1	1	1	1	1	1	1	1	1	1	1	1	1	1
Lesser Black-backed Gull	2																				
Herring Gull	1	1	1	1	1	1	1	1	1	1		1	1	1		1	1	1		1	1
Thayer's Gull	1																	1		1	1
California Gull	1					1	1	1	1	1	1	1	1	1	1	1	1	1	1	1	1
Ring-billed Gull	1					1	1	1	1	1	1	1	1	1	1	1	1	1	1	1	1
Mew Gull	1	1	1	1														1		1	1
Black-headed Gull	1																				
Laughing Gull	1																	1	1		
Franklin's Gull	1																				
Bonaparte's Gull	1	1	1	1		1		1	1	1		1	1					1	1	1	1
Little Gull	1																				
Heermann's Gull	1							1			1	1	1	1	1	1	1	1	1	1	1
Ivory Gull	1	1		1	1																
Black-legged Kittiwake	1	1	1	1	1	1	1	1	1	1		1	1	1		1	1	1		1	1
Red-legged Kittiwake	1	1	1	1	1																
Ross's Gull	1	1		1																	
Sabine's Gull	1	1	1	1		1		1													
Gull-billed Tern	1																	1	1	1	
Forster's Tern	1									1	1	1	1	1	1	1	1	1	1	1	1
Common Tern	1					1		1		1		1		1		1		1		1	

Species	Colorado				Arizona				Texas				Great Lakes				Mississippi			
	S	S	F	W	S	S	F	W	S	S	F	W	S	S	F	W	S	S	F	W
Black Turnstone																				
Wilson's Phalarope	1	1	1		1	1	1		1	1	1									
Northern Phalarope	1	1	1			1														
Red Phalarope																				
European Woodcock																				
American Woodcock									1		1	1	1	1	1		1	1	1	1
Common Snipe	1	1	1	1	1		1	1	1	1	1	1	1	1	1		1	1	1	1
European Jacksnipe																				
Short-billed Dowitcher									1	1	1	1	1	1	1		1	1	1	1
Long-billed Dowitcher	1	1	1		1	1	1	1	1	1	1	1	1	1	1			1	1	1
Surfbird																				
Great Knot																				
Red Knot									1	1	1	1	1	1	1		1	1	1	1
Sanderling									1	1	1	1	1	1	1		1	1	1	1
Semipalmated Sandpiper									1	1	1		1	1	1		1	1	1	
Western Sandpiper	1	1	1		1	1	1	1	1	1	1	1	1	1	1		1	1	1	1
Rufous-necked Stint																				
Little Stint																				
Temminck's Stint																				
Long-toed Stint																				
Least Sandpiper	1	1	1		1	1	1	1	1	1	1	1	1	1	1		1	1	1	1
White-rumped Sandpiper									1	1	1		1	1	1		1	1	1	
Baird's Sandpiper	1	1	1			1	1		1	1	1									
Pectoral Sandpiper									1	1	1		1	1	1		1	1	1	
Sharp-tailed Sandpiper																				
Purple Sandpiper																				
Rock Sandpiper																				
Dunlin	1	1	1		1		1		1	1	1	1	1	1	1		1	1	1	1
Curlew Sandpiper																				
Spoonbill Sandpiper																				
Broad-billed Sandpiper																				
Stilt Sandpiper									1	1	1	1		1	1			1	1	
Buff-breasted Sandpiper									1	1	1			1	1					
Ruff																				
Pomarine Jaeger											1									
Parasitic Jaeger											1									
Long-tailed Jaeger																				
Great Skua																				
South Polar Skua																				
Glaucous Gull															1	1				
Iceland Gull																6				
Glaucous-winged Gull																				
Great Black-backed Gull																				
Slaty-backed Gull																				
Western Gull																				
Lesser Black-backed Gull																				
Herring Gull	1		1	1					1	1	1	1	1	1	1	1	1	1	1	1
Thayer's Gull																				
California Gull	1	1	1																	
Ring-billed Gull	1	1	1	1	1		1	1	1	1	1	1	1	1	1	1	1	1	1	1
Mew Gull																				
Black-headed Gull																				
Laughing Gull									1	1	1	1					1	1	1	1
Franklin's Gull	1	1	1						1	1	1		1	1	1					
Bonaparte's Gull	1	1	1						1		1	1	1	1	1	1	1		1	1
Little Gull													1	1	1					
Heermann's Gull																				
Ivory Gull																				
Black-legged Kittiwake																				
Red-legged Kittiwake																				
Ross's Gull																				
Sabine's Gull																				
Gull-billed Tern																				
Forster's Tern	1	1	1		1	1	1		1	1	1	1	1	1	1		1	1	1	1
Common Tern	1		1			1			1		1		1		1		1		1	1

Species	South Florida				New England				Maine Pelagic				N. Carolina Pelagic				Florida Pelagic			
	S	S	F	W	S	S	F	W	S	S	F	W	S	S	F	W	S	S	F	W
Black Turnstone																				
Wilson's Phalarope																				
Northern Phalarope									1	1			1	1	1					
Red Phalarope									1	1	1		1	1	1					
European Woodcock							7	7												
American Woodcock					1	1	1													
Common Snipe					1	1	1	1												
European Jacksnipe																				
Short-billed Dowitcher	1	1	1	1	1	1	1													
Long-billed Dowitcher	1		1	1			1													
Surfbird																				
Great Knot																				
Red Knot	1		1	1	1	1	1	1												
Sanderling	1	1	1	1	1	1	1	1												
Semipalmated Sandpiper	1	1	1	1	1	1	1													
Western Sandpiper	1	1	1	1	1	1	1													
Rufous-necked Stint																				
Little Stint																				
Temminck's Stint																				
Long-toed Stint																				
Least Sandpiper	1	1	1	1	1	1	1													
White-rumped Sandpiper	1	1	1		1	1	1													
Baird's Sandpiper																				
Pectoral Sandpiper	1	1	1		1	1	1													
Sharp-tailed Sandpiper																				
Purple Sandpiper					1		1	1												
Rock Sandpiper																				
Dunlin	1	1	1	1	1	1	1	1												
Curlew Sandpiper					2	3	5													
Spoonbill Sandpiper																				
Broad-billed Sandpiper																				
Stilt Sandpiper		1	1			1	1													
Buff-breasted Sandpiper						1	1													
Ruff						2	2													
Pomarine Jaeger									1	1	1		1	1	1		1		1	1
Parasitic Jaeger							1		1	1	1		1	1	1		1		1	1
Long-tailed Jaeger																				
Great Skua										2	2									
South Polar Skua													2	2						
Glaucous Gull								1												
Iceland Gull					1		1	1												
Glaucous-winged Gull																				
Great Black-backed Gull					1	1	1	1	1	1	1	1	1		1	1				
Slaty-backed Gull																				
Western Gull																				
Lesser Black-backed Gull			2	2	2		2	2												
Herring Gull	1	1	1	1	1	1	1	1	1	1	1	1	1	1	1	1	1		1	1
Thayer's Gull																				
California Gull																				
Ring-billed Gull	1	1	1	1	1	1	1	1					1	1	1	1	1	1	1	1
Mew Gull																				
Black-headed Gull					1		1	1												
Laughing Gull	1	1	1	1	1	1	1						1	1	1	1	1	1	1	1
Franklin's Gull																				
Bonaparte's Gull					1	1	1	1					1		1	1	1		1	1
Little Gull					1	1	1													
Heermann's Gull																				
Ivory Gull																				
Black-legged Kittiwake					1		1	1	1		1	1	1		1	1				
Red-legged Kittiwake																				
Ross's Gull																				
Sabine's Gull																				
Gull-billed Tern																				
Forster's Tern	1	1	1	1									1	1	1	1	1	1	1	1
Common Tern	1	1	1		1	1							1		1		1			

Species	Occ. Class	Alaska S	Alaska S	Alaska F	Alaska W	Westport Pelagic S	Westport Pelagic S	Westport Pelagic F	Westport Pelagic W	Monterey Pelagic S	Monterey Pelagic S	Monterey Pelagic F	Monterey Pelagic W	San Diego Pelagic S	San Diego Pelagic S	San Diego Pelagic F	San Diego Pelagic W	California S	California S	California F	California W	Colorado S	Colorado S	Colorado F	Colorado W	Arizona S	Arizona S	Arizona F	Arizona W	Texas S	Texas S	Texas F	Texas W	Great Lakes S	Great Lakes S	Great Lakes F	Great Lakes W	Mississippi S	Mississippi S	Mississippi F	Mississippi W	South Florida S	South Florida S	South Florida F	South Florida W	New England S	New England S	New England F	New England W	Maine Pelagic S	Maine Pelagic S	Maine Pelagic F	Maine Pelagic W	N. Carolina Pelagic S	N. Carolina Pelagic S	N. Carolina Pelagic F	N. Carolina Pelagic W	Florida Pelagic S	Florida Pelagic S	Florida Pelagic F	Florida Pelagic W
Arctic Tern	1	1	1			1		1				1																																		1	1			1	1										
Roseate Tern	1																																									1	1			1	1	1													
Aleutian Tern	1	1	1																																																										
Sooty Tern	1																																									1	1															1	1		
Bridled Tern	1																																																					1	1	1		1	1	1	
Little Tern	1																	1	1	1										1	1	1						1	1	1		1	1	1		1	1	1						1	1	1		1	1	1	
Royal Tern	1													1	1	1	1	1	1	1	1									1	1	1	1					1	1	1	1	1	1	1	1									1	1	1	1	1	1	1	1
Elegant Tern	1										1	1		1	1	1	1	1	1	1	1																																								
Sandwich Tern	1																													1	1	1							1			1	1	1	1									1	1	1		1	1	1	1
Caspian Tern	1									1	1	1		1	1	1	1	1	1	1	1	1	1	1			1	1		1	1	1	1	1	1	1		1	1	1	1	1	1	1	1									1	1	1					
Black Tern	1																	1	1	1		1	1	1		1	1	1		1	1	1		1	1	1		1	1	1		1	1	1		1	1	1							1	1					
White-winged Black Tern	4																																																												
Brown Noddy	1																																									1	1	1														1	1	1	
Black Noddy	4																																									4	4																		
Black Skimmer	1																	1	1	1	1									1	1	1	1					1	1	1	1	1	1	1	1	1	1	1						1	1	1	1				
Razorbill	1																																													1	1														
Thin-billed Murre	1	1	1	1	1	1	1	1	1	1	1	1	1					1	1	1	1																																								
Thick-billed Murre	1	1	1	1																																														1		1	1								
Dovekie	1	2	2																																															1		1	1								
Black Guillemot	1	1	1	1	1																																													1	1	1	1								
Pigeon Guillemot	1	1	1	1	1	1	1	1	1	1	1	1	1					1	1	1	1																																								
Marbled Murrelet	1	1	1	1	1	1	1	1	1									1	1																																										
Kittlitz's Murrelet	1	1	1	1	1																																																								
Xantus's Murrelet	1													1	1																																														
Craveri's Murrelet	2														2	2																																													
Ancient Murrelet	1	1	1	1	1	1		1	1	1		1	1																																																
Cassin's Auklet	1	1	1	1	1	1		1		1		1	1					1	1	1	1																																								
Parakeet Auklet	1	1	1																																																										
Crested Auklet	1	1	1																																																										
Least Auklet	1	1	1																																																										
Whiskered Auklet	1	1	1																																																										
Rhinoceros Auklet	1	1	1			1		1	1	1		1	1					1		1	1																																								
Atlantic Puffin	1																																													1	1														
Horned Puffin	1	1	1																																																										
Tufted Puffin	1	1	1	1	1	1		1	1									1	1																																										
White-crowned Pigeon	1																												1													1	1																		
Scaly-naped Pigeon	7																																									7		7	7																
Band-tailed Pigeon	1																	1	1	1		1	1	1		1	1	1		1	1	1																													
Red-billed Pigeon	2																													2	2																														
Rock Dove	1																	1	1	1	1	1	1	1	1	1	1	1	1	1	1	1	1	1	1	1	1	1	1	1	1	1	1	1	1	1	1	1	1												
Zenaida Dove	7																																									7		7	7																
White-winged Dove	1																	1	1	1						1	1	1		1	1	1	1									1		1	1																
Mourning Dove	1																	1	1	1	1	1	1	1	1	1	1	1	1	1	1	1	1	1	1	1	1	1	1	1	1	1	1	1	1	1	1	1	1												
Spotted Dove	1																	1	1*	1	1																																								
Ringed Turtle Dove	1																	1	1*	1	1					1	1*	1	1													1	1*	1	1																
Common Ground Dove	1																	1	1	1	1					1	1	1	1	1	1	1	1					1	1	1	1	1	1	1	1																
Ruddy Ground Dove	7																													7		7	7																												
Inca Dove	1																	1	1	1	1					1	1	1	1	1	1	1	1																												
White-tipped Dove	1																													1	1	1	1																												
Key West Quail Dove	7																																									7		7	7																
Ruddy Quail Dove	7																																									7		7	7																
Thick-billed Parrot	7																									7	7	7	7																																
Yellow-headed Parrot	1																	1	1*	1	1																																								
Budgerigar	1																																									1	1*	1	1																
Common Cuckoo	4	4	4																																																										
Oriental Cuckoo	7	7	7	7																																																									
Mangrove Cuckoo	1																																									1	1																		
Yellow-billed Cuckoo	1																	1	1			1	1			1	1			1	1			1	1			1	1			1	1			1	1														
Black-billed Cuckoo	1																													1				1	1											1	1														
Greater Roadrunner	1																	1	1	1	1					1	1	1	1	1	1	1	1																												
Smooth-billed Ani	1																																									1	1	1	1																
Groove-billed Ani	1																													1	1	1	1																												
Barn Owl	1																	1	1	1	1	1	1	1	1	1	1	1	1	1	1	1	1	1	1	1		1	1	1	1	1		1	1	1	1	1	1												
Common Screech Owl	1																	1	1	1	1	1	1	1	1	1	1	1	1	1	1	1	1	1	1	1	1	1	1	1	1	1	1	1	1	1	1	1	1												
Whiskered Screech Owl	1																									1	1	2	2																																

Species	Occ. Class	Alaska S	Alaska S	Alaska F	Alaska W	Westport Pelagic S	Westport Pelagic S	Westport Pelagic F	Westport Pelagic W	Monterey Pelagic S	Monterey Pelagic S	Monterey Pelagic F	Monterey Pelagic W	San Diego Pelagic S	San Diego Pelagic S	San Diego Pelagic F	San Diego Pelagic W	California S	California S	California F	California W	Colorado S	Colorado S	Colorado F	Colorado W	Arizona S	Arizona S	Arizona F	Arizona W	Texas S	Texas S	Texas F	Texas W	Great Lakes S	Great Lakes S	Great Lakes F	Great Lakes W	Mississippi S	Mississippi S	Mississippi F	Mississippi W	South Florida S	South Florida S	South Florida F	South Florida W	New England S	New England S	New England F	New England W	Maine Pelagic S	Maine Pelagic S	Maine Pelagic F	Maine Pelagic W	N. Carolina Pelagic S	N. Carolina Pelagic S	N. Carolina Pelagic F	N. Carolina Pelagic W	Florida Pelagic S	Florida Pelagic S	Florida Pelagic F	Florida Pelagic W
Flammulated Screech Owl	1																	1	1			1	1			1	1			1	1																														
Great Horned Owl	1	1	1	1	1													1	1	1	1	1	1	1	1	1	1	1	1	1	1	1	1	1	1	1	1	1	1	1	1	1	1	1	1	1	1	1	1												
Snowy Owl	1	1	1	1	1																																																								
Hawk Owl	1	1	1	1	1																															1	1												1	1											
Northern Pygmy Owl	1																	1	1			1	1			2	2	2	2																																
Ferruginous Pygmy Owl	2																									2	2			2	2																														
Elf Owl	1																									1	1			1	1																														
Burrowing Owl	1																	1	1	1	1	1	1	1	1	1	1	1	1	1	1	1	1									1	1	1	1																
Barred Owl	1																													1	1	1	1	1	1	1	1	1	1	1	1	1	1	1	1	1	1	1	1												
Spotted Owl	1																	1	1							1	1																																		
Great Gray Owl	2																	2	2	2																	2																								
Long-eared Owl	1																	1		1	1													1		1	1									1		1	1												
Short-eared Owl	1	1	1	1														1	1	1	1	1		1	1	1		1	1	1		1	1	1		1	1	1		1	1					1		1	1												
Boreal Owl	1	1	1																																																										
Saw-whet Owl	1																	1	1			1	1			1	1			1	1			1	1	1	1									1	1	1	1												
Jungle Nightjar	7	7	7																																																										
Chuck-will's-widow	1																													1	1			1	1			1	1			1	1																		
Whip-poor-will	1																					1	1			1	1			1	1			1	1			1	1																						
Buff-collared Nightjar	2																									2	2																																		
Poor-will	1																	1	1			1	1			1	1			1	1																														
Pauraque	1																													1	1	1	1																												
Common Nighthawk	1																	1	1	1		1	1	1		1	1	1		1	1	1		1	1	1		1	1	1		1	1	1		1	1	1													
Lesser Nighthawk	1																	1	1	1						1	1	1		1	1	1																													
Wh.-throated N.-tailed Swift	7	7	7																																																										
Black Swift	1																	1	1			1	1																																						
Chimney Swift	1																													1	1	1		1	1	1		1	1	1		1	1	1		1	1	1													
Vaux's Swift	1																	1	1	1																																									
Fork-tailed Swift	4		7	4																																																										
Common Swift	7	7	7	7																																																										
White-throated Swift	1																	1	1	1	1					1	1	1	1	1	1	1	1																												
Antillean Palm Swift	7																																									7		7	7																
Green Violet-ear	7																															7	7																												
Cuban Emerald	7																																									7	7		7																
Lucifer Hummingbird	1																													1	1	1	1																												
Ruby-throated Hummingbird	1																													1	1	1		1	1	1		1	1	1		1		1		1	1	1													
Black-chinned Hummingbird	1																	1	1	1		1	1	1		1	1	1		1	1	1																													
Bahama Woodstar	7																																									7		7	7																
Costa's Hummingbird	1																	1	1	1	1					1	1		1	1	1	1																													
Anna's Hummingbird	1																	1	1	1	1					1	1	1	1																																
Broad-tailed Hummingbird	1																	1	1	1		1	1	1		1	1	1		1	1	1																													
Rufous Hummingbird	1	1	1															1	1			1	1				1			1	1		1																												
Allen's Hummingbird	1																	1	1	1	1						2																																		
Bumblebee Hummingbird	7																										7																																		
Calliope Hummingbird	1																	1	1			1	1																																						
Magnificent Hummingbird	1																									1	1	1																																	
Plain-capped Starthroat	6																									6	6	6	6																																
Blue-throated Hummingbird	1																									1	1	1		1	1	1																													
Buff-bellied Hummingbird	1																													1	1	1	1																												
Violet-crowned Hummingbird	1																									1	1	1																																	
Berylline Hummingbird	3																									5	3	6																																	
White-eared Hummingbird	3																									5	3	5																																	
Broad-billed Hummingbird	1																									1	1	1																																	
Eared Trogon	6																											6																																	
Elegant Trogon	1																									1	1	1																																	
Belted Kingfisher	1	1	1	1														1	1	1	1	1	1	1	1	1	1	1	1	1	1	1	1	1	1	1	1	1	1	1	1	1		1	1	1	1	1	1												
Ringed Kingfisher	1																													1	1	1	1																												
Green Kingfisher	1																													1	1	1	1																												
Hoopoe	7			7																																																									
Eurasian Wryneck	7			7																																																									
Common Flicker	1	1	1	1														1	1	1	1	1	1	1	1	1	1	1	1	1	1	1	1	1	1	1		1	1	1	1	1		1	1	1	1	1													
Pileated Woodpecker	1																	1	1	1										1	1	1	1	1	1	1		1	1	1	1	1	1	1	1	1	1	1	1												
Red-bellied Woodpecker	1																													1	1	1	1	1	1	1	1	1	1	1	1	1	1	1	1																
Golden-fronted Woodpecker	1																													1	1	1	1																												
Gila Woodpecker	1																									1	1	1	1																																
Red-headed Woodpecker	1																																																												

Species	Occ. Class	Alaska				Westport Pelagic				Monterey Pelagic				San Diego Pelagic			
		S	S	F	W	S	S	F	W	S	S	F	W	S	S	F	W
Acorn Woodpecker	1																
Lewis's Woodpecker	1																
Yellow-bellied Sapsucker	1																
Williamson's Sapsucker	1																
Hairy Woodpecker	1																
Downy Woodpecker	1																
Ladder-backed Woodpecker	1																
Nuttall's Woodpecker	1																
Brown-backed Woodpecker	1																
Red-cockaded Woodpecker	1																
White-headed Woodpecker	1																
Bl.-backed Three-toed W'pecker	1																
Northern Three-toed W'pecker	1	1	1	1	1												
Rose-throated Becard	1																
Eastern Kingbird	1																
Loggerhead Kingbird	6																
Gray Kingbird	1																
Tropical Kingbird	1																
Western Kingbird	1																
Cassin's Kingbird	1																
Thick-billed Kingbird	1																
Fork-tailed Flycatcher	4																
Scissor-tailed Flycatcher	1																
Greater Kiskadee	1																
Sulphur-bellied Flycatcher	1																
Great Crested Flycatcher	1																
Wied's Crested Flycatcher	1																
Ash-throated Flycatcher	1																
Olivaceous Flycatcher	1																
Nutting's Flycatcher	7																
Stolid Flycatcher	7																
Eastern Phoebe	1																
Black Phoebe	1																
Say's Phoebe	1	1	1	1													
Yellow-bellied Flycatcher	1																
Acadian Flycatcher	1																
Willow Flycatcher	1																
Alder Flycatcher	1	1	1														
Least Flycatcher	1																
Hammond's Flycatcher	1	1	1														
Dusky Flycatcher	1																
Gray Flycatcher	1																
Western Flycatcher	1																
Buff-breasted Flycatcher	1																
Coues' Flycatcher	1																
Eastern Pewee	1																
Western Pewee	1	1	1														
Olive-sided Flycatcher	1	1	1														
Vermilion Flycatcher	1																
Northern Beardless Flycatcher	1																
Common Skylark	1	2		3		1	1*	1	1								
Horned Lark	1	1	1														
Bahama Swallow	4																
Violet-green Swallow	1	1	1														
Tree Swallow	1	1	1														
Bank Swallow	1	1	1														
Rough-winged Swallow	1																
Common House Martin	7		7														
Barn Swallow	1																
Cliff Swallow	1	1	1														
Cave Swallow	1																
Purple Martin	1																
Cuban Martin	7																
Gray-breasted Martin	7																
Gray Jay	1	1	1	1	1												

Species	California				Colorado				Arizona				Texas			
	S	S	F	W	S	S	F	W	S	S	F	W	S	S	F	W
Acorn Woodpecker	1	1	1	1					1	1	1	1	1	1	1	1
Lewis's Woodpecker	1	1	1	1	1	1	1	1	1		1	1				
Yellow-bellied Sapsucker	1	1	1	1	1	1	1	1	1	1	1	1	1	1	1	1
Williamson's Sapsucker	1	1	1	1	1	1	1	1	1	1	1	1				
Hairy Woodpecker	1	1	1	1	1	1	1	1	1	1	1	1	1	1	1	1
Downy Woodpecker	1	1	1	1					1	1	1	1	1	1	1	1
Ladder-backed Woodpecker	1	1	1	1	1	1	1	1	1	1	1	1	1	1	1	1
Nuttall's Woodpecker	1	1	1	1												
Brown-backed Woodpecker									1	1	1	1				
Red-cockaded Woodpecker													1	1	1	1
White-headed Woodpecker	1	1	1	1												
Bl.-backed Three-toed W'pecker	1	1	1													
Northern Three-toed W'pecker					1	1	1	1								
Rose-throated Becard									1	1						
Eastern Kingbird					1	1	1						1	1	1	
Loggerhead Kingbird																
Gray Kingbird																
Tropical Kingbird									1	1	1		1	1	1	1
Western Kingbird	1	1	1		1	1	1		1	1	1		1	1	1	
Cassin's Kingbird	1	1	1	1					1	1	1		1	1	1	
Thick-billed Kingbird									1	1	1					
Fork-tailed Flycatcher																
Scissor-tailed Flycatcher													1	1	1	
Greater Kiskadee													1	1	1	1
Sulphur-bellied Flycatcher									1	1						
Great Crested Flycatcher													1	1	1	
Wied's Crested Flycatcher									1	1	1		1	1	1	
Ash-throated Flycatcher	1	1	1		1	1	1		1	1	1	1	1	1	1	
Olivaceous Flycatcher									1	1	1					
Nutting's Flycatcher									7	7	7	7				
Stolid Flycatcher																
Eastern Phoebe													1	1	1	1
Black Phoebe	1	1	1	1					1	1	1	1	1	1	1	1
Say's Phoebe	1	1	1	1	1	1	1		1	1	1	1	1	1	1	1
Yellow-bellied Flycatcher																
Acadian Flycatcher																
Willow Flycatcher	1	1			1	1			1	1			1	1		
Alder Flycatcher																
Least Flycatcher																
Hammond's Flycatcher	1	1			1	1			2		1	2				
Dusky Flycatcher	1	1			1	1			1	1	2	2				
Gray Flycatcher	1	1			1	1			1	1	1	1				
Western Flycatcher	1	1			1	1			1	1			1	1		
Buff-breasted Flycatcher									2	2						
Coues' Flycatcher									1	1						
Eastern Pewee													1	1	1	
Western Pewee	1	1	1		1	1	1		1	1	1		1	1	1	
Olive-sided Flycatcher	1	1			1	1			1	1						
Vermilion Flycatcher	1	1	1	1					1	1	1	1	1	1	1	1
Northern Beardless Flycatcher									1	1						
Common Skylark																
Horned Lark	1	1	1	1	1	1	1	1	1	1	1	1	1	1	1	1
Bahama Swallow																
Violet-green Swallow	1	1	1		1	1	1		1	1	1		1	1	1	
Tree Swallow	1	1	1	1	1	1	1		1	1	1	1	1	1	1	1
Bank Swallow	1	1			1	1			1	1			1	1		
Rough-winged Swallow	1	1	1	1	1	1			1	1	1		1	1	1	1
Common House Martin																
Barn Swallow	1	1	1		1	1	1		1	1	1		1	1	1	
Cliff Swallow	1	1			1	1			1	1			1	1		
Cave Swallow													1	1		
Purple Martin	1	1			1	1			1	1			1	1		
Cuban Martin																
Gray-breasted Martin															7	7
Gray Jay					1	1	1	1	1	1	1	1				

Species	Great Lakes				Mississippi				South Florida				New England				Maine Pelagic				N. Carolina Pelagic				Florida Pelagic			
	S	S	F	W	S	S	F	W	S	S	F	W	S	S	F	W	S	S	F	W	S	S	F	W	S	S	F	W
Acorn Woodpecker																												
Lewis's Woodpecker																												
Yellow-bellied Sapsucker	1	1	1		1		1	1					1	1	1													
Williamson's Sapsucker																												
Hairy Woodpecker	1	1	1	1	1	1	1	1					1	1	1	1												
Downy Woodpecker	1	1	1	1	1	1	1	1					1	1	1	1												
Ladder-backed Woodpecker																												
Nuttall's Woodpecker																												
Brown-backed Woodpecker																												
Red-cockaded Woodpecker					1	1	1	1																				
White-headed Woodpecker																												
Bl.-backed Three-toed W'pecker	1	1	1	1									1	1	1	1												
Northern Three-toed W'pecker	1	1	1	1																								
Rose-throated Becard																												
Eastern Kingbird	1	1	1		1	1	1		1		1		1	1	1	1												
Loggerhead Kingbird									6		6	6																
Gray Kingbird					1	1	1																					
Tropical Kingbird																												
Western Kingbird									1		1	1																
Cassin's Kingbird																												
Thick-billed Kingbird																												
Fork-tailed Flycatcher															4													
Scissor-tailed Flycatcher									1		1	1																
Greater Kiskadee																												
Sulphur-bellied Flycatcher																												
Great Crested Flycatcher	1	1	1		1	1	1		1	1	1	1																
Wied's Crested Flycatcher																												
Ash-throated Flycatcher																												
Olivaceous Flycatcher																												
Nutting's Flycatcher																												
Stolid Flycatcher									7		7	7																
Eastern Phoebe	1	1	1		1	1	1	1	1		1	1	1	1	1													
Black Phoebe																												
Say's Phoebe																												
Yellow-bellied Flycatcher	1	1											1	1														
Acadian Flycatcher	1	1			1	1							1	1														
Willow Flycatcher	1	1			1	1							1	1														
Alder Flycatcher	1	1											1	1														
Least Flycatcher	1	1											1	1														
Hammond's Flycatcher																												
Dusky Flycatcher																												
Gray Flycatcher																												
Western Flycatcher																												
Buff-breasted Flycatcher																												
Coues' Flycatcher																												
Eastern Pewee	1	1	1		1	1	1		1		1		1	1	1													
Western Pewee																												
Olive-sided Flycatcher	1	1											1	1														
Vermilion Flycatcher																												
Northern Beardless Flycatcher																												
Common Skylark																												
Horned Lark	1	1	1	1	1	1	1	1					1	1	1	1												
Bahama Swallow									4	4																		
Violet-green Swallow																												
Tree Swallow	1	1	1		1	1	1	1	1		1	1	1	1	1	1												
Bank Swallow	1	1			1	1	1						1	1														
Rough-winged Swallow	1	1			1	1	1		1		1	1	1	1														
Common House Martin																												
Barn Swallow	1	1	1		1	1	1						1	1	1													
Cliff Swallow	1	1			1		1						1	1														
Cave Swallow																												
Purple Martin	1	1			1	1			1	1			1	1														
Cuban Martin									7		7	7																
Gray-breasted Martin																												
Gray Jay	1	1	1	1									1	1	1	1												

Species	Occ. Class	Alaska				Westport Pelagic				Monterey Pelagic				San Diego Pelagic				California				Colorado				Arizona				Texas				Great Lakes				Mississippi				South Florida				New England				Maine Pelagic				N. Carolina Pelagic				Florida Pelagic			
		S	S	F	W	S	S	F	W	S	S	F	W	S	S	F	W	S	S	F	W	S	S	F	W	S	S	F	W	S	S	F	W	S	S	F	W	S	S	F	W	S	S	F	W	S	S	F	W	S	S	F	W	S	S	F	W	S	S	F	W
Blue Jay	1																													1	1	1	1	1	1	1	1	1	1	1	1	1	1	1	1	1	1	1	1												
Steller's Jay	1	1	1	1	1													1	1	1	1	1	1	1	1	1	1	1	1	1	1	1	1																												
Scrub Jay	1																	1	1	1	1	1	1	1	1	1	1	1	1	1	1	1	1									1	1	1	1																
Gray-breasted Jay	1																									1	1	1	1	1	1	1	1																												
Green Jay	1																													1	1	1	1																												
Brown Jay	1																													1	1	1	1																												
Black-billed Magpie	1	1	1	1	1													1	1	1	1																																								
Yellow-billed Magpie	1																	1	1	1	1																																								
Northern Raven	1	1	1	1	1													1	1	1	1	1	1	1	1	1	1	1	1	1	1	1	1	1	1	1	1									1	1	1	1												
White-necked Raven	1																									1	1	1	1	1	1	1	1																												
American Crow	1																	1	1	1	1	1	1	1	1	1	1	1	1	1	1	1	1	1	1	1	1	1	1	1	1					1	1	1	1												
Northwestern Crow	1	1	1	1	1																																																								
Fish Crow	1																													1	1	1	1					1	1	1	1	1	1	1	1																
Mexican Crow	1																													1	1	1	1																												
Pinyon Jay	1																	1	1	1	1	1	1	1	1	1	1	1	1																																
Clark's Nutcracker	1																	1	1	1	1	1	1	1	1	1	1	1	1																																
Black-capped Chickadee	1	1	1	1	1													1	1	1	1	1	1	1	1									1	1	1	1									1	1	1	1												
Carolina Chickadee	1																																					1	1	1	1	1	1	1	1																
Mexican Chickadee	1																									1	1	1	1																																
Mountain Chickadee	1																	1	1	1	1	1	1	1	1	1	1	1	1	1	1	1	1																												
Siberian Chickadee	2	2	2	2	2																																																								
Boreal Chickadee	1	1	1	1	1																													1	1	1	1									1	1	1	1												
Chestnut-backed Chickadee	1	1	1	1	1													1	1	1	1																																								
Tufted Titmouse	1																													1	1	1	1	1	1	1	1	1	1	1	1	1	1	1	1	1	1	1	1												
Plain Titmouse	1																	1	1	1	1	1	1	1	1	1	1	1	1	1	1	1	1																												
Bridled Titmouse	1																									1	1	1	1																																
Verdin	1																	1	1	1	1					1	1	1	1	1	1	1	1																												
Bushtit	1																	1	1	1	1	1	1	1	1	1	1	1	1	1	1	1	1																												
White-breasted Nuthatch	1																	1	1	1	1	1	1	1	1	1	1	1	1	1	1	1	1	1	1	1	1	1	1	1	1					1	1	1	1												
Red-breasted Nuthatch	1	2	2	2	2													1	1	1	1	1	1	1	1	1	1	1	1					1	1	1	1									1	1	1	1												
Brown-headed Nuthatch	1																													1	1	1	1					1	1	1	1	1	1	1	1																
Pygmy Nuthatch	1																	1	1	1	1	1	1	1	1	1	1	1	1	1	1	1	1																												
Brown Creeper	1	1	1	1	1													1	1	1	1	1	1	1	1	1	1	1	1	1	1	1	1	1	1	1	1	1		1	1					1	1	1	1												
Wrentit	1																	1	1	1	1																																								
Red-whiskered Bulbul	1																																									1	1*	1	1																
North American Dipper	1	1	1	1	1													1	1	1	1	1	1	1	1	1	1	1	1																																
House Wren	1																	1	1	1	1	1	1	1		1	1	1	1	1	1	1	1	1	1	1		1	1	1	1	1		1	1	1	1	1													
Brown-throated Wren	1																									1	1	1																																	
Winter Wren	1	1	1	1	1													1	1	1	1	1	1	1	1					1		1	1	1	1	1		1		1	1					1	1	1													
Bewick's Wren	1																	1	1	1	1	1	1	1	1	1	1	1	1	1	1	1	1					1	1	1	1																				
Carolina Wren	1																													1	1	1	1	1	1	1	1	1	1	1	1	1	1	1	1	1	1	1	1												
Cactus Wren	1																	1	1	1	1					1	1	1	1	1	1	1	1																												
Marsh Wren	1																	1	1	1	1	1	1	1	1	1	1	1	1	1	1	1	1	1	1	1		1	1	1	1	1		1	1	1	1	1													
Sedge Wren	1																													1		1	1	1	1											1	1														
Canyon Wren	1																	1	1	1	1					1	1	1	1																																
Rock Wren	1																	1	1	1	1	1	1	1		1	1	1	1	1	1	1	1																												
Northern Mockingbird	1																	1	1	1	1	1	1	1	1	1	1	1	1	1	1	1	1	1	1	1	1	1	1	1	1	1	1	1	1	1	1	1	1												
Bahama Mockingbird	7																																									7	7																		
Gray Catbird	1																					1	1			1	1			1	1	1	1	1	1	1		1	1	1	1	1	1	1	1	1	1	1													
Brown Thrasher	1																					1	1							1	1	1	1	1	1	1		1	1	1	1	1	1	1	1	1	1	1													
Long-billed Thrasher	1																													1	1	1	1																												
Bendire's Thrasher	1																	1	1	1						1	1	1	1																																
Curve-billed Thrasher	1																									1	1	1	1	1	1	1	1																												
California Thrasher	1																	1	1	1	1																																								
Le Conte's Thrasher	1																	1	1	1	1					1	1	1	1																																
Crissal Thrasher	1																	1	1	1	1					1	1	1	1	1	1	1	1																												
Sage Thrasher	1																	1	1	1	1					1	1	1	1	1	1	1	1																												
American Robin	1	1	1	1	1													1	1	1	1	1	1	1	1	1	1	1	1	1	1	1	1	1	1	1	1	1	1	1	1	1	1	1	1	1	1	1	1												
Fieldfare	7																																															7	7												
Rufous-backed Thrush	3																			6	6					4		3	3			6	6																												
Clay-colored Thrush	4																															4	4																												
Dusky Thrush	4	4	4																																																										
Eye-browed Thrush	3	3	3																																																										
Varied Thrush	1	1	1	1	1													1	1	1	1																																								

Species	Occ. Class	Alaska				Pelagic				Pelagic				Pelagic				California				Colorado				Arizona				Texas				Great Lakes				Mississippi				Florida				England				Pelagic				Pelagic				Pelagic			
		S	S	F	W	S	S	F	W	S	S	F	W	S	S	F	W	S	S	F	W	S	S	F	W	S	S	F	W	S	S	F	W	S	S	F	W	S	S	F	W	S	S	F	W	S	S	F	W	S	S	F	W	S	S	F	W	S	S	F	W
Wood Thrush	1																													1	1	1		1	1	1		1	1	1						1	1	1													
Hermit Thrush	1	1	1	1													1	1	1	1	1	1	1	1	1	1	1	1	1	1	1	1	1	1	1		1		1	1	1		1	1	1	1	1	1												
Swainson's Thrush	1	1	1	1													1	1	1		1	1	1										1	1	1		1		1						1	1	1													
Gray-cheeked Thrush	1	1	1																															1	1			1		1						1	1														
Veery	1																					1	1											1	1											1	1														
Eastern Bluebird	1																					1	1	1		1	1	1	1	1	1	1	1	1	1	1	1	1	1	1	1	1	1	1	1	1	1	1	1												
Western Bluebird	1																	1	1	1	1	1	1	1	1	1	1	1	1	1	1	1	1																												
Mountain Bluebird	1																	1	1	1	1	1	1	1	1	1	1	1	1	1		1	1																												
Northern Wheatear	1	1	1																																																										
Bluethroat	2	2	2																																																										
Siberian Rubythroat	4	4	4	4																																																									
Townsend's Solitaire	1	1	1	1													1	1	1	1	1	1	1	1	1	1	1	1	1	1	1	1																												
Willow Warbler	7	7	7	7																																																									
Dusky Warbler	5	5	5	5																																																									
Arctic Warbler	1	1	1																																																										
M'dorff's Grasshop. Warb.	6			6																																																								
Blue-gray Gnatcatcher	1																	1	1	1	1	1	1	1		1	1	1	1	1	1	1	1	1	1			1	1	1	1	1	1	1	1	1	1														
Black-capped Gnatcatcher	6																									6	5	6	6																												
Black-tailed Gnatcatcher	1																	1	1	1	1					1	1	1	1	1	1	1	1																												
Golden-crowned Kinglet	1	1	1	1	1													1	1	1	1	1	1	1	1	1	1	1	1	1	1	1	1	1	1	1	1	1		1	1					1	1	1	1												
Ruby-crowned Kinglet	1	1	1															1	1	1	1	1	1	1	1	1	1	1	1	1	1	1	1	1	1	1		1		1	1	1		1	1	1	1	1													
Red-breasted Flycatcher	5	5	5																																																										
Gray-spotted Flycatcher	4	4	4																																																										
Siberian Accentor	5			5																																																									
White Wagtail	2	2	2																																																										
Gray Wagtail	5	5	5																																																										
Yellow Wagtail	1	1	1																																																										
Water Pipit	1	1	1															1		1	1	1	1	1	1	1	1	1	1	1		1	1	1		1		1		1	1	1		1	1	1		1													
Pechora Pipit	6	6	6																																																										
Indian Tree Pipit	3	3	5	3																																																									
Red-throated Pipit	1	1	1																																																										
Sprague's Pipit	1																									1		1	1	1		1	1																												
Bohemian Waxwing	1	1	1																																												1													
Cedar Waxwing	1																	1	1	1	1	1	1	1	1	1		1	1	1		1	1	1	1	1		1		1	1	1		1	1	1	1	1													
Phainopepla	1																	1	1	1						1	1	1	1	1		1	1																												
Brown Shrike	6	6	6	6																																																									
Northern Shrike	1	1	1	1													1		1	1													1		1	1									1		1	1												
Loggerhead Shrike	1																	1	1	1	1	1	1	1	1	1	1	1	1	1	1	1	1					1	1	1	1	1	1	1	1																
European Starling	1	1	1	1	1													1	1	1	1	1	1	1	1	1	1	1	1	1	1	1	1	1	1	1	1	1	1	1	1	1	1	1	1	1	1	1	1												
Crested Myna	1					1	1*	1	1																																																				
Black-capped Vireo	1																													1	1																										
White-eyed Vireo	1																													1	1	1		1	1			1	1	1		1	1	1	1																
Hutton's Vireo	1																	1	1	1	1					1	1	1	1	1	1	1	1																												
Bell's Vireo	1																	1	1			1	1			1	1			1	1																												
Thick-billed Vireo	7																																											7		7	7																
Gray Vireo	1																	1	1							1	1																																				
Yellow-throated Vireo	1																													1	1			1	1			1	1			1	1	1		1	1														
Solitary Vireo	1																	1	1	1		1	1			1	1	1	1	1	1				1																										
Black-whiskered Vireo	1																																											1	1																		
Yellow-green Vireo	3																			5						5	6			?	?																												
Red-eyed Vireo	1																					1	1							1	1	1		1	1	1		1	1	1		1	1	1		1	1	1													
Philadelphia Vireo	1																																	1	1											1	1														
Warbling Vireo	1																	1	1			1	1			1	1			1	1			1	1			1	1							1	1														
Bananaquit	4																																											4		4	4																
Black-and-White Warbler	1																													1	1			1	1	1		1		1		1		1	1	1	1	1													
Prothonotary Warbler	1																													1	1			1	1			1	1			1	1																		
Swainson's Warbler	1																													1	1							1	1			1	1	1																	
Worm-eating Warbler	1																													1	1			1	1			1	1			1				1	1														
Golden-winged Warbler	1																																	1	1																										
Blue-winged Warbler	1																																	1	1											1	1														
Bachman's Warbler	6																																																												
Tennessee Warbler	1																																	1	1			1	1			1		1		1	1														
Orange-crowned Warbler	1	1	1															1	1	1	1	1	1	1		1	1	1	1	1	1	1	1							1	1	1		1	1																
Nashville Warbler	1																									1		1						1	1							1		1		1	1														
Virginia's Warbler	1																	1	1			1	1			1	1																																

Species	Occ. Class	Alaska				Westport Pelagic				Monterey Pelagic				San Diego Pelagic				California				Colorado				Arizona			
		S	S	F	W	S	S	F	W	S	S	F	W	S	S	F	W	S	S	F	W	S	S	F	W	S	S	F	W
Colima Warbler	1																												
Lucy's Warbler	1																	1	1			1	1			1	1		
Northern Parula Warbler	1																												
Tropical Parula Warbler	3																												
Olive Warbler	1																									1	1	1	2
Yellow Warbler	1	1	1															1	1	1	1	1	1			1	1		
Magnolia Warbler	1																												
Cape May Warbler	1																												
Black-throated Blue Warbler	1																												
Yellow-rumped Warbler	1	1	1															1	1	1	1	1	1	1	1	1	1	1	1
Black-throated Gray Warbler	1																	1	1	1	1	1	1			1	1	1	1
Townsend's Warbler	1	1	1															1		1	1					1		1	
Black-throated Green Warbler	1																												
Golden-cheeked Warbler	1																												
Hermit Warbler	1																	1	1	1						1	1	1	
Cerulean Warbler	1																												
Blackburnian Warbler	1																												
Yellow-throated Warbler	1																												
Grace's Warbler	1																					1	1			1	1		
Chestnut-sided Warbler	1																												
Bay-breasted Warbler	1																												
Blackpoll Warbler	1	1	1																										
Pine Warbler	1																												
Kirtland's Warbler	1																												
Prairie Warbler	1																												
Palm Warbler	1																												
Ovenbird	1																					1	1						
Northern Waterthrush	1	1	1																										
Louisiana Waterthrush	1																												
Kentucky Warbler	1																												
Connecticut Warbler	1																												
Mourning Warbler	1																												
MacGillivray's Warbler	1																	1	1			1	1			1	1	1	
Common Yellowthroat	1																	1	1	1	1	1	1	1		1	1	1	1
Gray-crowned Yellowthroat	7																												
Yellow-breasted Chat	1																	1	1			1	1			1	1		
Fan-tailed Warbler	7																									7		7	7
Red-faced Warbler	1																									1	1		
Hooded Warbler	1																												
Wilson's Warbler	1	1	1															1	1	1		1	1	1		1	1		
Canada Warbler	1																												
American Redstart	1																	1	1			1	1						
Painted Redstart	1																									1	1		
Slate-throated Redstart	6																									6	6		
Rufous-capped Warbler	4																									5	5		
House Sparrow	1																	1	1	1	1	1	1	1	1	1	1	1	1
Eurasian Tree Sparrow	1																												
Bobolink	1																					1	1						
Eastern Meadowlark	1																									1	1	1	1
Western Meadowlark	1																	1	1	1	1	1	1	1	1	1	1	1	1
Yellow-headed Blackbird	1																	1	1	1	1	1	1	1		1	1	1	1
Red-winged Blackbird	1																	1	1	1	1	1	1	1	1	1	1	1	1
Tricolored Blackbird	1																	1	1	1	1								
Tawny-shouldered Blackbird	7																												
Orchard Oriole	1																												
Black-headed Oriole	1																												
Spotted Oriole	1																												
Hooded Oriole	1																	1	1							1	1		
Altamira Oriole	1																												
Scarlet-headed Oriole	5																									6	6	5	5
Black-vented Oriole	6																												
Scott's Oriole	1																	1	1							1	1		
Northern Oriole	1																	1	1	1	1	1	1			1	1		

Species	Texas				Great Lakes				Mississippi				South Florida				New England				Maine Pelagic				N. Carolina Pelagic				Florida Pelagic			
	S	S	F	W	S	S	F	W	S	S	F	W	S	S	F	W	S	S	F	W	S	S	F	W	S	S	F	W	S	S	F	W
Colima Warbler	1	1																														
Lucy's Warbler																																
Northern Parula Warbler	1	1			1	1			1	1	1						1	1														
Tropical Parula Warbler	3	3	4	4																												
Olive Warbler																																
Yellow Warbler	1	1			1	1	1		1		1		1	1	1	1	1	1	1													
Magnolia Warbler					1	1			1		1						1	1														
Cape May Warbler					1	1							1		1	1	1	1	1													
Black-throated Blue Warbler					1	1							1		1		1	1														
Yellow-rumped Warbler	1		1	1	1	1	1		1		1	1	1		1	1	1	1	1	1												
Black-throated Gray Warbler	1		1																													
Townsend's Warbler																																
Black-throated Green Warbler					1	1			1		1						1	1														
Golden-cheeked Warbler	1	1																														
Hermit Warbler																																
Cerulean Warbler					1	1			1	1	1																					
Blackburnian Warbler					1	1			1		1						1	1														
Yellow-throated Warbler	1	1			1	1			1	1	1		1		1	1																
Grace's Warbler																																
Chestnut-sided Warbler					1	1			1		1						1	1														
Bay-breasted Warbler					1	1			1		1						1	1														
Blackpoll Warbler						1			1		1		1				1	1														
Pine Warbler	1	1	1	1	1	1			1	1	1	1	1	1	1	1	1	1														
Kirtland's Warbler					1	1*																										
Prairie Warbler					1	1			1	1	1		1	1	1	1	1	1														
Palm Warbler					1	1			1		1	1	1		1	1	1	1														
Ovenbird					1	1			1		1						1	1														
Northern Waterthrush					1	1			1		1		1		1	1	1	1														
Louisiana Waterthrush	1	1			1	1			1	1							1	1														
Kentucky Warbler	1	1			1	1			1	1	1																					
Connecticut Warbler					1	1																										
Mourning Warbler					1	1											1	1														
MacGillivray's Warbler																																
Common Yellowthroat	1	1	1	1	1	1	1		1	1	1	1	1	1	1	1	1	1	1													
Gray-crowned Yellowthroat	7		7	7																												
Yellow-breasted Chat	1	1			1	1			1	1	1						1	1														
Fan-tailed Warbler	7		7	7																												
Red-faced Warbler																																
Hooded Warbler	1	1			1	1			1	1	1																					
Wilson's Warbler					1	1			1		1						1	1														
Canada Warbler					1	1			1		1						1	1														
American Redstart	1	1			1	1			1	1	1						1	1														
Painted Redstart	1	1																														
Slate-throated Redstart																																
Rufous-capped Warbler	4	4																														
House Sparrow	1	1	1	1	1	1	1	1	1	1	1	1	1	1	1	1	1	1	1	1												
Eurasian Tree Sparrow					1	1*	1	1																								
Bobolink					1	1			1				1		1		1	1	1													
Eastern Meadowlark	1	1	1	1	1	1	1	1	1	1	1	1	1		1	1																
Western Meadowlark	1	1	1	1	1	1	1	1																								
Yellow-headed Blackbird	1	1	1	1	1	1																										
Red-winged Blackbird	1	1	1	1	1	1	1	1	1	1	1	1	1	1	1	1	1	1	1	1												
Tricolored Blackbird																																
Tawny-shouldered Blackbird													7		7	7																
Orchard Oriole	1	1			1	1			1	1			1				1	1														
Black-headed Oriole	1		1	1																												
Spotted Oriole													1	1	1	1																
Hooded Oriole	1	1	1	1																												
Altamira Oriole	1	1	1	1																												
Scarlet-headed Oriole																																
Black-vented Oriole	6	6																														
Scott's Oriole	1	1																														
Northern Oriole	1	1			1	1			1	1							1	1														

Species	Occ. Class	Alaska				Pelagic				Pelagic				Pelagic				California				Colorado				Arizona				Texas				Great Lakes				Mississippi				Florida				England				Pelagic				Pelagic				Pelagic			
		S	S	F	W	S	S	F	W	S	S	F	W	S	S	F	W	S	S	F	W	S	S	F	W	S	S	F	W	S	S	F	W	S	S	F	W	S	S	F	W	S	S	F	W	S	S	F	W	S	S	F	W	S	S	F	W	S	S	F	W
Great-tailed Grackle	1																	1	1	1	1					1	1	1	1	1	1	1	1																												
Boat-tailed Grackle	1																																					1	1	1	1	1	1	1	1																
Common Grackle	1																													1	1	1	1	1	1	1	1	1	1	1	1	1	1	1	1	1	1	1	1												
Brown-headed Cowbird	1																	1	1	1	1	1	1	1	1	1	1	1	1	1	1	1	1	1	1	1	1	1	1	1	1	1	1	1	1	1	1	1	1												
Bronzed Cowbird	1																									1	1	1	1	1	1	1	1																												
Western Tanager	1																	1	1	1	1	1	1	1		1	1	1		1	1																														
Scarlet Tanager	1																																	1	1											1	1														
Hepatic Tanager	1																									1	1			1	1																														
Summer Tanager	1																	1	1			1	1			1	1			1	1							1	1			1	1																		
Stripe-headed Tanager	3																																									3		3	3																
Blue-gray Tanager	7																																									7	7	7	7																
Northern Cardinal	1																									1	1	1	1	1	1	1	1	1	1	1	1	1	1	1	1	1	1	1	1	1	1	1	1												
Pyrrhuloxia	1																									1	1	1	1	1	1	1	1																												
Rose-breasted Grosbeak	1																																	1	1											1	1														
Black-headed Grosbeak	1																	1	1			1	1			1	1			1	1																														
Blue Grosbeak	1																	1	1			1	1			1	1	1		1	1							1	1																						
Indigo Bunting	1																									1				1	1			1	1			1	1							1	1														
Lazuli Bunting	1																	1	1			1	1			1	1	1	1																																
Varied Bunting	1																									1	1																																		
Painted Bunting	1																													1	1							1	1			1	1	1	1																
Black-faced Grassquit	7																																									7		7	7																
Melodious Grassquit	7																																									7		7	7																
Dickcissel	1																													1	1			1	1			1	1																						
Brambling	2	2	2	2																																																									
Hawfinch	4	4	4																																																										
Evening Grosbeak	1																	1	1			1	1		1	1	1							1	1	1	1									1	1	1	1												
Eurasian Bullfinch	4	4	4	4																														1			1																								
Purple Finch	1																	1	1	1	1																1																								
Cassin's Finch	1																	1	1	1	1	1	1	1	1																																				
House Finch	1																	1	1	1	1	1	1	1	1	1	1	1	1	1	1	1	1													1	1	1	1												
Common Rosefinch	3	3	3																																																											
White-collared Seedeater	4																													4		4	4																												
Pine Grosbeak	1	1	1	1	1													1	1	1	1	1	1	1										1	1	1	1									1	1	1	1												
Gray-crowned Rosy Finch	1	1	1	1	1													1	1	1		1	1	1	1																																				
Black Rosy Finch	1																					1	1	1	1																																				
Brown-capped Rosy Finch	1																					1	1	1	1																																				
Oriental Greenfinch	4	5	5	4																																																									
Hoary Redpoll	1	1	1	1	1																																																								
Common Redpoll	1	1	1	1	1																													1		1	1																								
Pine Siskin	1																	1	1	1	1	1	1	1		1	1	1	1	1	1	1		1	1	1	1									1	1	1													
American Goldfinch	1																	1	1	1	1	1	1	1	1					1	1	1	1	1	1	1	1	1	1	1	1					1	1	1	1												
Lesser Goldfinch	1																	1	1	1	1	1	1	1	1	1	1	1	1	1	1	1	1																												
Lawrence's Goldfinch	1																	1	1																																										
Red Crossbill	1																	1	1	1	1	1	1	1	1	1	1	1	1					1	1	1	1									1	1	1	1												
White-winged Crossbill	1	1	1																															1	1	1	1									1	1	1	1												
Olive Sparrow	1																													1	1	1	1																												
Green-tailed Towhee	1																	1	1			1	1			1	1	1	1	1		1	1																												
Rufous-sided Towhee	1																	1	1	1	1	1	1	1	1	1	1	1	1	1	1	1	1	1	1	1	1	1	1	1	1					1	1	1	1												
Brown Towhee	1																	1	1	1	1	1	1	1	1	1	1	1	1	1	1	1	1																												
Abert's Towhee	1																	1	1	1	1					1	1	1	1																																
Lark Bunting	1																					1	1	1		1		1	1	1	1	1	1																												
Savannah Sparrow	1	1	1	1														1	1	1	1	1	1	1	1	1	1	1	1	1	1	1	1	1	1	1		1		1	1	1		1	1	1	1	1	1												
Grasshopper Sparrow	1																	1	1			1	1			1	1	1	1	1	1	1	1	1	1							1		1	1	1	1														
Baird's Sparrow	1																									1			1						1																										
Henslow's Sparrow	1																													1	1	1	1	1	1											1	1														
Le Conte's Sparrow	1																													1		1	1	1	1			1		1	1																				
Sharp-tailed Sparrow	1																													1	1	1	1	1	1			1		1	1	1		1	1	1	1	1	1												
Seaside Sparrow	1																													1	1	1	1					1	1	1	1	1	1	1	1	1	1	1	1												
Vesper Sparrow	1																	1	1	1	1	1	1	1	1	1	1	1	1	1	1	1	1	1	1											1	1														
Lark Sparrow	1																	1	1	1	1	1	1	1	1	1	1	1	1	1	1	1	1	1	1																										
Five-striped Sparrow	1																									1	1	1																																	
Rufous-winged Sparrow	1																									1	1	1	1																																
Rufous-crowned Sparrow	1																	1	1	1	1	1	1	1	1	1	1	1	1																																
Bachman's Sparrow	1																																					1	1	1	1																				
Botteri's Sparrow	1																									1	1			1	1	1																													

Species	Occ. Class	Alaska				Westport Pelagic				Monterey Pelagic				San Diego Pelagic				California				Colorado				Arizona			
		S	S	F	W	S	S	F	W	S	S	F	W	S	S	F	W	S	S	F	W	S	S	F	W	S	S	F	W
Cassin's Sparrow	1																					1	1			1	1	1	1
Black-throated Sparrow	1																	1	1	1	1	1	1			1	1	1	1
Sage Sparrow	1																	1	1	1	1	1	1			1	1	1	1
Northern Junco	1	1	1	1														1	1	1	1	1	1	1	1	1	1	1	1
Gray-headed Junco	1																					1	1	1	1	1	1	1	1
Mexican Junco	1																									1	1	1	1
American Tree Sparrow	1	1	1	1														1		1	1	1		1	1				
Chipping Sparrow	1																	1	1	1	1	1	1	1		1	1	1	1
Clay-colored Sparrow	1																					1	1						
Brewer's Sparrow	1																	1	1	1	1	1	1			1	1	1	1
Field Sparrow	1																												
Black-chinned Sparrow	1																	1	1							1	1	1	1
Harris's Sparrow	1																					1		1	1				
White-crowned Sparrow	1	1	1	1	1													1	1	1	1	1	1	1	1	1		1	1
Golden-crowned Sparrow	1	1	1	1														1		1	1								
White-throated Sparrow	1																												
Fox Sparrow	1	1	1	1														1	1	1	1	1	1	1	1	1		1	1
Lincoln's Sparrow	1	1	1															1	1	1	1	1	1	1	1	1	1	1	1
Swamp Sparrow	1																												
Song Sparrow	1	1	1	1	1													1	1	1	1	1	1	1	1	1	1	1	1
McCown's Longspur	1																					1	1	1	1				
Lapland Longspur	1	1	1	1																		1		1	1				
Smith's Longspur	1	1	1																										
Chestnut-collared Longspur	1																	1		1	1	1	1	1		1		1	1
Snow Bunting	1	1	1	1	1																								
McKay's Bunting	1	1	1	1	1																								
Little Bunting	6	6	6	6																									
Rustic Bunting	3	3	3	3																									
Gray Bunting	6	6	6	6																									
Pallas' Reed Bunting	6	6	6	6																									
Common Reed Bunting	5	5	5	5																									

Species	Texas				Great Lakes				Mississippi				South Florida				New England				Maine Pelagic				N. Carolina Pelagic				Florida Pelagic			
	S	S	F	W	S	S	F	W	S	S	F	W	S	S	F	W	S	S	F	W	S	S	F	W	S	S	F	W	S	S	F	W
Cassin's Sparrow	1	1	1	1																												
Black-throated Sparrow	1	1	1	1																												
Sage Sparrow																																
Northern Junco	1	1	1	1	1	1	1	1	1		1	1					1	1	1	1												
Gray-headed Junco	1	1	1	1																												
Mexican Junco																																
American Tree Sparrow	1		1	1	1		1	1									1		1	1												
Chipping Sparrow	1	1	1	1	1	1			1	1	1	1	1		1	1	1	1														
Clay-colored Sparrow	1	1	1	1	1	1																										
Brewer's Sparrow	1		1	1																												
Field Sparrow	1	1	1	1	1	1	1	1	1	1	1	1					1	1	1	1												
Black-chinned Sparrow	1	1																														
Harris's Sparrow	1		1	1																												
White-crowned Sparrow	1		1	1	1		1	1																								
Golden-crowned Sparrow																																
White-throated Sparrow	1		1	1	1	1	1	1	1		1	1					1	1	1	1												
Fox Sparrow	1	1	1	1	1	1	1		1		1	1					1		1	1												
Lincoln's Sparrow	1		1	1	1	1			1		1						1	1														
Swamp Sparrow	1		1	1	1	1	1		1		1	1					1	1	1	1												
Song Sparrow	1	1	1	1	1	1	1	1	1	1	1	1					1	1	1	1												
McCown's Longspur	1		1	1																												
Lapland Longspur	1		1	1	1		1	1				1					1		1	1												
Smith's Longspur	1		1	1								1																				
Chestnut-collared Longspur	1		1	1																												
Snow Bunting					1		1	1									1		1	1												
McKay's Bunting																																
Little Bunting																																
Rustic Bunting																																
Gray Bunting																																
Pallas' Reed Bunting																																
Common Reed Bunting																																

APPENDIX B

Species	Date	Place	Witness
Common Loon	1/1/79	Florida Bay	John B. Edson
Yellow-billed Loon	May 21, 79	Attu, Alaska	Joseph C. Burgiel
Arctic Loon	1/19	Moss Landing Ca.	Rich Stallcup
Red-throated Loon	1/18	Pt. Reyes Ca.	Rich Stallcup
Red-necked Grebe	27 Jan 79	Maces Bay, N.B.	Davis Finch
Horned Grebe	1/3/79	Port Canaveral, Fla.	JBE
Eared Grebe	1/18	Bolinas, Ca.	Rich Stallcup
Least Grebe	2/10	Santa Anna, Tx.	Steve W. Blacklock
Western Grebe	1/18	Stinson Beach Ca	Rich Stallcup
Pied-billed Grebe	1/1/79	Nine Mile Pond EVERGlades Nat. Park	J. B. E
Wandering Albatross			
Short-tailed Albatross			
Black-footed Albatross	9/10/79	Westport, WA	Jim Lane
Laysan Albatross			
Shy Albatross			
Yellow-nosed Albatross			
Cape Petrel			
Northern Fulmar	28 Jan 79	Gulf of Maine	Davis Finch
Cory's Shearwater	11 Aug	Gulf of Maine	Will Russell
Pink-footed Shearwater	8 Sept	San Diego, CA	Donna L. Dittmann
Flesh-footed Shearwater	7 Oct.	Westport, WA	Wayne C. Weber
Greater Shearwater	11 Aug	Gulf of Maine	Will Russell
Buller's Shearwater	10 Sept. 79	Westport, Wash.	Peter D. Vickery
Sooty Shearwater	2 Aug. 79	Gulf of Alaska	Thede Tobish
Short-tailed Shearwater	6/10/79	Gambell, Alaska	Paul G. DuMont
Manx Shearwater (my 600th species)	1/19	Pacific Grove Ca	Rich Stallcup
Little Shearwater			
Audubon's Shearwater	5/3/79	OFF Ponce De Leon Inlet, Fla.	Paul W. Sykes Jr.
Streaked Shearwater			
Black-capped Petrel	5/3/79	Daytona Beach, FL	Paul W. Sykes Jr. Guy McCaskie [illegible] Olive W. Scott

Species	Date	Place	Witness
Scaled Petrel			
South Trinidad Petrel			
White-faced Storm Petrel			
Fork-tailed Storm Petrel	6/17/79	Seward-Kodiak Ferry	Tania Bailey
Leach's Storm Petrel	11 Aug	Gulf of Maine	Will Russell
Ashy Storm Petrel	13 Oct	Monterey Bay	Alan Baldridge
Band-rumped Storm Petrel			
Galapagos Storm Petrel			
Black Storm Petrel	8 Sept	Off San Diego	Guy McCaskie
Least Storm Petrel	8 Sept	Off San Diego	Guy McCaskie
Wilson's Storm Petrel	May 3	Daytona Beach, Fla.	[illegible]
British Storm Petrel			
Red-billed Tropicbird			
White-tailed Tropicbird			
American White Pelican	1/1/79	Flamingo, ENP, Fla.	J. B. E.
Brown Pelican	1/1/79	" " "	J. B. E.
Masked Booby	5/5/79	Dry Tortugas	Rich Bias Alan Anderson Homer H. Eshbaugh
Blue-footed Booby			
Brown Booby	5-5-79	Dry Tortugas	Oliver K. Scott Alan Anderson
Red-footed Booby	5/5/79	Dry Tortugas	Rich Bias Homer H. Eshbaugh
Northern Gannet	28 Jan 79	Gulf of Maine	Davis Finch
Great Cormorant	27 Jan 79	Saint John, N.B.	Davis Finch
Double-crested Cormorant	1/1/79	Nine Mile Pond near Flamingo, ENP, Fla	J. B. E.
Olivaceous Cormorant	2/10	Santa Anna NWR	Steve W. Blacklock
Brandt's Cormorant	1/19	Pacific Grove Ca.	Rich Stallcup
Pelagic Cormorant	1/18	Pt. Reyes Ca.	Rich Stallcup
Red-faced Cormorant	5/19/79	Attu, Alaska	Joseph C Burgiel
American Anhinga	1/1/79	Anhinga Trail, ENP, Fla.	J. B. E.
Magnificent Frigatebird	5-5-79	Dry Tortugas	Oliver K. Scott
Lesser Frigatebird			

Species	Date	Place	Witness
Great Blue Heron	1/1/79	Flamingo, ENP, Fla.	J.B.E.
Green Heron	1/1/79	Anhinga Trail, ENP, Fla.	JBE
Little Blue Heron	1/1/79	Royal Palm Hammock, Fla.	J.B.E.
Cattle Egret	1/1/79	Homestead, Fla	J.B.E.
Reddish Egret	2/11/79	Cameron Co., Tx.	Steve W. Blacklock
Great Egret	1/1/79	Nine Mile Pond, ENP, Fla.	JBE
Snowy Egret	1/1/79	" " " " "	JBE
Little Egret			
Chinese Egret			
Louisiana Heron	1/1/79	W. of Homestead, Fla.	JBE
Black-crowned Night Heron	1/2/79	Shark Valley area by Tamiami Trail, Fla.	JBE
Yellow-crowned Night Heron	1/3/79	Port Canaveral, Fla.	JBE
Least Bittern	3/10/79	Loxahatchee N.W.R., Fla.	Paul W. Sykes Jr.
American Bittern	2/28/79	Laguna Atascosa NWR, TX	John C. Arvin
Wood Stork	1/1/79	Royal Palm Hammock, Fla.	JBE
Glossy Ibis	1/1/79	Flamingo, Fla.	JBE
White-faced Ibis	2/9/79	Calhoun Co., Tx.	Steve W. Blacklock
White Ibis	1/1/79	Royal Palm Hammock, Fla.	JBE
Roseate Spoonbill	1/1/79	Flamingo, Fla.	JBE
American Flamingo	1/1/79	4 in Florida Bay E of Bowie Key	JBE
Mute Swan	29 Jan 79	Ipswich, Mass.	Davis Finch
Whooper Swan	16 March 79	Oakville, Ontario	Davis Finch
Bewick's Swan			
Whistling Swan	1/17/79	Butte Sink, Calif.	Walter R. Anderson
Trumpeter Swan tied Robinson record	7-12-79	Christian L. Grand Teton Nat. Park	Oliver K. Scott
Canada Goose	13 Jan 79	Foss Reservoir, Okla	Warren D. Harden
Brant	1/19	Moss Landing Ca	Rich Stallcup
Barnacle Goose			
Emperor Goose	6/6/79	Gambell, Alaska	R. Martin Smith
Greater White-fronted Goose	1/17/79	Colusa NWR, Cal	W R Anderson

Species	Date	Place	Witness
Bean Goose			
Snow Goose	13 Jan 79	Foss Reservoir, Okla	Warren D Harden
Ross' Goose	1/17/79	Gray Lodge, CA	Walt Anderson
Black-bellied Whistling Duck	2/10/79	Hidalgo Co., Tx.	Steve W. Blacklock
Fulvous Whistling Duck	26 Apr	Winnie, TX	John L [illegible]
Mallard	13 Jan 79	Foss Reservoir, Okla	Warren D Harden
Mexican Duck	8 July 79	PALOMINAS, ARIZ	KENN KAUFMAN
American Black Duck	27 Jan 79	Maces Bay, N.B.	Davis Finch
Mottled Duck	2/9/79	Refugio Co., Tx.	Steve W. Blacklock
Spot-billed Duck	17 May 1979	Attu Island, Alaska	Davis Finch
Gadwall	1/17/79	Butte Sink, CA	Walt Anderson
Common Pintail	1/3/79	Port Canaveral, Fla.	JBE
White-cheeked Pintail	4/10/79	LAGUNA ATASCOSA NWR, TX	JOHN C ARVIN
Falcated Teal			
Green-winged Teal	1/3/79	Lakeland, Fla.	JBE
Baikal Teal			
Blue-winged Teal	2/10/79	ARANSAS CO., TX.	Steve W. Blacklock
Cinnamon Teal	1/18	Drakes Bay Ca.	Rich Stallcup
Garganey	13 Sept. 79	Attu Is Alaska	Thede Tobish
Eurasian Wigeon	16 Jan 79	Ft Collins City Park Lake, Colo	Clait E. Braun
American Wigeon	1/15/79	Guanella Pass, Colo.	R.A. Ryder
Northern Shoveler	1/3/79	McKay Bay, Tampa, Fla.	JBE
Wood Duck	1/15/79	Denver, Colo.	R.A. Ryder
Redhead	1/20	Palo Alto, Ca.	Rich Stallcup
Common Pochard	6/3/79	Attu Island	Jon Dunn
Ring-necked Duck	1/2/79	Tamarack, Fla.	JBE
Canvasback	1/15/79	Denver, Colo.	R.A. Ryder
Greater Scaup	1/18	Bolinas, Ca	Rich Stallcup
Lesser Scaup	1/3/79	Port Canaveral, Fla.	JBE
Tufted Duck	1/19	Tiburon, Ca	Rich Stallcup

Species	Date	Place	Witness
Common Goldeneye	13 Jan 79	Lake Hefner, OKC, Okla	[illegible]
Barrow's Goldeneye	1/18	Tiburon, Ca.	Rich Stallcup
Bufflehead	1/17/79	Gray Lodge, Cal.	Walt Anderson
Oldsquaw	27 Jan 79	Maces Bay, N.B.	Davis Finch
Harlequin Duck	19 May 79	Attu I., Alaska	Davis Finch
Steller's Eider	6 June 79	Gambell, St. Lawrence Island, Alaska	Ellen Lee Rich Stallcup
Common Eider	27 Jan 79	Point Lepreau, N.B.	Davis Finch
King Eider	23 May 79	Attu Island, AK	George E. "Terry" Hall
Spectacled Eider	6 June 79	St. Lawrence Is. Gambell, Alaska	Rich Stallcup
White-winged Scoter	1/18	Tiburon, Ca	Rich Stallcup
Surf Scoter	1/18	Stinson Beach Ca.	Rich Stallcup
Black Scoter	1/18	Pt. Reyes, Ca.	Rich Stallcup
Ruddy Duck	1/3/79	McKay Bay, Tampa, Fla.	JBE
Masked Duck	3/10/79	Loxahatchee N.W.R., Fla.	Paul W. [illegible] Jr.
Hooded Merganser	13 Jan 79	[illegible] Reservoir, Okla	[illegible]
Smew	17 May 79	Attu	Madeline Smith
Common Merganser	15 Jan 79	Lake Hefner, OKC, Okla	[illegible]
Red-breasted Merganser	1/1/79	Coot Bay Pond, ENP, Fla.	JBE
Turkey Vulture	1/1/79	Homestead, Fla.	JBE
Black Vulture	1/1/79	Royal Palm Hammock, ENP, Fla.	JBE
California Condor	9/7/79	near Mt. Pinos, Calif.	[illegible]
White-tailed Kite	1/17/79	Colusa NWR, Cal.	Walt Anderson
Swallow-tailed Kite	5-7-79	[illegible] Nat. Pk.	[illegible] K. [illegible]
Hook-billed Kite	4/11/79	Santa Ana NWR, TX	John Arvin
Mississippi Kite	6/27/79	Natchez Trace S.	Frances Wills
Snail Kite	1/2/79	8 birds in Shark Valley area of Tamiami Trail, Fla.	JBE
Northern Goshawk	8 July 79	Carr Canyon, Huachucas, AZ	Kenn Kaufman
Sharp-shinned Hawk	1/1/79	resting on pole W. of Homestead, Fla.	JBE
Cooper's Hawk	1/17/79	Gray Lodge, CA	Walt Anderson
Red-tailed Hawk	1/1/79	near Long Pine Key, ENP, Fla.	JBE

Species	Date	Place	Witness
Red-shouldered Hawk	1/1/79	Royal Palm Hammock, ENP, Fla.	JBE
Broad-winged Hawk	4/10	NEAR Cambellton, TX	John CARVIN
Swainson's Hawk	1/1/79	"Farm Rd" in ENP, Fla.	JBE
Zone-tailed Hawk	4/28/79	Chisos Mts, Big Bend NP, TX	David E. Wolf
White-tailed Hawk	2/10/79	REFUGIO Co., Tx.	Steve W. Blacklock
Short-tailed Hawk	1/1/79	2 at Royal Palm Hammock + 2 near Flamingo, ENP, Fla. 4	JBE
Rough-legged Hawk	14 Jan 79	Palo Duro Canyon, Texas	Warren D. [illegible]
Ferruginous Hawk	14 Jan 79	East of Canyon, Texas	Warren D [illegible]
Gray Hawk	10 July 79	PATAGONIA, ARIZ.	KENN KAUFMAN
Harris' Hawk	2/10/79	Hidalgo Co., Tx.	Steve W. Blacklock
Lesser Black Hawk	11 July	VERDE RIVER, ARIZ	KENN KAUFMAN
Golden Eagle	14 Jan 79	Palo Duro Canyon, Texas	Warren D [illegible]
White-tailed Eagle	23 May 79	Attu Island, AK	George E. "Terry" Hall
Bald Eagle	1/1/79	over Coot Bay Pond, ENP, Fla.	JBE
Steller's Sea Eagle			
Northern Harrier	1/1/79	N. of Homestead, Fla.	JBE
Osprey	1/1/79	near Coot Bay, Fla.	JBE
Crested Caracara	2/9/79	Refugio Co., Tx.	Steve W. Blacklock
Gyrfalcon	13 JUNE '79	KOUGAROK ROAD NOME, ALASKA	Michael David Greene, Cindra Greene
Prairie Falcon	4/20/79	Daniels Park, CO	George Clayton, Jane H. Clayton, Clait E Braun
Peregrine Falcon	5/23/79	Attu Island, Alaska	[illegible]
Aplomado Falcon			
Merlin	16 Jan 79	near Cobb Lake, Colo	Clait E. Braun
Eurasian Kestrel			
American Kestrel	1/1/79	50+ Homestead area, Fla.	JBE
Plain Chachalaca	2/10/79	Hidalgo Co., Tx.	Steve W. Blacklock
Blue Grouse	4/20/79	Green Mtn. CO	George Clayton, Jane H Clayton
Spruce Grouse	8 March 79	nr Cynthia, Alberta	Davis W. Finch
Ruffed Grouse	08 NOV / 12 Aug	Mi 330 Parks Hiway, AK / Otter Pt, Bar Hbr, Me.	Jennifer [illegible] / Will Russell
Willow Ptarmigan	12 JUNE '79	KOUGAROK ROAD NOME, ALASKA	Michael David Greene, Cindra Greene

Species	Date	Place	Witness
Rock Ptarmigan	19 May 79	Attu	Macklin Smith
White-tailed Ptarmigan	15 Jan 79	Guanella Pass, Colo	Clait E. Braun
Greater Prairie Chicken	9 April 79	Attwater P.C. Refuge	Wayne A. Shifflett
Lesser Prairie Chicken	21 April 79	SE of Campo, CO Comanche Nat'l Grasslands	Clait E. Braun, Jane Clayton, George Clayton
Sharp-tailed Grouse	21 Apr. 79	SE of Castlerock, CO	Clait E. Braun, Jane H. Clayton, George Clayton
Sage Grouse	20 April 79	No of Kremmling, CO	Clait E. Braun, Jane H. Clayton, George Clayton
Common Bobwhite	13 Jan 79	Washita NWR, Okla	[illegible]
Scaled Quail	21 April 79	Two Buttes Res. CO	Clait E. Braun, Jane H. Clayton, George Clayton
California Quail	1/17/79	Colusa NWR, Cal	Walt Anderson
Gambel's Quail	24 Feb	Continental, AZ	Kenn Kaufman
Mountain Quail	14 May	Chinquapin station Yosemite, Ca.	Rich Stallcup
Montezuma Quail	14 Aug	Paradise Road, Ariz.	Kenn Kaufman
Ring-necked Pheasant	1/17/79	Colusa NWR, Cal.	Walt Anderson
Chukar	9-11-79	Wenatchee WA.	Howard E. Ozwood
Gray Partridge	7 Mar. 1979	Edmonton, Alta.	Wayne Nelly, Cleo Mitchell
Black Francolin	4/23/79	Gum Cove, LA	John M Lead
Wild Turkey	2/9/79	Aransas Co., Tx.	Steve W. Blacklock
Common Crane			
Whooping Crane	2/9/79	Aransas NWF Aransas Co., Tx.	Steve W. Blacklock
Sandhill Crane	1/17/79	Butte Sink, Cal	Walt Anderson
Limpkin	1/3/79	Lakeland, Fla.	JBE
King Rail	4/23/79	Gum Cove, LA	John M Lead
Clapper Rail	2/9/79	Nueces Co., Tx.	Steve W. Blacklock
Virginia Rail	1/17/79	Gray Lodge, Cal	Walt Anderson
Spotted Rail			
Sora	1/19	Tiburon, Ca	Rich Stallcup
Yellow Rail	4/25	Anahuac N. W. Refuge	Rose Ann Rowlett
Black Rail	4/25	Anahuac Refuge	Rose Ann Rowlett
Corn Crake			
Paint-billed Crake			

Species	Date	Place	Witness
Purple Gallinule	3/10/79	Loxahatchee N.W.R., Fla.	[illegible signature]
Common Gallinule	1/2/79	Tamiami Trail, Fla.	JBE
European Coot			
American Coot	1/1/79	Everglades Nat. Park	JBE
Caribbean Coot	1/3/79	XMAS count bird at Port St. Lucie, Fla.	JBE
North American Jacana			
American Oystercatcher	1/3/79	St. Petersburg, Fla.	JBE
Black Oystercatcher	1/19	Pacific Grove Ca	Rich Stallcup
Black-necked Stilt	1/19	Moss Landing	Rich Stallcup
American Avocet	1/3/79	(108) birds at McKay Bay, Tampa, Fla.	JBE
Double-striped Thick-knee			
Northern Lapwing			
Ringed Plover	6 June 79	St. Lawrence Is. Gambell, Alaska	Rich Stallcup
Semipalmated Plover	1/1/79	Flamingo, Fla.	JBE
Little Ringed Plover			
Wilson's Plover	1/1/79	Flamingo, Fla.	JBE
Killdeer	1/1/79	Homestead, Fla.	JBE
Piping Plover	4/25/79	Bolivar Flats, Texas	Victor L. Emanuel
Snowy Plover	1/19	Moss Landing Ca.	Rich Stallcup
Mongolian Plover	6/6/79	Gambell, ALAS	PA Buckley
Mountain Plover	4/21/79	two Buttes Res. C.O.	Jane G. Clayton, George Clayton, Walt E. Brown
Greater Golden Plover			
Lesser Golden Plover	4/25/79	Anahuac NWR, Texas	Victor L. Emanuel
Black-bellied Plover	1/1/79	Flamingo, Fla.	JBE
Dotterel			
Black-tailed Godwit	10/24/79	TINICUM AREA	John C. Miller
Hudsonian Godwit	26 Apr	Anahuac NWR, TX	John L. Rowlett
Bar-tailed Godwit	26 May	ATTU, Alaska	Jon Dunn
Marbled Godwit	1/1/79	Flamingo, Fla.	JBE
Eskimo Curlew			

Species	Date	Place	Witness
Whimbrel	1/19	Pacific Grove Ca	Rich Stallcup
Bristle-thighed Curlew			
Eurasian Curlew			
Far Eastern Curlew			
Long-billed Curlew	1/18	Bolinas Ca.	Rich Stallcup
Upland Sandpiper	4/25	Anahuac NWR, Texas	Victor L. Emanuel
Spotted Redshank	MAY 21, '79	ATTU IS. ALASKA	H. Granville Smith
Marsh Sandpiper			
Greenshank	May 20 79	ATTU IS. Alaska	Gerald Rosenband
Greater Yellowlegs	1/17/79	Colusa NWR, Cal	Walt Anderson
Lesser Yellowlegs	2/11/79	Cameron Co., Tx	Steve W. Blacklock
Solitary Sandpiper	4/11/79	Santa Ana NWR, TX	John C Arvin
Wood Sandpiper	MAY 19/79	Attu, Alaska	[illegible]
Willet	1/1/79	Flamingo, Fla	JBE
Terek Sandpiper	6/6/79	Gambell, AK.	W.H. Russell
Common Sandpiper	MAY 21 '79	Attu Is. Alaska	Thede Tobish
Spotted Sandpiper	2/10/79	Hidalgo Co., Tx.	Steve W. Blacklock
Gray-tailed Tattler	14 Sept. 79	Attu Is. Alaska	Thede Tobish
Wandering Tattler	1/19	Pacific Grove Ca	Rich Stallcup
Ruddy Turnstone	1/1/79	Flamingo, Fla.	JBE
Black Turnstone	1/18	Bolinas, Ca	Rich Stallcup
Wilson's Phalarope	4/10	Laguna Atascosa NWR, TX	John C Arvin
Northern Phalarope	5/16	Anchorage, Alaska	David W Sonneborn
Red Phalarope	1/19	Pacific Grove	Rich Stallcup
European Woodcock			
American Woodcock	1/27	Lake Calumet, Chicago	Burleigh Hines, Jerry Rosenband, Larry Balch
Common Snipe	16 Jan 79	near Cobb Lake, Colo	Clait E. Braun
European Jacksnipe			
Short-billed Dowitcher	1/1/79	Flamingo, Fla.	JBE
Long-billed Dowitcher	1/17/79	Colusa NWR Cal	Walt Anderson

Species	Date	Place	Witness
Surfbird	1/19	Pescadero, Ca.	Rich Stallcup
Great Knot			
Red Knot	9/9/79	Nueces Co., Tx.	Gene O. Blacklock
Sanderling	1/3/79	Vero Beach, Fla.	JBE
Semipalmated Sandpiper	22 April 79	Neenoshe Res., Kiowa Co	Clait E. Braun, George Clayton, Jan Clayton
Western Sandpiper	1/1/79	Flamingo, Fla.	JBE
Rufous-necked Stint	5/20/79	Attu, Alaska	Michael David Greene
Little Stint	5/17/79	Attu, Alaska	Paul H. Lehman Jr., Jon Dunn
Temminck's Stint	5/22/79	Attu, Alaska	Benton Basham
Long-toed Stint	5/22/79	Attu, Alaska	Michael David Greene
Least Sandpiper	1/17/79	Colusa NWR, Cal	Walt Anderson
White-rumped Sandpiper	5-3-79	St. Petersburg, Fla	Oliver K. Scott
Baird's Sandpiper	18 April 79	Neenoshe Res., Kiowa Co	Clait E. Braun, George Clayton, Jan Clayton
Pectoral Sandpiper	4/25/79	Anahuac NWR, Texas	[illegible]
Sharp-tailed Sandpiper	9/17/79	Attu, Alaska	Lisa J. Oakley
Purple Sandpiper	27 Jan 79	Maces Bay, N.B.	Davis Finch
Rock Sandpiper	5/17/79	Attu, Alaska	Joseph C Burgiel
Dunlin	1/1/79	Flamingo, Fla.	JBE
Curlew Sandpiper	8/18/79	Jamaica Bay WR., NY.	Tom Davis, Robert [illegible]
Spoonbill Sandpiper			
Broad-billed Sandpiper			
Stilt Sandpiper	9/11/79	Cameron Co., Tx.	Gene O. Blacklock
Buff-breasted Sandpiper	26 Apr	Anahuac NWR, TX	John L. Rowlett
Ruff	30 May 79	Attu Island, AK	George E. "Terry" Hall
Pomarine Jaeger	May 3	Daytona Beach, Fla	Jon Dunn
Parasitic Jaeger	27 May 79	Attu Island, AK	George E "Terry" Hall
Long-tailed Jaeger	6 June 79	Gambell, St. Lawrence Is.	Dolores [illegible]
Great Skua	30 Dec 79	off Maryland - Baltimore Canyon	Lawrence G. Balch, Richard A. Rowlett
South Polar Skua	10 Sept 79	off Westport WA	Terry Wahl
Glaucous Gull	13 Jan 79	Lake Hefner, OKC, Okla	[illegible]

Species	Date	Place	Witness
Iceland Gull	27 Jan 79	Maces Bay, N.B.	Davis Finch
Glaucous-winged Gull	1/18	Stinson Beach Ca.	Rich Stallcup
Great Black-backed Gull	27 Jan 79	Maces Bay, N.B.	Davis Finch
Slaty-backed Gull	11/1/79	Elmendorf AFB Dump Anchorage, Alaska	David W Sonneborn
Western Gull	1/18	Bolinas, Ca	Rich Stallcup
Lesser Black-backed Gull	27 Jan 79	Digby, N.S.	Davis Finch
Herring Gull	1/1/79	Flamingo, Fla.	JBE
Thayer's Gull	1/18	Pt. Reyes, Ca	Rich Stallcup
California Gull	1/18	Inverness, Ca	Rich Stallcup
Ring-billed Gull	1/1/79	Flamingo, Fla.	JBE
Mew Gull	1/18	Inverness, Ca	Rich Stallcup
Black-headed Gull	20 May 79	Attu Isl., AK	George "Terry" Hall
Laughing Gull	1/1/79	Flamingo, Fla.	JBE
Franklin's Gull	7/1/79	Sand Lake NWR, S.D.	Kim Eckert
Bonaparte's Gull	1/3/79	Sebastian Inlet, Fla.	JBE
Little Gull	6/30/79	Woodland Dunes Nature Center Two Rivers Wis.	James F. Steffen
Heermann's Gull	1/19	Moss Landing	Rich Stallcup
Ivory Gull	8 June 79	Gambell, AK	Macklin Smith
Black-legged Kittiwake	27 Jan 79	Saint John, N.B.	Davis Finch
Red-legged Kittiwake	15 June 79	St. Paul, Pribilofs AK	Robert O. Paxton
Ross' Gull	10 June 79	Gambell, AK	Robert [illegible] / Macklin Smith
Sabine's Gull	June 11, 1979	Gambell, Alaska	Larry Peavler
Gull-billed Tern	2/11/79	Cameron Co., Tx.	Steve W. Blacklock
Forster's Tern	1/3/79	Lakeland, Fla.	JBE
Common Tern	1/3/79	Port Canaveral, Fla.	JBE
Arctic Tern	5-3-79	Guy McCaskie	Daytona Beach, Fla.
Roseate Tern	5-5-79	Dry Tortugas, Fla.	Oliver K. Scott
Aleutian Tern	22-5-79	Attu Alaska	J. Kelln Aspide
Sooty Tern	5/6/79	Rit Barry / Frederick M Barry	Dry Tortugas, Fla.
Bridled Tern	5-3-79	Off Daytona Beach	Oliver K Scott

Species	Date	Place	Witness
Little Tern	25/4-79	HIGH ISLAND	[illegible]
Royal Tern	1/1/79	Flamingo, Fla.	JBE
Elegant Tern	8 Sept.	San Diego	Guy McCaskie
Sandwich Tern	1/3/79	Mullet Key, Fla.	JBE
Caspian Tern	1/1/79	Nine Mile Pond, ENP, Fla.	JBE
Black Tern	4/25/79	Bolivar flats, Tex	Michael C Lanier
White-winged Black Tern			
Brown Noddy	5/6/79	Dry Tortugas, Fla.	Bil Barry
Black Noddy	5/6/79	Dry Tortugas Fla.	Will Russell & Maude Russell
Black Skimmer	1/1/79	Flamingo, Fla.	JBE
Razorbill	27 Jan 79	Digby, N.S.	Davis Finch
Thin-billed Murre	1/19	Monterey, Ca	Rich Stallcup
Thick-billed Murre	27 Jan 79	Bay of Fundy near Saint John, N.B.	Davis Finch
Dovekie	27 Jan 79	Bay of Fundy between Saint John, N.B. + Digby, N.S.	Davis Finch
Black Guillemot	27 Jan 79	Ferry between Freeport and Westport, N.S.	Davis Finch
Pigeon Guillemot	1/19	Monterey, Ca	Rich Stallcup
Marbled Murrelet	1/19	Pigeon Point Ca	Rich Stallcup
Kittlitz's Murrelet	29 May 79	Attu I., Alaska	Davis Finch
Xantus' Murrelet	7 Oct. 79	off Westport, WA	Dennis Paulson
Craveri's Murrelet			
Ancient Murrelet	7 June 79	Gambell, St Lawrence I., Alaska	Davis Finch
Cassin's Auklet	10 Sept 79	20 MILES off Westport WA	Wm. Harrington-Tweit
Parakeet Auklet	6/6	Gambell, Alaska	Bill Boyle
Crested Auklet	6 June 79	St. Lawrence Is. Gambell, Alaska	Rich Stallcup
Least Auklet	6/6	Gambell, Alaska	Fritz Scheider
Whiskered Auklet	30 July 79	Igitkin Pass, Alaska	Thede Tobish
Rhinoceros Auklet	1/19	Monterey, Ca	Rich Stallcup
Atlantic Puffin	28 Jan 79	Gulf of Maine	Davis Finch
Horned Puffin	25 May 79	Attu I., Alaska	Davis Finch
Tufted Puffin	5-17-79	ATTU	Larry Peavler

Species	Date	Place	Witness
White-crowned Pigeon	4-9-79	[illegible]	[illegible]
Scaly-naped Pigeon			
Band-tailed Pigeon	1/20	Carmel, Ca.	Rich Stallcup
Red-billed Pigeon	4/11/79	Starr Co., TX	John C Arvin
Rock Dove	1/2/79	Miami, Fla.	JBE
Zenaida Dove			
White-winged Dove	1/1/79	Flamingo, Fla.	JBE
Mourning Dove	1/1/79	Homestead, Fla.	JBE
Spotted Dove	3-29-79	Los Angeles Arboretum	Dorothy [illegible], Virginia A. Patterson, [illegible] Smith
Ringed Turtle Dove	1/3/79	St. Petersburg, Fla.	JBE
Common Ground Dove	1/2/79	Tamarack, Fla.	JBE
Ruddy Ground Dove			
Inca Dove	4/9/79	Refugio Co., Tx.	Steve W. Blacklock
White-tipped Dove	4/10/79	Hidalgo Co., Tx.	Steve W. Blacklock
Key West Quail Dove	2-4-79	Everglades nat park Snake Bite, Fla.	[illegible]
Ruddy Quail Dove			
Thick-billed Parrot			
Yellow-headed Parrot	9-6-79	Los Angeles Ca.	Kimball Garrett, Pete Peterson, Jon Dunn
Budgerigar	1/3/79	St. Petersburg, Fla.	JBE
Common Cuckoo			
Oriental Cuckoo			
Mangrove Cuckoo	5-5-79	Sugarloaf Key, Fla.	Oliver K. Scott
Yellow-billed Cuckoo	4/11/79	Santa Ana NWR, TX	John C Arvin
Black-billed Cuckoo	24 Apr	High Island, TX	John L Rowlett
Greater Roadrunner	14 Jan 79	Palo Duro Canyon, Texas	[illegible]
Smooth-billed Ani	1/1/79	Homestead, Fla.	JBE
Groove-billed Ani	2/28/79	Laguna Atascosa NWR TX	John C Arvin
Barn Owl	1/1/79	1 sec. after midnight, New years Eve Florida City, Fla.	JBE
Common Screech Owl	4/10/79	Hidalgo Co., Tx.	Steve W. Blacklock
Whiskered Screech Owl	7 July 79	Carr Canyon, Ariz	Kenn Kaufman

Species	Date	Place	Witness
Flammulated Screech Owl	14 MAY	Henness Ridge Yosemite N.P.	Richard W. Stallcup
Great Horned Owl	1/17/79	Colusa, CA	Walt Anderson
Snowy Owl	29 Jan 79	Salisbury, Mass.	Davis Finch
Hawk Owl	3 Nov 79	20 miles west of Ester, Alaska	Daniel A. Gibson
Northern Pygmy Owl	8 July 79	South Fork of Cave Creek Canyon, Ariz.	Kenn Kaufman
Ferruginous Pygmy Owl	5-10-79	Falcon Dam, TX	Bob Farris / John C Arvin
Elf Owl	5/9/79	Bentsen State Park, TX	John C Arvin
Burrowing Owl	1/2/79	Pembroke Pines, Fla.	JBE
Barred Owl	2/11/79	Welder Wildlife Refuge	Steve W. Blacklock
Spotted Owl	8 July 79	South Fork of Cave Creek Canyon, Ariz.	Kenn Kaufman
Great Gray Owl	29 Jan 79	Topsfield, Mass.	Davis Finch
Long-eared Owl	29 Jan 79	Salisbury, Mass.	Davis Finch
Short-eared Owl	29 Jan 79	Salisbury, Mass.	Davis Finch
Boreal Owl	5/16/79	Anchorage, AK Rabbit Creek	Pat Abrams / Donna Prator
Saw-whet Owl	10/14/79	Rich Stallcup ↔	Inverness, California
Jungle Nightjar			
Chuck-will's-widow	3/9/79	Delray Beach, Fla.	Paul W. Sykes Jr.
Whip-poor-will	6/30/79	Tomahawk Trail, Lake Co., Minn.	Kim Eckert
Buff-collared Nightjar	10 July	Guadalupe Canyon, Ariz.	Kenn Kaufman
Poor-will	4/27/79	35 mi. S of Alpine, TX	David E. Wolf
Pauraque	2/10/79	Hidalgo Co., Tx.	Steve W. Blacklock
Common Nighthawk	4/23/79	Gum Cove, LA	John McReed
Lesser Nighthawk	5/9/79	Near Rio Grande City, TX	John C Arvin
White-throated Needle-tailed Swift			
Black Swift	14 MAY	Yosemite Valley	Rich Stallcup
Chimney Swift	4/16	San Antonio, TX	John C Arvin
Vaux's Swift	79/7/28	West Vancouver, B.C.	Bruce A. Macdonald
Fork-tailed Swift			
Common Swift			
White-throated Swift	24 Feb	Tucson, AZ	Kenn Kaufman

Species	Date	Place	Witness
Antillean Palm Swift			
Green Violet-ear			
Cuban Emerald			
Lucifer Hummingbird	6/24/79	Big Bend NP, Tex	Peter Scott
Ruby-throated Hummingbird	24-4-79	High Island TX.	Norm Mellor
Black-chinned Hummingbird	4/11/79	McAllen, TX	John C Arvin
Bahama Woodstar			
Costa's Hummingbird	2/25	Sun City, Ariz.	[illegible]
Anna's Hummingbird	1/18	Stinson Beach, Ca	Rich Stallcup
Broad-tailed Hummingbird	24 May 79	Big Bend Nat'l Park, TX	John C Arvin
Rufous Hummingbird	8 July	Carr Canyon, Ariz	Kenn Kaufman
Allen's Hummingbird	13 May	Berkeley, Ca.	Rich Stallcup
Bumblebee Hummingbird			
Calliope Hummingbird	14 May	Yosemite Valley	Rich Stallcup
Magnificent Hummingbird	8 July	Ramsey Canyon, Ariz	Kenn Kaufman
Plain-capped Starthroat			
Blue-throated Hummingbird	24 May 79	Big Bend Nat'l Park, TX	John C Arvin
Buff-bellied Hummingbird	5/9/79	Brownsville, Tx.	Steve [illegible]
Violet-crowned Hummingbird	8 July	Ramsey Canyon, Ariz	Kenn Kaufman
Berylline Hummingbird			
White-eared Hummingbird	9 July	Summerhaven, Ariz	Kenn Kaufman
Broad-billed Hummingbird	8 July	Carr Canyon, Ariz	Kenn Kaufman
Eared Trogon			
Elegant Trogon	9 July	Cave Creek Canyon, Ariz	Kenn Kaufman
Belted Kingfisher	1/1/79	Everglades Nat. Park	JBE
Ringed Kingfisher	4/11/79	Starr Co., TX	John C Arvin
Green Kingfisher	5/10/79	Starr County, TX	John C Arvin
Hoopoe			
Eurasian Wryneck			
Common Flicker	13 Jan 79	Washita NWR, Okla	[illegible]

Species	Date	Place	Witness
Pileated Woodpecker	1/1/79	Everglades Nat. Park, Fla.	JBE
Red-bellied Woodpecker	1/1/79	Homestead, Fla.	JBE
Golden-fronted Woodpecker	4 Jan 79	[illegible], Texas	[illegible]
Gila Woodpecker	23 FEB	SONOITA CREEK, AZ	KENN KAUFMAN
Red-headed Woodpecker	2/1/79	Jackson, Miss	Frances Wills
Acorn Woodpecker	1/17/79	Colusa, CA	Walt Anderson
Lewis' Woodpecker	1/17/79	Sutter Buttes, CA	Walt Anderson
Yellow-bellied Sapsucker	1/24/79	Frances Wills	Jackson Miss.
Williamson's Sapsucker	14 MAY	Periguoy Yosemite, Calif.	Rich Stallcup
Hairy Woodpecker	1/19	Pacific Grove, Ca	Rich Stallcup
Downy Woodpecker	1/15/79	Guanella Pass, Colo.	RA Ryder
Ladder-backed Woodpecker	2/10/79	Hidalgo Co., Tx.	Steve W. Blacklock
Nuttall's Woodpecker	1/17/79	Colusa, CA	Walt Anderson
Brown-backed Woodpecker	23 FEB	PATAGONIA MTS, AZ	KENN KAUFMAN
Red-cockaded Woodpecker	24 Apr	Silsbee, Texas	John L Rowlett
White-headed Woodpecker	14 MAY	Yosemite Valley	Rich Stallcup
Black-backed Three-toed Woodpecker	6/30/79	Isabella, Minn.	Kim Eckert
Northern Three-toed Woodpecker	6/17/79	ALASKA CHUGACH NAT'L FOREST	Marian A. Cressman James L Cressman
Rose-throated Becard	9 JULY	SONOITA CREEK, ARIZ	KENN KAUFMAN
Eastern Kingbird	4/23/79	Gum Cove, LA	John McLeod
Loggerhead Kingbird			
Gray Kingbird	5-4-79	Key Biscayne, Fla.	Oliver K. Scott
Tropical Kingbird	2/10/79	Hidalgo Co., Tx.	Steve W. Blacklock
Western Kingbird	Mar. 29	Riverside, CA	Donna P. Johnson
Cassin's Kingbird	4/27/79	8 mi. S of Alpine, TX	David E. Wolf
Thick-billed Kingbird	9 JULY	SONOITA CREEK, ARIZ	KENN KAUFMAN
Fork-tailed Flycatcher			
Scissor-tailed Flycatcher	9 April, 79	Attwater P.C. Refuge	Wayne [illegible]
Greater Kiskadee	2/10/79	Hidalgo Co., Tx.	Steve W. Blacklock
Sulphur-bellied Flycatcher	5/10/79	STARR Co., TX	JOHN CARVIN

Species	Date	Place	Witness
Great Crested Flycatcher	1/1/79	Homestead, Fla.	JBE
Wied's Crested Flycatcher	4/11/79	Santa Ana NWR, TX	John C Arvin
Ash-throated Flycatcher	4/28/79	Big Bend NP, TX	David E. Wolf
Olivaceous Flycatcher	8 July	Carr Canyon, Ariz	Kenn Kaufman
Nutting's Flycatcher			
Stolid Flycatcher			
Eastern Phoebe	1/1/79	Homestead, Fla.	JBE
Black Phoebe	1/17/79	Colusa NWR, Cal	Walt Anderson
Say's Phoebe	1/17/79	Sutter Buttes, Cal	Walt Anderson
Yellow-bellied Flycatcher	5/10/79	Starr Co., TX	John C Arvin
Acadian Flycatcher	4/25	High Island, Texas	Victor L. Emanuel
Willow Flycatcher	6/28/79	St. Charles, Mo.	Phoebe Snetsinger Carmen Patterson
Alder Flycatcher	6/15/79	Anchorage, Alaska	Joel Greenberg Leonard Graf
Least Flycatcher	6/30/79	Woodland Dunes Nature Center, Two Rivers, Wis	Bernard N. Brouchoud
Hammond's Flycatcher	23 Feb	Sonoita Creek AZ	Kenn Kaufman
Dusky Flycatcher	14 May	Henness Ridge Yosemite N.P.	Rich Stallcup
Gray Flycatcher	7-12-79	Rock Springs uplift, Wyo.	Oliver K. Scott
Western Flycatcher	4/28/79	Chisos Mts, Big Bend NP, TX	David E. Wolf
Buff-breasted Flycatcher	8 July	Carr Canyon, Ariz	Kenn Kaufman
Coues' Flycatcher	8 July	Carr Canyon, Ariz	Kenn Kaufman
Eastern Pewee	24 Apr	High Island, TX	John L. Rowlett
Western Pewee	13 May	Berkeley, Ca	Rich Stallcup
Olive-sided Flycatcher	5/10/79	Santa Ana NWR, TX	John C Arvin
Vermilion Flycatcher	24 Feb	Tucson, AZ	Kenn Kaufman
Northern Beardless Flycatcher	10 July	Guadalupe Canyon, Ariz	Kenn Kaufman
Common Skylark	1/18	Pt. Reyes, Ca.	Rich Stallcup
Horned Lark	13 Jan 79	Lake Arbuckle, OKG, Okla	Warren D. Harden
Bahama Swallow			
Violet-green Swallow	23 Feb	Near Nogales, AZ	Kenn Kaufman
Tree Swallow	1/1/79	Homestead, Fla	JBE

Species	Date	Place	Witness
Bank Swallow	4/11/79	Starr Co., TX	John C Arvin
Rough-winged Swallow	24 Feb	Tucson, AZ	Kenn Kaufman
Common House Martin			
Barn Swallow	3/29	Riverside, CA	Donna P. Johnson
Cliff Swallow	4/9	San Antonio, TX	John C. Arvin
Cave Swallow	4/9	20 mi S. Jourdanton, TX	John C Arvin
Purple Martin	2/10/79	Aransas Co., Tx.	Steve O. Blacklock
Cuban Martin			
Gray-breasted Martin			
Gray Jay	1/15/79	Squaw Mtn., Colo.	R A Ryder
Blue Jay	1/1/79	Homestead, Fla	JBE
Steller's Jay	1/15/79	Guanella Pass, Colo.	R A Ryder
Scrub Jay	4 Jan 79	Palo Duro Canyon, Texas	Warren D Harden
Gray-breasted Jay	23 Feb	Patagonia Mts., AZ	Kenn Kaufman
Green Jay	2/10/79	Hidalgo Co., Tx.	Steve O. Blacklock
Brown Jay	4/11/79	Starr Co., TX	John C Arvin
Black-billed Magpie	1/15/79	Golden, Colo.	R A Ryder
Yellow-billed Magpie	1/17/79	Colusa, Cal	Walt Anderson
Northern Raven	1/15/79	Guanella Pass, Colo.	R A Ryder
White-necked Raven	2/11/79	Cameron Co., Tx.	Steve O. Blacklock
American Crow	1/1/79	Royal Palm Hammock, ENP, Fla.	JBE
Northwestern Crow	79/7/28	Vancouver, B.C.	Bruce A. Macdonald
Fish Crow	1/2/79	Tamarack, Fla.	JBE
Mexican Crow	2/11/79	Cameron Co., Tx.	Steve O. Blacklock
Pinyon Jay	23 Feb	Patagonia Mts., AZ	Kenn Kaufman
Clark's Nutcracker	1/15/79	Guanella Pass, Co.	R A Ryder
Black-capped Chickadee	16 Jan 79	Ft Collins, Colo.	Clait E. Braun
Carolina Chickadee	13 Jan 79	Norman, Okla	Warren D Harden
Mexican Chickadee	9 July	Chiricahua Mts., Ariz	Kenn Kaufman
Mountain Chickadee	1/15/79	Guanella Pass, Colo	R A Ryder

Species	Date	Place	Witness
Siberian Chickadee			
Boreal Chickadee	5/16/79	Anchorage Alaska	David W Sonneborn
Chestnut-backed Chickadee	1/18	Muir Woods	Rich Stallcup
Tufted Titmouse	14 Jan 79	Palo Duro Canyon, Texas	Warren [illegible]
Plain Titmouse	1/17/79	Colusa, Cal.	Walt Anderson
Bridled Titmouse	23 FEB	Sonoita Creek, AZ	Kenn Kaufman
Verdin	23 FEB	Sonoita Creek, AZ	Kenn Kaufman
Bushtit	1/18	Muir Woods, Ca	Rich Stallcup
White-breasted Nuthatch	27 JAN 79	Hampton, N.H.	Dennis Abbott
Red-breasted Titmouse	1/15/79	R.A. Ryder @ Guanella Pass, Colo.	
Brown-headed Nuthatch	4/6/79	Jackson, MS	Ruth E. Downey
Pygmy Nuthatch	16 Jan 79	Rist Canyon Ft. Collins, Colo	Clait E. Braun
Brown Creeper	1/20	Carmel Valley Ca.	Rich Stallcup
Wrentit	1/18	Bolinas, Ca	Rich Stallcup
Red-whiskered Bulbul	2/4	Kendall, Fla.	Benton Basham
North American Dipper	1/15/79	Guanella Pass, Colo.	R.A. Ryder
House Wren	1/1/79	Homestead, Fla.	JBE
Brown-throated Wren	8 July	Carr Canyon, Ariz	Kenn Kaufman
Winter Wren	1/18	Muir Woods Ca.	Rich Stallcup
Bewick's Wren	14 Jan 79	Palo Duro Canyon, Texas	Warren [illegible]
Carolina Wren	1/24/79	Jackson, Miss.	Frances Wills
Cactus Wren	2/11/79	Cameron, Co., Tx	Steve O. Blacklock
Marsh Wren	1/17/79	Gray Lodge, CA	Walt Anderson
Sedge Wren	4/25/79	Anahuac Refuge	Rose Ann Rowlett
Canyon Wren	14 Jan 79	Palo Duro Canyon, Texas	Warren [illegible]
Rock Wren	1/17/79	Sutter Buttes, Cal	Walt Anderson
Northern Mockingbird	1/1/79	Homestead, Fla.	JBE
Bahama Mockingbird			
Gray Catbird	1/1/79	Homestead, Fla.	JBE
Brown Thrasher	1/24/79	Jackson Miss	Frances Wills

Species	Date	Place	Witness
Long-billed Thrasher	2/10/79	Hidalgo Co., Tx.	Steve W. Blacklock
Bendire's Thrasher	25 FEB	PHOENIX, AZ	KENN KAUFMAN
Curve-billed Thrasher	14 Jan 79	Palo Duro Canyon, Tucson	Warren D. [illegible]
California Thrasher	1/20	Carmel Valley, Ca	Rich Stallcup
Le Conte's Thrasher	25 FEB	PHOENIX, AZ	KENN KAUFMAN
Crissal Thrasher	25 FEB	PHOENIX, AZ	KENN KAUFMAN
Sage Thrasher	20 April 79	Junction Butte, CO	Clait E. Braun, George Clayton, Jane H. Clayton
American Robin	1/1/79	Everglades Nat. Park, Fla.	JBC
Fieldfare			
Rufous-backed Thrush			
Clay-colored Thrush			
Dusky Thrush			
Eye-browed Thrush	5/29/79	Attu Isl. Alaska	[illegible] Basham
Varied Thrush	1/17/79	Sutter Buttes, CA	Walt Anderson
Aztec Thrush			
Wood Thrush	4/6/79	Jackson, MS	Ruth E. Downey
Hermit Thrush	1/17/79	Sutter Buttes, CA	Walt Anderson
Swainson's Thrush	24 Apr	High Island, TX	John L Rowlett
Gray-cheeked Thrush	24 Apr	High Island, TX	John L Rowlett
Veery	24 Apr	High Island, TX	John L Rowlett
Eastern Bluebird	14 Jan 79	[illegible] Canyon, Tucson	Warren D. [illegible]
Western Bluebird	1/18	Olema, Ca.	Rich Stallcup
Mountain Bluebird	14 Jan 79	Palo Duro Canyon, Tucson	Warren D. [illegible]
Northern Wheatear	4 June 1979	Gambell, Alaska	Max Parker, H. P. Langridge
Bluethroat	6 June 79	St. Lawrence Is. Gambell, AK	Rich Stallcup
Siberian Rubythroat	28 May 79	~~[illegible]~~ Attu, AK.	Thede Tobish
Townsend's Solitaire	14 Jan 79	Palo Duro Canyon, Tucson	Warren D. [illegible]
Willow Warbler			
Dusky Warbler			
Arctic Warbler	9 JUNE '79	Gambell, Alaska	Michael Greene, Cindy Greene

Species	Date	Place	Witness
Middendorff's Grasshopper Warbler	18 Sept. 79	Attu Is. Alaska	[illegible]
Blue-gray Gnatcatcher	2/4	Flamingo E.N.P. Fla	Kenton Basham
Black-capped Gnatcatcher			
Black-tailed Gnatcatcher	25 FEB	Phoenix, AZ	Kenn Kaufman
Golden-crowned Kinglet	14 Jan 79	Palo Duro Canyon, Texas	[illegible]
Ruby-crowned Kinglet	1/17/79	Colusa, CA	Walt Anderson
Red-breasted Flycatcher			
Gray-spotted Flycatcher			
Siberian Accentor			
White Wagtail	5 June 79	Gambell, St. Lawrence I., Alaska	Davis Finch
Gray Wagtail	5		
Yellow Wagtail	21 May 79	Attu I. Alaska	Davis W. Finch
Water Pipit	1/17/79	Colusa, CA	Walt Anderson
Pechora Pipit	5/22/79	Attu AK	Ben King
Indian Tree Pipit	20 May 79	Attu I., Alaska	Davis W. Finch
Red-throated Pipit	20 May 79	Attu I., Alaska	Davis W. Finch
Sprague's Pipit	8/11/79	San Patricio Co., Tx.	Steve O. Blacklock
Bohemian Waxwing	1/15/79	Denver, Colo.	[illegible]
Cedar Waxwing	2/1/79	Jackson Miss	Frances Wills
Phainopepla	1/17/79	Sutter Buttes, CA	Walt Anderson
Brown Shrike			
Northern Shrike	1/22/79	Long Island (Dighy Neck) N.S.	Peter Vickery
Loggerhead Shrike	1/1/79	West of Florida City, Fla.	JBE
European Starling	1/4/79	St. Andrews Church Jackson, Miss.	[illegible] Clark
Crested Myna	79/7/25	Vancouver, B.C.	Bruce A. Macdonald
Black-capped Vireo	4/10	San Antonio, TX	John C Arvin
White-eyed Vireo	1/1/79	Flamingo, Fla.	JBE
Hutton's Vireo	1/18	5 Brooks, Ca	Rich Stallcup
Bell's Vireo	4/28/79	Santa Elena Canyon, Big Bend, TX	David E. Wolf
Thick-billed Vireo			

Species	Date	Place	Witness
Gray Vireo	11 July	Slate Creek Divide, Ariz	Kenn Kaufman
Yellow-throated Vireo	24 Apr	High Island, TX	John L Rowlett
Solitary Vireo	2/28/79	Santa Ana NWR TX	John C Arvin
Black-whiskered Vireo	5-4-79	Key Biscayne, Fla.	Oliver K. Scott
Yellow-green Vireo			
Red-eyed Vireo	4/6/79	Jackson, MS	Ruth E Downey
Philadelphia Vireo	4/25/79	High Island, Texas	Victor L. Emanuel
Warbling Vireo	13 MAY	Berkeley, Ca	Rich Stallcup
Bananaquit			
Black-and-White Warbler	1/18	Stinson Beach Ca.	Rich Stallcup
Prothonotary Warbler	4/6/79	Jackson, MS	Ruth E Downey
Swainson's Warbler	5/2/79	Jackson Miss	Frances Wills
Worm-eating Warbler	24 Apr	High Island, TX	John L Rowlett
Golden-winged Warbler	4/25/79	High Island, TX	Victor L. Emanuel
Blue-winged Warbler	24 Apr	High Island, TX	John L Rowlett
Bachman's Warbler			
Tennessee Warbler	24 Apr	High Island, TX	John L Rowlett
Orange-crowned Warbler	1/17/79	Colusa, CA	Walt Anderson
Nashville Warbler	4/10/79	San Antonio, TX	John C Arvin
Virginia's Warbler	9 July	Near Onion Saddle, Ariz	Kenn Kaufman
Colima Warbler	4/28/79	Chisos Mts, Big Bend, TX	David E. Wolf
Lucy's Warbler	9 July	Sonoita Creek, Ariz	Kenn Kaufman
Northern Parula Warbler	2/4	Royal Palm E.N.P. Fla	Benton Basham
Tropical Parula Warbler	2/29/79	Santa Ana NWR TX	John C Arvin
Olive Warbler	9 July	Rose Canyon, Mt. Lemmon, Ariz	Kenn Kaufman
Yellow Warbler	4/25/79	High Island, Texas	Victor L. Emanuel
Magnolia Warbler	4/25/79	High Island Tx	Victor L. Emanuel
Cape May Warbler	5-4-79	Key Biscayne, Fla.	Oliver K. Scott
Black-throated Blue Warbler	5-4-79	Key Biscayne, Fla.	Oliver K. Scott
Yellow-rumped Warbler	1/1/79	Homestead, Fla	JBE

Species	Date	Place	Witness
Black-throated Gray Warbler	13 MAY	Berkeley, Ca.	Rich Stallcup
Townsend's Warbler	1/18	Five Brooks, Ca	Rich Stallcup
Black-throated Green Warbler	2/28/79	SANTA ANA NWR, TX	John C Arvin
Golden-cheeked Warbler	4/10	SAN ANTONIO, TX	JOHN C ARVIN
Hermit Warbler	1/19	Jack's Peak, Ca	Rich Stallcup
Cerulean Warbler	4/25	High Island, Tx	Margaret H. Allan
Blackburnian Warbler	24 Apr	High Island, TX	John L Rowlett
Yellow-throated Warbler	4/6	Jackson Miss	Frances Wills
Grace's Warbler	9 JULY	ROSE CANYON, MT. LEMMON, ARIZ	KENN KAUFMAN
Chestnut-sided Warbler	24 Apr	High Island, Tx	John L Rowlett
Bay-breasted Warbler	24 Apr	High Island, TX	John L Rowlett
Blackpoll Warbler	24 Apr	High Island, TX	John L Rowlett
Pine Warbler	4/6/79	Jackson, MS	Ruth E. Downey
Kirtland's Warbler	6/29/79	Mio, Michigan	Barbara [illegible] / Larry [illegible]
Prairie Warbler	[illegible]	[illegible]	[illegible]
Palm Warbler	1/1/79	Homestead, Fla.	JBE
Ovenbird	1/1/79	Homestead, Fla.	JBE
Northern Waterthrush	24-4-79	HIGH ISLAND, TX.	Norm Mellor
Louisiana Waterthrush	6/17/79	Natchez Trace S.	Frances Wills
Kentucky Warbler	24 Apr	Silsbee, Texas	John L Rowlett
Connecticut Warbler	7/1/79	Nickerson bog, Minn.	Kim Eckert
Mourning Warbler	5/8/79	SABAL PALM SANCTUARY CAMERON CO, TX	John C Arvin
MacGillivray's Warbler	14 MAY	Yosemite N.P.	Rich Stallcup
Common Yellowthroat	1/1/79	Homestead, Fla.	JBE
Gray-crowned Yellowthroat			
Yellow-breasted Chat	4/24/79	Silsbee, TEXAS	Victor L. Emanuel
Fan-tailed Warbler			
Red-faced Warbler	9 JULY	ROSE CANYON, MT. LEMMON, ARIZ	KENN KAUFMAN
Hooded Warbler	4/24/79	Silsbee, TEXAS	Victor L. Emanuel
Wilson's Warbler	5/8/79	SABAL PALM SANCTUARY CAMERON CO, TX	JOHN C ARVIN

Species	Date	Place	Witness
Canada Warbler	5/8/79	Sabal Palm Sanctuary Cameron Co, TX	John C Arvin
American Redstart	4/27/79	High Island, Texas	Margaret J Miller
Painted Redstart	8 July	South Fork of Cave Creek Canyon, Ariz	Kenn Kaufman
Slate-throated Redstart			
Rufous-capped Warbler	4/28/79	Santa Elena Canyon, Big Bend, TX	David E. Wolf
House Sparrow	1/1/79	Flamingo, Fla.	JBE
Eurasian Tree Sparrow	6/28/79	St Louis, Mo	Phoebe Snetsinger Carmen Patterson Joel Greenberg
Bobolink	5/7/79	[illegible]	John B. Edscorn
Eastern Meadowlark	1/1/79	W. of Homestead, Fla.	JBE
Western Meadowlark	16 Jan 79	Ft Collins, Poudre Canyon Colo	Clait E. Braun
Yellow-headed Blackbird	1/17/79	Colusa NWR, CA	Walt Anderson
Red-winged Blackbird	1/1/79	Homestead, Fla.	JBE
Tricolored Blackbird	1/17/79	Colusa NWR, Cal	Walt Anderson
Tawny-shouldered Blackbird			
Orchard Oriole	4/23/79	Gum Cove, LA	John M. Good
Black-headed Oriole	4/11/79	Starr Co, TX	John C Arvin
Spotted Oriole	3/10/79	Delray Beach, Fla.	Paul W. Sykes Jr.
Hooded Oriole	10 July	Ruby Road, Ariz	Kenn Kaufman
Altamira Oriole	2/10/79	Hidalgo Co., Tx.	Steve W. Blacklock
Scarlet-headed Oriole	10/2/79	Tucson, AZ	Sally F. Monson Gale Monson
Black-vented Oriole			
Scott's Oriole	4/27/79	36 mi N of Alpine, TX	David E. Wolf
Northern Oriole	3/29/79	Arcadia, CA	Edwin [illegible] Johnson
Rusty Blackbird	5/16	"Virginia Patterson Anchorage, Alaska	David W Sonneborn
Brewer's Blackbird	14 Jan 79	West of Canyon, Texas	Warren D Harden
Great-tailed Grackle	13 Jan 79	Lake Overholser, OKC, Okla	Warren D Harden
Boat-tailed Grackle	1/1/79	W of Homestead, Fla.	JBE
Common Grackle	1/1/79	" " " "	JBE
Brown-headed Cowbird	1/1/79	" " " "	JBE
Bronzed Cowbird	2/11/79	Cameron Co., Tx.	Steve W. Blacklock

Species	Date	Place	Witness
Western Tanager	13 MAY	Berkeley, Ca	Rich Stallcup
Scarlet Tanager	24 Apr	High Island, TX	John L. Rowlett
Hepatic Tanager	4/28/79	Chisos Mts, Big Bend, TX	David E. Wolf
Summer Tanager	24 Apr	Silsbee, Texas	John L. Rowlett
Stripe-headed Tanager			
Blue-gray Tanager			
Northern Cardinal	1/1/79	Homestead, Fla.	J B E
Pyrrhuloxia	2/11/79	Welder Wildlife Refuge	Steve O. Stackfoot
Rose-breasted Grosbeak	4/24/79	High Island, Texas	Margaret J. Mellor
Black-headed Grosbeak	5.13.79	Berkeley, Ca.	Susan J. Swanson
Blue Grosbeak	24 Apr	Silsbee, Texas	John L. Rowlett
Indigo Bunting	2/4	Flamingo ENP Fla	Benton Basham
Lazuli Bunting	5.13.79	Del Puerto Canyon, Ca.	Susan J. Swanson
Varied Bunting	4/28/79	Old Ranch, Big Bend NP, TX	David E. Wolf
Painted Bunting	1/2/79	Kendall, Fla.	J B E
Black-faced Grassquit			
Melodious Grassquit			
Dickcissel	4/26/79	Anahuac NWR, TX	[illegible]
Brambling	5/20/79	Attu, Alaska	Arnold Small
Hawfinch			
Evening Grosbeak	16 Jan 79	Ft. Collins, Colo	Clait E. Braun
Eurasian Bullfinch			
Purple Finch	1/20	Carmel Valley, Ca	Rich Stallcup
Cassin's Finch	16 Jan 79	Ft. Collins, Colo	Clait E. Braun
House Finch	1/15/79	Denver, Colo.	R A Ryder
Common Rosefinch			
White-collared Seedeater	1/2/79	San Ygnacio TX	[illegible] / Don Garvin / [illegible]
Pine Grosbeak	27 Jan 79	Dipper Harbour, N.B.	Davis Finch
Gray-crowned Rosy Finch	15 Jan 79	Squaw Pass, Colo.	Clait E. Braun
Black Rosy Finch	15 Jan 79	Squaw Pass, Colo	Clait E. Braun

Species	Date	Place	Witness
Brown-capped Rosy Finch	15 Jan 79	Squaw Pass, Colo	Clait E. Braun
Oriental Greenfinch			
Hoary Redpoll	May 21 '79	ATTU ALASKA	[illegible]
Common Redpoll	8 March 79	nr Cynthia, Alberta	Davis W. Finch
Pine Siskin	14 Jan 79	West of Canyon, Texas	[illegible]
American Goldfinch	13 Jan 79	Norman, Okla	[illegible]
Lesser Goldfinch	1/17/79	Colusa, CA	Walt Anderson
Lawrence's Goldfinch	13 MAY	Digger Pine C.G. - Mines Road Ca.	Rich Stallcup
Red Crossbill	24 FEB	BEAR CANYON, SANTA CATALINA MTS., AZ	KENN KAUFMAN
White-winged Crossbill	27 Jan 79	Digby Neck, N.S.	Davis Finch
Olive Sparrow	9/10/79	Hidalgo Co., Tx.	Steve W. Blacklock
Green-tailed Towhee	23 FEB	SONOITA CREEK, AZ	KENN KAUFMAN
Rufous-sided Towhee	1/4/79	Jackson Ms	[illegible]
Brown Towhee	14 Jan 79	Palo Duro Canyon, Texas	[illegible]
Abert's Towhee	24 FEB	TUCSON, AZ	KENN KAUFMAN
Lark Bunting	14 Jan 79	West of Canyon, Texas	[illegible]
Savannah Sparrow	1/1/79	Flamingo, Fla.	J B E[illegible]
Grasshopper Sparrow	2/11/79	WELDER Wildlife Refuge	Steve W. Blacklock
Baird's Sparrow	7/2/79	Ordway Prairie, S.D.	Kevin Eckert
Henslow's Sparrow	[illegible]-27-79	Houston, Texas	Ernest [illegible] Stephens Zelda B. Stephens
Le Conte's Sparrow	2/11/79	WELDER Wildlife Refuge	Steve W. Blacklock
Sharp-tailed Sparrow	26 Apr	Bolivar Flats, TX	John L. Rowlett
Seaside Sparrow	18 Aug 79	Jamaica Bay, N.Y.C.	Robert O. Paxton
Vesper Sparrow	2/11/79	WELDER Wildlife Refuge	Steve W. Blacklock
Lark Sparrow	1/17/79	Butte Sink, Cal	Walt Anderson
Five-striped Sparrow My 650th	10 July	CALIFORNIA GULCH, ARIZONA	KENN KAUFMAN
Rufous-winged Sparrow	24 FEB	TUCSON, AZ	KENN KAUFMAN
Rufous-crowned Sparrow	1/17/79	Sutter Buttes, CA	Walt Anderson
Bachman's Sparrow	4/24/79	Silsbee, Texas	Victor L. Emanuel
Botteri's Sparrow	5/9/79	CAMERON CO., TX	John C Arvin

Species	Date	Place	Witness
Cassin's Sparrow	4/10	Laguna Atascosa NWR	John Carvin
Black-throated Sparrow	24 Feb	Tucson, AZ	Kenn Kaufman
Sage Sparrow	25 Feb	Phoenix, AZ	Kenn Kaufman
Northern Junco	13 Jan 79	Norman, Okla	Warren D Harden
Gray-headed Junco	16 Jan 79	Poudre Canyon El Collins Colo	Clait E. Braun
Mexican Junco	24 Feb	Bear Canyon, Santa Catalina Mts, AZ	Kenn Kaufman
American Tree Sparrow	13 Jan 79	Norman, Okla	Warren D Harden
Chipping Sparrow	23 Feb	Harshaw Canyon, AZ	Kenn Kaufman
Clay-colored Sparrow	29 June	Mio, Mich.	Larry Balch Barbara Hickey
Brewer's Sparrow	25 Feb	Phoenix, AZ	Kenn Kaufman
Field Sparrow	13 Jan 79	Oklahoma City, Okla	Warren D Harden
Black-chinned Sparrow	23 Feb	Harshaw Canyon, AZ	Kenn Kaufman
Harris' Sparrow	13 Jan 79	Norman, Okla	Warren D Harden
White-crowned Sparrow	14 Jan 79	West of Canyon, Texas	Warren D Harden
Golden-crowned Sparrow	1/17/79	Colusa NWR, Cal	Walt Anderson
White-throated Sparrow	1/4/79	Jackson Miss	[illegible]
Fox Sparrow	13 Jan 79	Oklahoma City, Okla	Warren D Harden
Lincoln's Sparrow	14 Jan 79	Palo Duro Canyon, Texas	Warren D Harden
Swamp Sparrow	2/10/79	Hidalgo Co., Tx.	Steve W. Blacklock
Song Sparrow	13 Jan 79	Oklahoma City, Okla	Warren D Harden
McCown's Longspur	14 Jan 79	West of Canyon, Texas	Warren D Harden
Lapland Longspur	13 Jan 79	along I-40 Western Okla	Warren D Harden
Smith's Longspur	13 Jan 79	Norman, Okla	Warren D Harden
Chestnut-collared Longspur	13 Jan 79	Norman, Okla	Warren D Harden
Snow Bunting	1/27/79	Maces Bay, N.B.	Peter D. Vickery
McKay's Bunting	6 June 79	St. Lawrence Is. Gambell, Alaska	Rich Stallcup
Little Bunting	____	____	____
Rustic Bunting	5/20/79	Attu, Alaska	Michael David Greene
Gray Bunting	____	____	____
Pallas' Reed Bunting	____	____	____

Species	Date	Place	Witness
Common Reed Bunting			
Canary-Winged Parakeet	1/2/79	Miami, Fla.	JBE
Scarlet Ibis	1/1/79	Flamingo, Fla.	JBE
Antillean Nighthawk	5-6-79	Dry Tortugas, Fla.	Oliver K. Scott
Green Sandpiper	5/22/79	Attu, AK	first verified N.A. record Ben King
Cuckoo (Cuculus sp.) (either Oriental or Common)	6/15/79	St. Paul, Pribilofs, AK	Will Russell
Tropical Kingbird (T. melancholicus)	10 July	near Nogales, Ariz	Kenn Kaufman
Cook's petrel	17 Nov.	Davidson Sea Mount	Debi Love Millich
Stejneger's Petrel	17 Nov.	~65 miles WSW Point Sur, California	Rich Stallcup

APPENDIX C

ELIGIBLE SPECIES FOR BIG YEAR 1979

Species seen appear in bold face

Common Loon	1
Yellow-billed Loon	1
Arctic Loon	1
Red-throated Loon	1
Red-necked Grebe	1
Horned Grebe	1
Eared Grebe	1
Least Grebe	1
Western Grebe	1
Pied-billed Grebe	1
Wandering Albatross	7
Short-tailed Albatross	7
Black-footed Albatross	1
Laysan Albatross	3
Shy Albatross	7
Yellow-nosed Albatross	6
Cape Petrel	7
Northern Fulmar	1
Cory's Shearwater	1
Pink-footed Shearwater	1
Flesh-footed Shearwater	2
Greater Shearwater	1
Buller's Shearwater	1
Sooty Shearwater	1
Short-tailed Shearwater	1
Manx Shearwater	1
Little Shearwater	7
Audubon's Shearwater	1
Streaked Shearwater	6
Black-capped Petrel	3
Scaled Petrel	4
South Trinidad Petrel	7
Cook's Petrel	7
Stejneger's Petrel	7
White-faced Storm Petrel	6
Fork-tailed Storm Petrel	1
Leach's Storm Petrel	1
Ashy Storm Petrel	1
Band-rumped Storm Petrel	7
Galapagos Storm Petrel	7
Black Storm Petrel	1
Least Storm Petrel	1
Wilson's Storm Petrel	1
British Storm Petrel	7
Red-billed Tropicbird	2
White-tailed Tropicbird	2
American White Pelican	1
Brown Pelican	1
Masked Booby	3
Blue-footed Booby	3
Brown Booby	1
Red-footed Booby	6
Northern Gannet	1
Great Cormorant	1
Double-crested Cormorant	1
Olivaceous Cormorant	1
Brandt's Cormorant	1
Pelagic Cormorant	1
Red-faced Cormorant	1
American Anninga	1
Magnificent Frigatebird	1
Lesser Frigatebird	7
Great Blue Heron	1
Green Heron	1
Little Blue Heron	1
Cattle Egret	1
Reddish Egret	1
Great Egret	1
Snowy Egret	1
Little Egret	7
Chinese Egret	7
Louisiana Heron	1
Black-crowned Night Heron	1
Yellow-crowned Night Heron	1
Least Bittern	1
American Bittern	1
Wood Stork	1
Glossy Ibis	1
White-faced Ibis	1
White Ibis	1
Roseate Spoonbill	1
American Flamingo	1
Mute Swan	1
Whooper Swan	2
Bewick's Swan	6
Whistling Swan	1
Trumpeter Swan	1
Canada Goose	1
Brant	1
Barnacle Goose	7
Emperor Goose	1
Greater White-fr. Goose	1
Bean Goose	3
Snow Goose	1
Ross's Goose	1
Black-bell. Whist. Duck	1
Fulvous Whistling Duck	1
Mallard	1
Mexican Duck	1
American Black Duck	1
Mottled Duck	1
Spot-billed Duck	7
Gadwall	1
Common Pintail	1
White-cheeked Pintail	5
Falcated Teal	4
Green-winged Teal	1
Baikal Teal	7
Blue-winged Teal	1
Cinnamon Teal	1
Garganey	3
Eurasian Wigeon	1
American Wigeon	1
Northern Shoveler	1
Wood Duck	1
Redhead	1
Common Pochard	2
Ring-necked Duck	1
Canvasback	1
Greater Scaup	1
Lesser Scaup	1
Tufted Duck	1
Common Goldeneye	1
Barrow's Goldeneye	1
Bufflehead	1
Oldsquaw	1
Harlequin Duck	1
Steller's Eider	1
Common Eider	1
King Eider	1
Spectacled Eider	1
White-winged Scoter	1
Surf Scoter	1
Ruddy Duck	1
Black Scoter	1
Masked Duck	2
Hooded Merganser	1
Smew	2
Common Merganser	1
Red-breasted Merganser	1
Turkey Vulture	1
Black Vulture	1
California Condor	2
White-tailed Kite	1
Swallow-tailed Kite	1
Hook-billed Kite	3
Mississippi Kite	1
Snail Kite	1
Northern Goshawk	1
Sharp-shinned Hawk	1
Cooper's Hawk	1
Red-tailed Hawk	1
Red-shouldered Hawk	1
Broad-winged Hawk	1
Swainson's Hawk	1
Zone-tailed Hawk	1
White-tailed Hawk	1
Short-tailed Hawk	1
Rough-legged Hawk	1
Ferruginous Hawk	1
Gray Hawk	1
Harris's Hawk	1
Lesser Black Hawk	1
Golden Eagle	1
White-tailed Eagle	3
Bald Eagle	1
Steller's Sea Eagle	7
Northern Harrier	1
Osprey	1
Crested Caracara	1
Gyrfalcon	1
Prairie Falcon	1
Peregrine Falcon	1
Aplomado Falcon	7
Merlin	1
Eurasian Kestrel	7
American Kestrel	1
Plain Chachalaca	1
Blue Grouse	1
Spruce Grouse	1
Ruffed Grouse	1
Willow Ptarmigan	1
Rock Ptarmigan	1
White-tailed Ptarmigan	1
Greater Prairie Chicken	1
Lesser Prairie Chicken	1
Sharp-tailed Grouse	1
Sage Grouse	1
Common Bobwhite	1
Scaled Quail	1
California Quail	1
Gambel's Quain	1
Mountain Quail	1
Montezuma Quail	1
Ring-necked Pheasant	1
Chukar	1
Gray Partridge	1
Black Francolin	1
Wild Turkey	1
Common Crane	7
Whooping Crane	1
Sandhill Crane	1
Limpkin	1
King Rail	1
Clapper Rail	1
Virginia Rail	1
Spotted Rail	7
Sora	1
Yellow Rail	1
Black Rail	1
Corn Crake	7
Paint-billed Crake	7
Purple Gallinule	1
Common Gallinule	1
European Coot	7
American Coot	1
Caribbean Coot	1
North American Jacana	4
American Oystercatcher	1
Black Oystercatcher	1
Black-necked Stilt	1
American Avocet	1
Double-striped Thick-knee	7
Northern Lapwing	7
Ringed Plover	5
Semipalmated Plover	1
Little Ringed Plover	7
Wilson's Plover	1
Killdeer	1
Piping Plover	1
Snowy Plover	1
Mongolian Plover	3
Mountain Plover	1
Greater Golden Plover	5
Lesser Golden Plover	1
Black-bellied Plover	1
Dotterel	5
Black-tailed Godwit	5
Hudsonian Godwit	1
Bar-tailed Godwit	1
Marbled Godwit	1
Eskimo Curlew	7
Whimbrel	1
Bristle-thighed Curlew	2
Eurasian Curlew	7
Far Eastern Curlew	6
Long-billed Curlew	1
Upland Sandpiper	1
Spotted Redshank	3
Marsh Sandpiper	7
Greenshank	3
Greater Yellowlegs	1
Lesser Yellowlegs	1
Solitary Sandpiper	1
Wood Sandpiper	1
Willet	1
Terek Sandpiper	5
Common Sandpiper	3
Spotted Sandpiper	1
Gray-tailed Tattler	2
Wandering Tattler	1
Ruddy Turnstone	1
Black Turnstone	1
Wilson's Phalarope	1
Northern Phalarope	1
Red Phalarope	1
Green Sandpiper	7
European Woodcock	7
American Woodcock	1
Common Snipe	1
European Jacksnipe	7
Short-billed Dowitcher	1

ELIGIBLE SPECIES FOR BIG YEAR 1979 (Continued)

- **Long-billed Dowitcher** 1
- **Surfbird** 1
- Great Knot 5
- **Red Knot** 1
- **Sanderling** 1
- **Semipalmated Sandpiper** 1
- **Western Sandpiper** 1
- **Rufous-necked Stint** 2
- **Little Stint** 7
- **Temminck's Stint** 3
- **Long-toed Stint** 2
- **Least Sandpiper** 1
- **White-rumped Sandpiper** 1
- **Baird's Sandpiper** 1
- **Pectoral Sandpiper** 1
- **Sharp-tailed Sandpiper** 2
- **Purple Sandpiper** 1
- **Rock Sandpiper** 1
- **Dunlin** 1
- **Curlew Sandpiper** 2
- Spoonbill Sandpiper 6
- Broad-billed Sandpiper 5
- **Stilt Sandpiper** 1
- **Buff-breasted Sandpiper** 1
- **Ruff** 2
- **Pomarine Jaeger** 1
- **Parasitic Jaeger** 1
- **Long-tailed Jaeger** 1
- **Great Skua** 2
- **South Polar Skua** 2
- **Glaucous Gull** 1
- **Iceland Gull** 1
- **Glaucous-winged Gull** 1
- **Great Black-backed Gull** 1
- **Slaty-backed Gull** 2
- **Western Gull** 1
- **Lesser Black-backed Gull** 2
- **Herring Gull** 1
- **Thayer's Gull** 1
- **California Gull** 1
- **Ring-billed Gull** 1
- **Mew Gull** 1
- **Black-headed Gull** 1
- **Laughing Gull** 1
- **Franklin's Gull** 1
- **Bonaparte's Gull** 1
- **Little Gull** 1
- **Heermann's Gull** 1
- **Ivory Gull** 1
- **Black-legged Kittiwake** 1
- **Red-legged Kittiwake** 1
- **Ross's Gull** 1
- **Sabine's Gull** 1
- **Gull-billed Tern** 1
- **Forster's Tern** 1
- **Common Tern** 1
- **Arctic Tern** 1
- **Roseate Tern** 1
- **Aleutian Tern** 1
- **Sooty Tern** 1
- **Bridled Tern** 1
- **Little Tern** 1
- **Royal Tern** 1
- **Elegant Tern** 1
- **Sandwich Tern** 1
- **Caspian Tern** 1
- **Black Tern** 1
- White-winged Black Tern 4
- **Brown Noddy** 1

- **Black Noddy** 4
- **Black Skimmer** 1
- **Razorbill** 1
- **Thin-billed Murre** 1
- **Thick-billed Murre** 1
- **Dovekie** 1
- **Black Guillemot** 1
- **Pigeon Guillemot** 1
- **Marbled Murrelet** 1
- **Kittlitz's Murrelet** 1
- **Xantus' Murrelet** 1
- Craveri's Murrelet 1
- **Ancient Murrelet** 1
- **Cassin's Auklet** 1
- **Parakeet Auklet** 1
- **Crested Auklet** 1
- **Least Auklet** 1
- **Whiskered Auklet** 1
- **Rhinoceros Auklet** 1
- **Atlantic Puffin** 1
- **Horned Puffin** 1
- **Tufted Puffin** 1
- **White-crowned Piegon** 1
- Scaly-naped Pigeon 7
- **Band-tailed Pigeon** 1
- **Red-billed Pigeon** 2
- **Rock Dove** 1
- Zenaida Dove 7
- **White-winged Dove** 1
- **Mourning Dove** 1
- **Spotted Dove** 1
- **Ringed Turtle Dove** 1
- **Common Ground Dove** 1
- Ruddy Ground Dove 7
- **Inca Dove** 1
- **White-tipped Dove** 1
- **Key West Quail Dove** 7
- Ruddy Quail Dove 7
- Thick-billed Parrot 7
- **Yellow-headed Parrot** 1
- **Budgerigar** 1
- Common Cuckoo 4
- Oriental Cuckoo 7
- **Cuculus Species**
- **Mangrove Cuckoo** 1
- **Yellow-billed Cuckoo** 1
- **Black-billed Cuckoo** 1
- **Greater Roadrunner** 1
- **Smooth-billed Ani** 1
- **Groove-billed Ani** 1
- **Barn Owl** 1
- **Common Screech Owl** 1
- **Whiskered Screech Owl** 1
- **Flammulated Screech Owl** 1
- **Great Horned Owl** 1
- **Snowy Owl** 1
- **Hawk Owl** 1
- **Northern Pygmy Owl** 1
- **Ferruginous Pygmy Owl** 2
- **Elf Owl** 1
- **Burrowing Owl** 1
- **Barred Owl** 1
- **Spotted Owl** 1
- **Great Gray Owl** 2
- **Long-eared Owl** 1
- **Short-eared Owl** 1
- **Boreal Owl** 1
- **Saw-whet Owl** 1
- Jungle Nightjar 7

- **Chuck-will's-widow** 1
- **Whip-poor-will** 1
- **Buff-collared Nightjar** 2
- **Poor-will** 1
- **Pauraque** 1
- **Common Nighthawk** 1
- **Lesser Nighthawk** 1
- Wh.-throated N.-tailed Swift 7
- **Black Swift** 1
- **Chimney Swift** 1
- **Vaux's Swift** 1
- Fork-tailed Swift 4
- Common Swift 7
- **White-throated Swift** 1
- Antillean Palm Swift 7
- Green Violet-ear 7
- Cuban Emerald 7
- **Lucifer Hummingbird** 1
- **Ruby-throated Hummingbird** 1
- **Black-chinned Hummingbird** 1
- Bahama Woodstar 7
- **Costa's Hummingbird** 1
- **Anna's Hummingbird** 1
- **Broad-tailed Hummingbird** 1
- **Rufous Hummingbird** 1
- **Allen's Hummingbird** 1
- Bumblebee Hummingbird 7
- **Calliope Hummingbird** 1
- **Magnificent Hummingbird** 1
- Plain-capped Starthroat 6
- **Blue-throated Hummingbird** 1
- **Buff-bellied Hummingbird** 1
- **Violet-crowned Hummingbird** 1
- Berylline Hummingbird 3
- **White-eared Hummingbird** 3
- **Broad-billed Hummingbird** 1
- Eared Trogon 6
- **Elegant Trogon** 1
- **Belted Kingfisher** 1
- **Ringed Kingfisher** 1
- **Green Kingfisher** 1
- Hoopoe 7
- Eurasian Wryneck 7
- **Common Flicker** 1
- **Pileated Woodpecker** 1
- **Red-bellied Woodpecker** 1
- **Golden-fronted Woodpecker** 1
- **Gila Woodpecker** 1
- **Red-headed Woodpecker** 1
- **Acorn Woodpecker** 1
- **Lewis's Woodpecker** 1
- **Yellow-bellied Sapsucker** 1
- **Williamson's Sapsucker** 1
- **Hairy Woodpecker** 1
- **Downy Woodpecker** 1
- **Ladder-backed Woodpecker** 1
- **Nuttall's Woodpecker** 1
- **Brown-backed Woodpecker** 1
- **Red-cockaded Woodpecker** 1
- **White-headed Woodpecker** 1
- **Bl.-backed Three-toed W'pec.** 1
- **Northern Three-toed W'pecker** 1
- **Rose-throated Becard** 1
- **Eastern Kingbird** 1
- Loggerhead Kingbird 6
- **Gray Kingbird** 1
- **Tropical Kingbird** 1
- **Western Kingbird** 1
- **Cassin's Kingbird** 1

- **Thick-billed Kingbird** 1
- Fork-tailed Flycatcher 4
- **Scissor-tailed Flycatcher** 1
- **Greater Kiskadee** 1
- **Sulphur-bellied Flycatcher** 1
- **Great Crested Flycatcher** 1
- **Wied's Crested Flycatcher** 1
- **Ash-throated Flycatcher** 1
- **Olivaceous Flycatcher** 1
- Nutting's Flycatcher 7
- Stolid Flycatcher 7
- **Eastern Phoebe** 1
- **Black Phoebe** 1
- **Say's Phoebe** 1
- **Yellow-bellied Flycatcher** 1
- **Acadian Flycatcher** 1
- **Willow Flycatcher** 1
- **Alder Flycatcher** 1
- **Least Flycatcher** 1
- **Hammond's Flycatcher** 1
- **Dusky Flycatcher** 1
- **Gray Flycatcher** 1
- **Western Flycatcher** 1
- **Buff-breasted Flycatcher** 1
- **Coues's Flycatcher** 1
- **Eastern Pewee** 1
- **Western Pewee** 1
- **Olive-sided Flycatcher** 1
- **Vermilion Flycatcher** 1
- **Northern Beardless Flycatcher** 1
- **Common Skylark** 1
- **Horned Lark** 1
- Bahama Swallow 4
- **Violet-green Swallow** 1
- **Tree Swallow** 1
- **Bank Swallow** 1
- **Rough-winged Swallow** 1
- Common House Martin 7
- **Barn Swallow** 1
- **Cliff Swallow** 1
- **Cave Swallow** 1
- **Purple Martin** 1
- Cuban Martin 7
- Gray-breasted Martin 7
- **Gray Jay** 1
- **Blue Jay** 1
- **Steller's Jay** 1
- **Scrub Jay** 1
- **Gray-breasted Jay** 1
- **Green Jay** 1
- **Brown Jay** 1
- **Black-billed Magpie** 1
- **Yellow-billed Magpie** 1
- **Northern Raven** 1
- **White-necked Raven** 1
- **American Crow** 1
- **Northwestern Crow** 1
- **Fish Crow** 1
- **Mexican Crow** 1
- **Pinyon Jay** 1
- **Clark's Nutcracker** 1
- **Black-capped Chickadee** 1
- **Carolina Chickadee** 1
- **Mexican Chickadee** 1
- **Mountain Chickadee** 1
- Siberian Chickadee 2
- **Boreal Chickadee** 1
- **Chestnut-backed Chickadee** 1
- **Tufted Titmouse** 1

ELIGIBLE SPECIES FOR BIG YEAR 1979 (Continued)

Plain Titmouse 1
Bridled Titmouse 1
Verdin 1
Bushtit 1
White-breasted Nuthatch 1
Red-breasted Nuthatch 1
Brown-headed Nuthatch 1
Pygmy Nuthatch 1
Brown Creeper 1
Wrentit 1
Red-whiskered Bulbul 1
North American Dipper 1
House Wren 1
Brown-throated Wren 1
Winter Wren 1
Bewick's Wren 1
Carolina Wren 1
Cactus Wren 1
Marsh Wren 1
Sedge Wren 1
Canyon Wren 1
Rock Wren 1
Northern Mockingbird 1
Bahama Mockingbird 7
Gray Catbird 1
Brown Thrasher 1
Long-billed Thrasher 1
Bendire's Thrasher 1
Curve-billed Thrasher 1
California Thrasher 1
Le Conte's Thrasher 1
Crissal Thrasher 1
Sage Thrasher 1
American Robin 1
Fieldfare 7
Rufous-backed Thrush 3
Clay-colored Thrush 4
Dusky Thrush 4
Eye-browed Thrush 3
Varied Thrush 1
Aztec Thrush 6
Wood Thrush 1
Hermit Thrush 1
Swainson's Thrush 1
Gray-cheeked Thrush 1
Veery 1
Eastern Bluebird 1
Western Bluebird 1
Mountain Bluebird 1
Northern Wheatear 1
Bluethroat 2
Siberian Rubythroat 4
Townsend's Solitaire 1
Willow Warbler 7
Dusky Warbler 5
Arctic Warbler 1
M'dorff's Grasshop. Warb. 6
Blue-gray Gnatcatcher 1
Black-capped Gnatcatcher 6
Black-tailed Gnatcatcher 1
Golden-crowned Kinglet 1
Ruby-crowned Kinglet 1
Red-breasted Flycatcher 5
Gray-spotted Flycatcher 4
Siberian Accentor 5
White Wagtail 2
Gray Wagtail 5
Yellow Wagtail 1
Water Pipit 1
Pechora Pipit 6
Indian Tree Pipit 3
Red-throated Pipit 1
Sprague's Pipit 1
Bohemian Waxwing 1
Cedar Waxwing 1
Phainopepla 1
Brown Shrike 6
Northern Shrike 1
Loggerhead Shrike 1
European Starling 1
Crested Myna 1
Black-capped Vireo 1
White-eyed Vireo 1
Hutton's Vireo 1
Bell's Vireo 1
Thick-billed Vireo 7
Gray Vireo 1
Yellow-throated Vireo 1
Solitary Vireo 1
Black-whiskered Vireo 1
Yellow-green Vireo 3
Red-eyed Vireo 1
Philadelphia Vireo 1
Warbling Vireo 1
Bananaquit 4
Black-and-White Warbler 1
Prothonotary Warbler 1
Swainson's Warbler 1
Worm-eating Warbler 1
Golden-winged Warbler 1
Blue-winged Warbler 1
Bachman's Warbler 6
Tennessee Warbler 1
Orange-crowned Warbler 1
Nashville Warbler 1
Virginia's Warbler 1
Colima Warbler 1
Lucy's Warbler 1
Northern Parula Warbler 1
Tropical Parula Warbler 3
Olive Warbler 1
Yellow Warbler 1
Magnolia Warbler 1
Cape May Warbler 1
Black-throated Blue Warbler 1
Yellow-rumped Warbler 1
Black-throated Gray Warbler 1
Townsend's Warbler 1
Black-throated Green Warbler 1
Golden-cheeked Warbler 1
Hermit Warbler 1
Cerulean Warbler 1
Blackburnian Warbler 1
Yellow-throated Warbler 1
Grace's Warbler 1
Chestnut-sided Warbler 1
Bay-breasted Warbler 1
Blackpoll Warbler 1
Pine Warbler 1
Kirtland's Warbler 1
Prairie Warbler 1
Palm Warbler 1
Ovenbird 1
Northern Waterthrush 1
Louisiana Waterthrush 1
Kentucky Warbler 1
Connecticut Warbler 1
Mourning Warbler 1
MacGillivray's Warbler 1
Common Yellowthroat 1
Gray-crowned Yellowthroat 7
Yellow-breasted Chat 1
Fan-tailed Warbler 7
Red-faced Warbler 1
Hooded Warbler 1
Wilson's Warbler 1
Canada Warbler 1
American Redstart 1
Painted Redstart 1
Slate-throated Redstart 6
Rufous-capped Warbler 4
House Sparrow 1
Eurasian Tree Sparrow 1
Bobolink 1
Eastern Meadowlark 1
Western Meadowlark 1
Yellow-headed Blackbird 1
Red-winged Blackbird 1
Tricolored Blackbird 1
Tawny-shouldered Blackbird 7
Orchard Oriole 1
Black-headed Oriole 1
Spotted Oriole 1
Hooded Oriole 1
Altamira Oriole 1
Scarlet-headed Oriole 5
Black-vented Oriole 6
Scott's Oriole 1
Northern Oriole 1
Rusty Blackbird 1
Brewer's Blackbird 1
Great-tailed Grackle 1
Boat-tailed Grackle 1
Common Grackle 1
Brown-headed Cowbird 1
Bronzed Cowbird 1
Western Tanager 1
Scarlet Tanager 1
Hepatic Tanager 1
Summer Tanager 1
Stripe-headed Tanager 3
Blue-gray Tanager 7
Northern Cardinal 1
Pyrrhuloxia 1
Rose-breasted Grosbeak 1
Black-headed Grosbeak 1
Blue Grosbeak 1
Indigo Bunting 1
Lazuli Bunting 1
Varied Bunting 1
Painted Bunting 1
Black-faced Grassquit 7
Melodious Grassquit 7
Dickcissel 1
Brambling 2
Hawfinch 4
Evening Grosbeak 1
Eurasian Bullfinch 4
Purple Finch 1
Cassin's Finch 1
House Finch 1
Common Rosefinch 3
White-collared Seedeater 4
Pine Grosbeak 1
Gray-crowned Rosy Finch 1
Black Rosy Finch 1
Brown-capped Rosy Finch 1
Oriental Greenfinch 4
Hoary Redpoll 1
Common Redpoll 1
Pine Siskin 1
American Goldfinch 1
Lesser Goldfinch 1
Lawrence's Goldfinch 1
Red Crossbill 1
White-winged Crossbill 1
Olive Sparrow 1
Green-tailed Towhee 1
Rufous-sided Towhee 1
Brown Towhee 1
Abert's Towhee 1
Lark Bunting 1
Savannah Sparrow 1
Grasshopper Sparrow 1
Baird's Sparrow 1
Henslow's Sparrow 1
Le Conte's Sparrow 1
Sharp-tailed Sparrow 1
Seaside Sparrow 1
Vesper Sparrow 1
Lark Sparrow 1
Five-striped Sparrow 1
Rufous-winged Sparrow 1
Rufous-crowned Sparrow 1
Bachman's Sparrow 1
Botteri's Sparrow 1
Cassin's Sparrow 1
Black-throated Sparrow 1
Sage Sparrow 1
Northern Junco 1
Gray-headed Junco 1
Mexican Junco 1
American Tree Sparrow 1
Chipping Sparrow 1
Clay-colored Sparrow 1
Brewer's Sparrow 1
Field Sparrow 1
Black-chinned Sparrow 1
Harris's Sparrow 1
White-crowned Sparrow 1
Golden-crowned Sparrow 1
White-throated Sparrow 1
Fox Sparrow 1
Lincoln's Sparrow 1
Swamp Sparrow 1
Song Sparrow 1
McCown's Longspur 1
Lapland Longspur 1
Smith's Longspur 1
Chestnut-collared Longspur 1
Snow Bunting 1
McKay's Bunting 1
Little Bunting 6
Rustic Bunting 3
Gray Bunting 6
Pallas's Reed Bunting 6
Common Reed Bunting 5

INELIGIBLE SPECIES NOT ON ABA LIST:

Canary-winged Parakeet
Scarlet Ibis
Antillean Nighthawk

INDEX